The Florida Citrus
Flavor Industry
1900–2000

ROBERT A. KRYGER

© 2024 by Robert A. Kryger.

Published by:
Emona Publishing
632 East Main Street, Suite 300
Lakeland, FL 33801
www.floridaflavorhistory.org

All Rights Reserved. No part of this book may be reproduced or transmitted in any form or by any means, electronic or mechanical, including photocopying, recording, or by any information storage and retrieval system, without written permission of the publisher.

The cover art is from "Valencia Morning" by Paul Schulz. ©Paul Schulz. Used By Permission.

ISBN: 979-8-218-45097-7 (hardback)
Library of Congress Control Number: 2024915759

Dedicated to my father, Allen Charles Kryger, who introduced me to the delightful world of citrus flavors.

Preface

In 1995, my father invited me to join him working in Florida's citrus flavor industry. We were not native Floridians, but he had been working with Florida citrus since the 1970s, a relative newcomer by citrus industry standards. Although I had grown up surrounded by bottles of citrus oils and terpenes around the house[1], I had left Florida in 1979, not intending to return. Once back, I was quickly captivated by the magical charm of citrus, and in particular, the fascinating mix of art, science and business that produces modern citrus flavors. Over time, I grew to appreciate the complex roles of growers, processors, byproduct businesses, regulatory agencies, research organizations, and others all working together to commercialize Florida citrus.

What particularly struck me about my colleagues in the citrus flavor industry was the pride they held in their work producing the citrus-flavored products enjoyed by so many around the world. And yet, it was mostly work hidden from the consumer's view. With few exceptions, the people enjoying these products rarely understood or appreciated the role played by the citrus flavor industry in their foods. But when industry insiders gathered together, fascinating stories of who did what when would come out, sometimes partially obscured to protect proprietary business information. Unfortunately, no one was capturing this oral history; preserving it was of little business value, nor was there much academic interest.

My effort to document the industry history began in the summer of 2020 as the Covid pandemic swept the world. I had retired from the citrus flavor industry a few years earlier and the idea of documenting the history of this fascinating "hidden" industry had been brewing in my mind for some time. Although I had heard many stories about the

---

[1] For preparing certain mixed drinks, firing up the charcoal grill, removing spots from clothes, and other cleaning tasks.

industry's founding by Dr. James Redd, I knew that little of this history was documented anywhere other than in the memories of his contemporaries, many of whom were deceased or elderly. If this history was ever to be properly documented, the effort would have to start soon. It was my hope that concerns about protecting proprietary information would be lessened for events that occurred quite some time ago. Once committed, perhaps my biggest surprise was how little of Florida's overall citrus history from the 20th century has been cohesively documented. Furthermore, the few academic studies of citrus history produced in the last 25 years seemed to be dominated by an anti-agribusiness perspective. I initially expected my effort to result in a long article. Soon, it became clear that this story was much larger than that.

The result is the present book. I have attempted to document the main factors instrumental in the formation of a citrus flavor industry in Florida and the subsequent development of the industry from Dr. Redd's eponymous company, Redd Laboratories. Although focused on citrus *flavor* history, I have nevertheless included quite a bit of information about citrus processing in Florida because of the integral importance of processing technology and economics to the business of citrus flavoring. Given my technical interests and background, I have paid particular attention to the technical developments that underpin the current industry. Less easy to discern were the business and sales strategies of the businessmen and companies involved; this type of information was closely guarded at the time, and rarely documented for historical considerations. As much as I could discern, usually from the recollections of key industry participants, I have included discussions of these strategies as well. I chose to limit my study to events prior to the year 2000, influenced both by the catastrophic effects of citrus greening, which began shortly after 2000, and the desire to minimize concerns about current proprietary information.

Should you have additional information or a different perspective about any topic in this book, please share it with me. I can be contacted through the website www.floridaflavorhistory.org.

Robert A. Kryger
Lakeland, FL
July, 2024

Acknowledgements

The completion of this project has been a long-standing personal goal and it would not have been possible without the encouragement, support and contributions of many people. Of these, a handful contributed particularly generously of their time, expertise and experience including: Tim Anglea, Ed Baranski, Beverly Bateman, Jeff Dodson, Gil Escobar, Luis Haro, Rex Harper, Don Hendrix, Paul Schulz, JD Vora, and Brett Welch. Other industry professionals who contributed important facts, memories, documents or interviews include: Randy Aulick, Elizabeth Baldwin, Wesley Beck, Eric Bennett, Niv BenYehuda, Hugo Bovill, Bob Braddock, Robert Brausch, Robin Bryant, Kristen Carlson, David Cline, Cathy Conway, Sean Frielich, Dan Gunter, Joe Johnson, Dennis Kujawski, Chris Li, Peary Marro, Susan Martin, David McKeithan, Carlos Odio, Sue Percival, Anne Plotto, Dave Rosen, Jerry Sachs, Colin Scott, Charles Thomas, Jan Van Iperen, David Walker, and Mark Walsh. I am very grateful to them also. It is my sincere hope that the final result meets their expectations and conveys their enthusiasm for the industry. I could never have properly completed this history without their help.

Several professional librarians and archivists also helped me including Jennifer Dawson at the Lake Alfred Citrus Research and Education Center, Marcia Hoecker at Florida Polytechnic University, LuAnn Mims at the Lakeland Public Library and Gerrianne Schaad at Florida Southern College. Their help was invaluable. Much appreciated also was the help of Florida Department of Citrus staff including the Executive Director Shannon Shepp, and the Scientific Research Director Rosa Walsh.

My assistant, Elizabeth Johnson, helped me extensively in the earliest phase of this project with organization and research. And my son, Sean, patiently provided proofreading and editing input. I am grateful to both. Gabriel Johnson provided additional editing, proofreading and indexing help as the manuscript neared completion. Despite their best efforts, all remaining mistakes are my responsibility. I further apologize for any factual errors or misunderstandings I incorporated into the book.

Finally, I would like to thank my wife Judy for her patience during this project. As far as she is concerned, I routinely over-promised and under-delivered. This is a debt I will likely take to my grave.

Contents

1 Introduction 1

2 The Florida Citrus Industry 1900–1940 7

3 The Invention of Frozen Concentrated OJ 43

4 Developments with the Growth of FCOJ 79

5 Essence Recovery 113

6 Birth of the Citrus Flavor Industry 1960–1982 153

7 The 1980s — The Flavor Industry Grows 197

8 The 1990s — The Golden Years 227

9 Looking Ahead into the Next Century 269

Index 273

1
Introduction

> *"Of all the plants spread by Nature upon the surface of the globe, there are none more beautiful than ... lemon and orange trees."*
>
> —M. George Gallesio, *A Treatise On The Citrus Family*, 1811[1].

Citrus is thought to have originated naturally in Southeast Asia, around China and India. Citrus trees grow in a wide range of tropical and sub-tropical conditions. The citrus genus forms hybrids and mutates easily, leading to significant natural variation. Some citrus varieties are known to have been cultivated in both China and India more than 2000 years ago. The modern name "orange" is derived from the Sanskrit name of the fruit *nagarunga*. The first citrus variety known in Europe was the citron, introduced via Persia around the time of Alexander the Great (ca. 300 BC). While the earliest arrival time of the more common citrus varieties to Europe remains unclear, it is known that Arabs brought oranges, lemons and pummelos to North Africa and Spain by 1150 AD. Oranges were widely cultivated around the Mediterranean by the 15th century, with the Portuguese particularly associated with sweet oranges at this time. Portuguese sailors, navigating by ship between India, the Far East, and Europe, likely facilitated the spread of citrus into Europe. Columbus is known to have brought orange, lemon and citron seeds to the New World on his second voyage (in 1483 AD). Subsequently, the Spanish introduced citrus throughout the Caribbean,

Central, and South America. Citrus reached North America by way of Florida in the mid 1500s. When the Spanish established St. Augustine, they planted oranges and lemons. Orange trees were soon growing wild in Florida. Grapefruits arrived in Florida in the early 1800s. Of all the common citrus fruits, only the grapefruit originated in the Western Hemisphere. First described in 1750 on the Caribbean island of Barbados, it is thought to have naturally formed as a hybrid from pummelo. In this manner, citrus was spread to all of the major continents, introducing people worldwide to this delightful fruit[2, 3, 4, 5, 6].

People living near citrus-growing regions quickly learned that sliced citrus fruits, and especially the peels or oils extracted from those peels, could be used to flavor foods and make perfumes and fragrances. Following the Middle Ages, with the advancement of chemistry, people began to employ distillation and solvent-based extraction techniques to natural essential oils and other fragrant materials, including citrus. The aim was to capture their essence, in aroma or taste, as a concentrated, usable ingredient. Over time, these discoveries were commercialized, giving rise to the flavor and fragrance industry, which in some ways intersected with the historic spice trade. By the 1800s, this flavor and fragrance industry was most technologically-advanced in Europe compared to other manufacturing locations. The European industry imported raw materials from around the globe and utilized the latest chemical know-how to produce highly-concentrated mixtures that conveyed the flavor or odor profile of natural products like fruits or flowers. These essences could be blended and incorporated into products to reinforce or enhance the sensory impact of a product, mimic a missing sensory character, or create brand-new sensory experiences. In contrast to spices, which were usually sold as food ingredients to be used by individuals during food preparation, flavors and fragrances were complex chemical compositions, designed by experts according to proprietary recipes, for incorporation into foods, beverages or other consumer products during manufacturing. Citrus products, often sourced nearby from Italy or Spain, were an important part of this European flavor and fragrance business, and in particular, citrus peel oils. These oils were extracted from the peels by physical pressing and possessed the characteristic aroma of the fresh fruit in a very concentrated form. They were easy to transport and did not decay or spoil like raw fruit or juice, making them valuable raw materials for flavor and fragrance products.

By the early 1900s, a small US-based flavor industry had emerged in the New York City area, mostly as subsidiaries of European companies taking advantage of shipping into NY ports to sell their products. Serving a growing population with increasing wealth, this US industry prospered throughout the 20th century, although it remained largely headquartered and concentrated in the Northeast. However, over the 100 years between 1900 and 2000, there was a fascinating shift in the global production of citrus flavors. While citrus-based fragrance manufacturing remained primarily in Europe, citrus flavor production largely relocated to Florida, a state with no history of sophisticated food or flavor production nor chemical industry[1]. The reasons behind the shift are complex and fascinating. Florida may have been an obvious place to grow citrus, but it was certainly not an obvious destination for a valued-added flavor industry. Just as other citrus growing regions had traditionally exported their citrus oils for processing elsewhere, Florida easily could have done the same.

Which brings us to the subject of the current study. How did Florida emerge as the epicenter of the world's natural citrus flavor production by the year 2000? By that year, three of the top 10 global flavor companies had established citrus flavor facilities in Florida, as did the largest soft-drink company in the world, Coca-Cola, which maintained a "secret" flavor production facility near Orlando. And supplementing these multinational companies were a handful of specialized local flavor companies. Together, employing approximately 500 people in total, these companies were responsible for producing a significant portion of the world's natural citrus flavors. This concentrated production continues in Florida to this day and these flavors are enjoyed worldwide in juices, fruit-flavored beverages, soft-drinks and various non-beverage food products such as candies, pastries and yogurts. The industry brings together a diverse array of professionals, including agricultural specialists, food and flavor experts, chemists, manufacturing and process engineers, businessmen, entrepreneurs and sales personnel. They collaborate to create, market and sell products that nearly everyone experiences through taste but seldom sees or touches directly.

Industry lore traces the genesis of this Florida industry to a single man, Dr. James Redd, and his company, Redd Laboratories, which

---

[1] During the same 100 years, the phosphate fertilizer industry was also developing in Florida.

was started in 1961. Furthermore, there is no doubt that over the next 40 years, the nexus of the world's natural citrus flavor manufacturing developed largely in the orbit of this unique company and the people trained there. Yet, Redd's important role has to be understood within the context of Florida's broader citrus industry. In fact, the story of how and why the citrus flavor industry developed and flourished in Florida, in parallel with the much larger orange juice industry, is a fascinating study of the development of a new industry from the interaction of innovative people working in private industry, public research organizations, and government agencies. While the industry's success was undoubtedly dependent on the tremendous growth of Florida orange juice, that success only made the flavor industry in Florida possible, not probable. Rather, a combination of favorable conditions, including market competition, public and private research investments, and commercial investments by enterprising and risk-tolerant individuals, made the outcome a reality. The objective of this work is to share this compelling story.

References

[1] M. George Gallesio. *A Treatise On The Citrus Family*. Trans. by S. D. Wilcox. Original in French, published 1811. Jacksonville, FL: The Florida Agriculturist, 1876.

[2] Francesco Calabrese. "Origin and History." In: *Citrus: The Genus Citrus*. Ed. by Giovanni Dugo and Angelo Di Giacomo. Vol. 26. New York, NY: Taylor & Francis, 2002. ISBN: 0-415-28491-0.

[3] Herbert John Webber. "History and Development of the Citrus Industry." In: *The Citrus Industry: History, Botany, and Breeding*. Ed. by Herbert John Webber and Leon Dexter Batchelor. Vol. 1. Berkeley, CA: University of California Press, 1943.

[4] Herbert John Webber, Walter Reuther, and Harry W. Lawton. "History and Development of the Citrus Industry." In: *The Citrus Industry: History, World Distribution, Botany, and Varieties*. Ed. by Herbert John Webber, Leon Dexter Batchelor, and Walter Reuther. Vol. 1. Berkeley, CA: University of California Press, 1967.

[5] S. Tolkowsky. *Hesperides: A History of the Culture and Use of Citrus Fruits*. London, U.K.: John Bale, Sons & Curnow, Ltd., 1938.

[6] T. Frederick Davis. *A History of the Orange in Florida 1575 - 1900*. Copy in the UF Special Collections Library. 1937.

2

The Florida Citrus Industry 1900–1940

> *"[The citrus industry] captures men with the deftness of an uncompromising maiden and thereafter refuses to set them free."*
>
> —J. T. Hopkins, *Fifty Years of Citrus: The Florida Citrus Exchange 1909–1959*[1].

Following the US Civil War, there were two main citrus growing regions in the United States, Florida and California. Citrus had arrived in Florida with the Spanish settlers in St. Augustine by 1579[2]. It came later to California, also with the Spanish. However, in both places commercial citrus farming only started in the 1800s. Florida primarily grew fruit for East Coast markets, with groves initially located near the St. John's River, Indian River and the Gulf Coast, where fruit could be shipped north by boat. California's fruit was mainly located near Los Angeles and was shipped to markets first in the Western part of the US, then expanding into the Midwest. The climates in both states were very different. Florida was semi-tropical with considerable rain and humidity. California's citrus regions were also warm, but considerably drier with a more Mediterranean-like climate. California primarily grew lemons and oranges, while Florida grew oranges, grapefruits and tangerines. In both places, fresh fruit had to be transported long distances to markets by relatively slow means. Fruit had to be picked early to be optimally ripe after transport, but not too early to be immature and taste sour or bitter. It was also important to carefully screen fruit for wounds or imperfections that could encourage decay during shipping. A common means to ship fresh Florida fruit at the time was in barrels packed with Spanish moss[3].

The US Department of Agriculture encouraged citrus growing, helped identify the best citrus fruit cultivars for each location, and studied best horticultural techniques. One important development at this time was grafting desired citrus varieties onto rootstocks, rather than growing those trees from seed. Rootstocks were compatible citrus varieties that grew well in the local soil, but did not produce desirable fruit. The desirable citrus variety was grafted on the base of the rootstock tree. After some time, all of the branches and fruit above the trunk would belong to the grafted cultivar. This process improved fruit yields and made it easier to standardize cultivars. The best trees could be selected for grafting, and the grafted trees were genetically identical to the parent. Additionally, in a severe freeze the rootstock was the last part of the tree to die and could sometimes be re-grafted. This new technique rapidly spread. Around the same time in the late 1800s, new railroad networks significantly opened up transportation possibilities to bring fresh citrus fruits to market more quickly in both Florida and California. However, cross country trains also opened the possibility of moving California's fresh fruit to the East Coast, competing with Florida fruit. Due to the drier California climate, the color and physical appearance of its fruit were generally better than Florida fruit. This posed a competitive problem for Florida growers because consumers associated better peel appearance with better tasting fruit. Nevertheless, Florida reached a production of 5 million boxes[1] of citrus fruits by the 1893/94 season[2], leading California's production of 2.2 million boxes[3].

Unfortunately for Florida, there was a series of very severe freezes in the late 1890s which devastated citrus in Florida. Freezes in Florida occurred occasionally and cool weather, in short bursts, actually helped to produce good tasting fruit. However, when temperatures fell into the low 20s °F for more than a few hours, the citrus trees would begin to die. These very low temperatures were rare in Florida, with the last major freeze happening in 1835[4, pg. 3]. However, on the morning

---

[1]Citrus fruits are measured in boxes. A standard box of oranges is 90 pounds. Other citrus varieties use slightly different weights.

[2]The citrus season in Florida runs from approximately October to June.

of December 29, 1894 temperatures dropped to 14°F in Jacksonville, 18°F in Orlando and 19°F in Tampa, barely warming above freezing the entire day. The next morning it dropped to 23°F in Tampa[4, pg. 30-37]. Combined with another severe freeze in February 1895, many trees were killed. By the 1900/01 season, Florida's citrus production had fallen to 0.35 million boxes, while California's production stood at 9.2 million. Florida would take about a decade to recover, and California's production would continue surpassing Florida for the next four decades[3].

Fresh Fruit

Up until the 1940s, the fresh fruit business dominated the Florida citrus industry. Growing the fruit was relatively easy; the difficulty lay in marketing it profitably. Professional growers planted large groves and set up packing houses to select the best fruit for shipping out of state for sale. Joining these larger growers were investors, both local and out-of-state. As a business investment, a commercial grove was relatively easy to set up. Appropriate land was acquired and decisions on fruit variety were made. Then budded rootstocks would be purchased from citrus nurseries and planted. A grove care-taking company would be hired for routine care and after about five years, fruit harvest could begin. Harvest companies were hired to manage the picking and selling of the fruit. The caretakers, harvesting companies and packing houses they used might be independent, but were often affiliated with larger professional growers. Alternatively, investors could simply purchase existing groves. In good years, it could be quite profitable. In bad years, the owner might decide to cut back on care-taking or harvesting expenses. The major risk was the very occasional freeze, which still left the land available for replanting or sale. Over time, many Floridians invested in citrus groves, typically ranging in size from 1 to 50 acres. Joining them were out-of-state investors, many of whom first saw citrus groves while vacationing in Florida. A 1930 study by Hawthorne and Turlington reported on the widespread nature of out-of-state growers[5].

The fruit supply was largely governed by the number of trees planted, varieties selected and weather, with a half-decade lag between planting and initial fruit harvest. Citrus in Florida matured between October and May, with different time frames for each variety. The exact dates

10 2. THE FLORIDA CITRUS INDUSTRY 1900–1940

varied year-to-year due to weather conditions. By variety, the fruit had to be harvested, assessed for suitability, packed, and shipped to points of sale up North. It was not possible to store fruit for more than a few weeks[3]. Fruit needed to move quickly to market or risk being lost. Distribution networks and marketing efforts had to respond promptly to get fruit to customers and advertise product availability. In good years with high fruit demand and prices, the business could be very profitable. In bad years, prices were low or little fruit was suitable for the fresh market.

As in many agricultural products, Florida citrus growers were both competitors and collaborators. Growing the overall market demand benefited everyone, but it relied on communal behavior to set up and share low-cost distribution networks, coordinate advertising efforts, and select only superior fruit for sale. Putting too much fruit on the market drove down returns for everyone. Furthermore, in a seasonal fruit market, the first fruit to market each season had a natural advantage. If immature fruit was delivered for sale, a particular grower might reap a windfall at the expense of unhappy customers, depressing future demand. Another constant stress for all Florida fruit sellers was oversupply, as new groves were planted following good economic years, increasing the future fruit supply. Without effort and investment, future demand was unlikely to match growing supply. It was a constant struggle for Florida growers to balance these cooperative and competitive stresses.

California had attempted to address this problem early by forming the Southern California Fruit Exchange as a cooperative of citrus growers in 1893. In 1905, it was renamed the California Fruit Growers Exchange and represented 45% of the fruit in California. By working together, the growers could create enforceable rules and collaborate to establish product standards, brand names, and advertising. The California Fruit Growers Exchange grew extremely powerful throughout this time period and acted very effectively to market California citrus products. By 1933, it was controlling about 85% of the citrus grown in California[6, pg. 2]. In many ways the Exchange was on the leading edge of what agricultural coop organizations could accomplish. The organization was renamed Sunkist Growers Inc. in 1952 and remains

---

[3]Lemons and limes could be stored longer than oranges, grapefruits and tangerines.

dominant in California even today. The history of the organization, its structure, and activities are fascinating, but beyond the scope of this work[7, 8, 9, 6]. However, it formed a very potent competitor for Florida's citrus industry.

Florida's growers recognized the advantages of such collaborative structures and attempted to create them, but the diversity of growers and their interests often pulled them apart. One of the most important early efforts was called the Florida Citrus Exchange (FCE), created from a coalition of growers in 1909, modeled directly on the activities of the California Fruit Growers Exchange[1, pg. 1-5]. The FCE would become the largest agricultural cooperative in Florida, and its collaborative activities would strongly influence the development of the citrus byproducts industry as it sought profitable use of its excess fruit. However, unlike in California, the FCE would never represent more than 35–40% of the fresh fruit marketed in the state, which limited their effectiveness[10]. Partly as a result, the FCE and others collaborated to establish the Florida Citrus Commission (FCC) in 1935, a state-chartered entity with authority "for the stabilization and protection of the reputation of the Florida citrus fruits, on inspection and grading, all under the Commission of Agriculture of the State of Florida[1, pg. 144-149][11, 12, 13]." The FCC would likewise play a significant role in the success of frozen concentrated orange juice, as discussed in the following chapter.

In this competitive environment, Florida growers faced many of the struggles common to agricultural products: insects, diseases, maintaining optimal tree health, fruit transportation and marketing troubles, competing for consumer food choice, changing preferences for citrus varieties, and fruit oversupply. In any given season, one or two issues were often the main struggle, while others temporarily receded in importance. The overall success of the industry was remarkable. Florida grew from producing 6.4 million boxes of citrus fruit in the 1909/10 season to 44 million boxes in the 1939/40 season. It helped that there were no freezes that killed trees like in 1895 during this time. California experienced similar growth. One measure of the marketing success achieved for citrus in the US was summarized by Crist[14]. Between 1918 and 1948, total per capita consumption of fresh fruits in the US changed little. However, citrus' share of the total rose substantially. Between 1918 and 1922, per capita citrus consumption was 24.0 pounds versus 51.3 pounds for apples. In 1944-48, citrus consumption had more than doubled to 57.6 pounds while apple consumption fell to 24.4 pounds.

As the Florida fresh fruit supply grew, so did the supply of excess or culled fruit which was unsuited for sale as fresh fruit. Not only did it represent lost profit, but disposal could also be a cost. Broader consumer exposure to fresh citrus was generating increased awareness and interest. Capitalizing on this exposure were entrepreneurs looking to generate value from the excess fruit. And it was from these efforts that citrus flavoring products eventually arose in Florida.

Processed Citrus Products

At the turn of the century, the main known byproducts produced from citrus fruits were raw and concentrated juice, essential oils from the peel, dried and candied peels, citric acid, pectin isolated from the peel, and citrate of lime. The latter product was a salt of citric acid produced by reacting the acid with the alkaline chemical lime. Of all these, the production of juice and essential oils proved most important to the development of the citrus flavor industry. Developments on both fronts, especially in Florida, are discussed here. For information on the early California byproduct industry the reader is referred to Will[15] or McNair[16].

In 1911, the Florida Citrus Exchange (FCE) financed a fellowship at the Mellon Institute of Pittsburgh to investigate possible commercial citrus byproducts. The bulk of this fruit in Florida was either oranges or grapefruits. The research project was carried out by F. Alex McDermott and lasted from 1911 to 1913. The results were apparently reported to the research sponsors, but were made more widely available in publications in 1916 and 1917[17, 18]. The project focused on four main fruit byproducts: juice, essential oils, fermentation of citrus juices to produce ethanol, and recovery of citric acid from the fruit. McDermott's work on juice targeted a bottled juice that could be stored without refrigeration for up to two years. This required pasteurization conditions that essentially sterilized the juice to prevent spoiling. However, in orange and grapefruit juice, this imparted a cooked off-flavor and caused the juice to darken after a few weeks. Additionally, the pulp and cloud of the juice fell out under storage, collecting in the bottom of the container. McDermott thought a clarified juice was best for commercial purposes and proposed removing as much pulp and cloud as possible before bottling, to minimize pulp settling. Through experimentation, he identified de-aeration as important to slow discoloration and found the lowest-temperature pasteurization conditions that seemed to sterilize the juice and produce minimal cooked off-notes[4]. Under these conditions, he reported being able to store juice for up to 18 months while retaining acceptable appearance and flavor. McDermott also discussed the importance of peel oil to the flavor of bottled juice. Leaving the peel on the fruit when juicing resulted in too much peel oil, causing additional off-flavors during storage. Conversely, removing the peel before juicing resulted in a bland product lacking flavor. Ultimately, for orange juice, he found that leaving the peel on about 10% of the fruit produced the best stored juice. However, for grapefruit, even a small amount of peel imparted very bitter notes, so he added some orange peel to the grapefruit during squeezing.

Over the next decade, commercial experimentation with glass-bottled ready-to-drink juice made progress. Despite McDermott's optimism, many practical problems had to be solved. First, pasteurization was accomplished after filling and sealing the bottles by immersion in hot water or steam. It was easy to over heat juice near the bottle walls, while under heating the interior juice. Overcooked juice suffered flavor deterioration and discoloration, while under-pasteurized juice risked spoiling and lost inventory. Furthermore, clarified juice was difficult to produce in commercial quantities and it was unclear whether consumers truly preferred it. Without clarification, pulp quickly settled in the bottled. Additionally, since no automatic juicing machine existed at this time, juicing was a mechanically-assisted manual process. Even with the best efforts, bottled juice neither looked or tasted like the fresh juice consumers could prepare themselves. Furthermore, the manufacturing cost of juicing the fruit, packaging and distribution was high. Nevertheless, some saw a market for ready-to-drink, easy-to-store bottled juices that could be consumed year-round either alone or as mixers with other ingredients in soft- or alcoholic-drinks. The earliest efforts focused mostly on grapefruit juice as it seemed to have less flavor deterioration under storage than orange juice.

Three authors have documented early Florida efforts to commercialize citrus juices. D. E. Timmons, a University of Florida agricultural

---

[4]McDermott recommended 63–65°C for 15–30 minutes, pasteurizing the juice after de-aeration in the bottle.

economist, provided a detailed account in a 1950 publication[19], drawing from information collected from citrus industry leaders. One of his sources was Seth Walker, a young chemist who worked at the Florida Agricultural Experimental Station in Gainesville, FL from 1912 to 1917 and went on to have a long career in citrus processing. Walker wrote a number of contemporaneous articles and later recorded a summarized account of early industry activity in a 1957 publication[20]. Additionally, a 1960 publication by Jack Shoemaker from the State of Florida Department of Agriculture titled "Commerical Canning in Florida" adds some additional facts[21]. These sources are supplemented here by other contemporary records.

In 1914, Claude E. Street was reported to be the first to experiment with commercially bottling grapefruit juice in glass bottles at a small facility in Avon Park, FL. Street's son, quoted by Timmons, provides a vivid description of the early work:

> The first experimental laboratory was established at Avon Park and constructed at the edge of a grapefruit grove during the late months of 1913. In this small building Mr. Claude E. Street conducted his experiments and produced a small amount of grapefruit juice during the winter of 1913 and throughout the year 1914. The initial work embodied experiments and study of methods to preserve the juice of the grapefruit in glass containers. Home preserving practices and kitchen methods were utilized as the basis for making a start. Laboratory technique and commercial practices were applied and studied.
>
> The problem of securing laboratory and semi-commercial equipment to be adapted to specific uses required endless effort. A small boiler was purchased from an old settler who was selling the remains of a sugar mill. Crude steam kettles with other small equipment were found and purchased at an abandoned jelly plant near Lake Panasoffkee ... Florida was farther removed from northern markets and central supply houses then, and money was less plentiful in those early days. Hence, the art of economy was practiced extensively.
>
> The grapefruit juice was pressed out by hand in this first laboratory and sealed in clear glass bottles. Crown caps were

used to close the bottles and were applied in the usual manner. Various methods were used of applying heat to sterilize the product and assure its keeping qualities. Batch after batch was prepared and samples were distributed among many of the town's people. Though [sic] the method of trial and error it was hoped that the work would succeed.

The juice was placed on sale in drug stores and over grocery counters in quart and pint bottles. The product was packed similar to grape juice and offered at the same price. Shipments were finally made by express to retail stores in nearby southern cities[19, pg. 8-9].

The effort was successful enough that Street (the father) built a small facility in Haines City, FL in 1915, bringing in outside investors in 1917 to construct a new building. The company was called Florida Fruit Products Company in 1915 [19, pg. 9][20] and perhaps later renamed Florida Grapefruit Juice Company according to Timmons[19, pg. 3]. Seth Walker was hired by Street in 1917 as his chief chemist and Walker reported that the process involved hand-squeezing the mechanically-sliced fruit on motor-driven reamers and pasteurizing the bottled juice in a steam-chamber for 30 minutes[20][19, pg. 9-10]. Street's son goes on to describe this operation:

> Grapefruit juice at the new plant was marketed under the brand name "Streets". The product was packed in bottles ranging in size from four ounce to forty-eight ounce. The two most popular sizes were pint bottles packed twenty-four to the case and the quart size packed twelve to the case. The juice was sold at the same standard price as Welch's grape juice.
>
> The Southern Drug Company of which Mr. F. C. Groover[5] was part owner handled the distribution of "Streets" grapefruit juice within the State of Florida and nearby markets.... Fifteen thousand cases of grapefruit juice were produced and marketed during the first operating season[19, pg. 10].

Street's son reported that his father was close friends with Dr. Paul R. Welch, the founder of Welch Grape Juice Company who manufac-

---

[5]Groover was an investor in Street's juice company.

tured grape juice in Poughkeepsie, NY. Welch was on hand in Haines City during the winter of 1915/16 helping Street[19, pg. 10]. Unfortunately, a freeze in late 1917 led to a supply of freeze-damaged fruit that the company owners decided to process anyway. The resulting bottled juice was quite inferior in quality, leading to unhappy customers. In 1918 following the turmoil, the company dissolved[20]. Following the turmoil, Street relocated to Bradenton, FL and turned his attention to canning citrus products in tin cans[21, pg. 33-34].

Another interesting and innovative person was Charles E. Langley who set up a company in Auburndale, FL named Dixie Canning and Preserving Company in late 1914[22]. Langley had been interested in utilizing culled citrus fruits that he had seen thrown away for a number of years. After spending two years in Minneapolis working with candy and syrup manufacturers, he developed a process to preserve grapefruit fruit or juice in enameled tin cans. The process used a proprietary preservative mixture added to the fruit or juice, followed by canning and a heat treatment in boiling water. Langley claimed the canned product lasted up to a year with little or no change in color or flavor. It is also noteworthy that Langley was the first to experiment with tin cans rather than glass bottles. He set up his company to commercialize the process and soon was offering products like *Langley's Special Processed Grapefruit, Langley's Special Fruit Salad, Grapefruit Extract for Flavoring Purposes, Guava Jelly, Orange Jelly, Orange Marmalade* and *Guava Marmalade*[23, 20][19, pg. 3]. Despite his claims that he could successfully can grapefruit juice, it seems that this product was not a priority for him. It is not clear how successful he was commercially. The company ran into legal trouble by 1918 and doesn't appear to have any activity after that[24, 25].

Another canning company called the Collins Canning Company announced a new plant in Lakeland, FL in 1917. Among other fruit products, they started manufacturing bottled clarified grapefruit juice[19, pg. 3][26, 27]. By March 1918 they were in full operation manufacturing 4000 quarts/day and selling the product under the *Southland* brand[28]. Walker described "the juice was more the color of coffee than of grapefruit juice, and tasted about as dark as it looked[20]." Shoemaker describes Collins producing a bottled, carbonated grapefruit juice perhaps as early as 1914, which was initially marketed locally and later out of state. It is not clear when his company began operations. Collins was a retired St. Paul printing-company owner with ties to the canning industry up north, who had moved to Lakeland. Here he saw an opportunity with the discarded fruit. The company name changed around 1922 to Southland Citrus Products Company [19, 29, pg. 5]. Unfortunately, the venture failed in 1924 after an ill-timed expansion and over committing to fruit purchases[21, pg. 32-33].

At this early time, there was still much to learn about fruit quality and the role of oxygen, enzyme activity, oil content, packaging interactions, and pasteurization techniques for producing an acceptable bottled juice product. There remained considerable debate regarding whether the best commercial product was clarified or cloudy like natural juice[30, 31]. And discoloration due to darkening remained a significant problem in either case. Far more commercial success was achieved in canned grapefruit segments during the 1920s which became a very successful product. Canned fruit soon became the primary use for excess grapefruit in Florida. More information on the early canned fruit industry can be found in references[32, 20, 19, 21].

Entrepreneurs continued their efforts to successfully market citrus juice. Ralph Polk Sr., the son of an early Indiana canner, attempted to bottle grapefruit juice in Miami, FL in 1920 before giving up due to discoloration and sedimentation problems and switching to canning grapefruit segments[21, pg. 33][19, pg. 6]. Polk would continue on with a long career in citrus canning. Walker describes the first commercial-scale packaging of citrus juice in tin cans (rather than glass) in Florida in 1923 at the Eagle Lake Cannery in Eagle Lake, FL[6]. Tin cans were cheaper and lighter than glass and shipped more efficiently, but the early general opinion was that the citric acid content of citrus juices would cause a metallic flavor from the can. This problem turned out to be less serious than first thought. The Eagle Lake Cannery was owned by the Florida Citrus Exchange (FCE) and their product was distributed locally to soda fountains[20]. Walker also describes a company he started himself in 1926 in Tampa to juice oranges inside a chilled industrial warehouse and distribute the fresh juice to nearby hotels and restaurants[20]. The idea of entrepreneurs buying fresh fruit around big cities to prepare fresh juice for local distribution was certainly not new. Timmons reports that another businessman Francis (Frank) Burkart of Eustis, FL claimed to commercially package the first shelf-stable canned

---

[6]Shoemaker states Street actually first canned grapefruit juice in 1921[21, pg. 33-34].

orange juice in Florida in 1924[19, pg. 5]. Burkart later filed a patent on his process which included calcium hydroxide (lime) as an ingredient in 1931[33]. J. Adams Bruce, who incorporated Bruce's Juices in 1928, was also involved in early juice production. During the course of a lawsuit in the 1950s, Bruce claimed to be selling citrus juice in milk bottles to customers in 1926[34]. Timmons reports that the company was bottling grapefruit juice in 1925 and canning orange juice in 1929[19, pg. 5]. Timmons further mentions that the Dr. P. Phillips Company in Orlando, FL was canning orange juice in the late 1920s.

Juice Innovations in the 1930s

By far the largest market for Florida citrus growers remained in fresh fruit sales but canned products were now well established. During the 1920s, orange fruit production in Florida was fairly stable averaging 10.2 million boxes while grapefruit increased from 5.8 million boxes in the 1920/21 season to 15.8 million boxes in the 1930/31 season[35]. Processed grapefruit had come to utilize 18% of the Florida crop in 1930/31 up from less than 1% in 1921/22[19, pg. 20]. Most of this was due to canned grapefruit segments, and to a smaller degree canned juice.

In December 1931, 10 grapefruit canners formed the Florida Grapefruit Canners Association. Later it was called the Florida Canners Association and then the Florida Citrus Canners Association. This organization was based in Tampa, FL and represented the interests of these producers of canned grapefruit fruit segments and juice[21, pg. 51]. Soon membership would include canners of orange products. Two important Florida canned-juice producers in the early 1930s were the Eagle Lake Cannery, originally affiliated with the Florida Citrus Exchange and producing product under the *Seald-Sweet* brand, and the Hill Bros. cannery in Bartow, FL using the Dromedary brand. Florida was the largest producer of canned grapefruit juice. In contrast, California was a larger producer of canned orange juice. Some of the California canned juice companies included Bireley's operating in Hollywood, CA having started as a fresh orange juice company back in 1923[36, 37], Natural Foods Products Company and the Santa Barbara Juice Company, both of Orange, CA[38].

The juice from Florida grapefruits and oranges, as any good Florida grower would attest, was better than from California fruit despite any cosmetic deficiencies of the peels. And it was very well understood that much of the fruit sold as fresh in the US was ultimately consumed as juice rather than as fruit segments, either juiced in restaurants and hotels for on-site service by consumers themselves, or by small, local distributors of fresh juice in various population centers. As popular as fresh citrus juices were, the refrigerated transportation barriers and shelf-life problems associated with spoilage and pulp sedimentation were challenging. And the only alternative source of ready-to-drink citrus juices was canned juice which everyone acknowledged was a poor substitute due to its processed off-flavors, at least based upon the existing process technology[39]. It did not take much imagination for citrus industry insiders, entrepreneurs and researchers to imagine a large market for convenient, fresh-tasting orange or grapefruit juice if delivered economically to the consumer. The only question was how to overcome the production, distribution, and convenience problems with the current state of the art. Within this environment, there was considerable enthusiasm for experimentation. This enthusiasm would continue for the next 15 years ultimately leading to the frozen conentrated orange juice (FCOJ) industry after World War II.

Among the many parallel efforts underway in the mid-1930s was experimentation by the manufacturers themselves. Whether in collaboration, as with the Florida Grapefruit Canners Association, or as individual producers, they were strongly motivated to improve their products. Generally small organizations, they produced products of varying quality and regularly experimented in-house with fruit selection and processing techniques as they saw fit. Some large national food companies, like General Foods or Borden, also sensed a business opportunity and sponsored research to create suitable products for national distribution. Growers' organizations like the Florida Citrus Exchange (FCE) or the California Fruit Growers Exchange, seeking to capitalize on new outlets for their fruit, also funded research. The USDA had long sponsored research in citrus breeding and crop management with facilities in California and Florida. Some of this research focused on citrus byproducts and in recognition of the growing byproducts markets in Florida, the USDA established a byproducts research group in 1932 in Winter Haven, Florida. The team was initially led by Harry von Loesecke and would go on to form a very important center for citrus byproduct research[40, 41]. Finally, university staff participated at facilities like the University of Florida Citrus Experiment Station, established in 1920[42] or the University of Berkeley Fruit Products Laboratory[43, 44, 45]. Major areas of juice-related research included mechanical processing technologies, the chemistry of fresh citrus flavors and how off-notes were created by processing or under storage, the role of fruit picking, handling and juicing in the production of good-tasting juice, how to prevent color and cloud deterioration, the prevention of microbial spoilage, the usage of food additives such as sugar or sulfites to combat some of these problems, and understanding the effects of processing and storage on vitamin C which was understood as one of the healthy benefits of citrus juices. There was also interest in concentrating citrus juices as it could help solve storage and distribution problems.

Considerable progress was made on mechanical juice extractors. Extracting juice from oranges or grapefruits was a complex process and was done only inefficiently by hand. Although labor-intensive, hand-squeezing was quite effective at producing juice with the desired level of pulp and peel oil. Various mechanical tools had been invented to speed up the process, but complete automation posed challenges. First, the equipment had to manage the different fruit sizes which could vary considerably. Second, controlling the pressure applied during juicing was critical as excessive pressure lead to an excess of peel oil and other peel components mixing with the juice, while too little pressure risked lower juice yields. The optimal pressure depended on factors such as the fruit ripeness, variety and condition of the peel. Third, the equipment needed to be designed with hygiene in mind, as it came into direct contact with the sugary juice and could support bacterial growth and contaminate the juice if not cleaned properly. Finally, of course, speed and cost were critical. It was a complex problem to solve.

Prior to 1930 in Florida, fruit was juiced using simple mechanical squeezing. M. M. Slayton describes manually-operated presses used to squeeze manually-sliced grapefruit halves, as well as a hopper press where whole fruits were squeezed by a mechanical paddle. These devices were later replaced by the invention of what he called a "rotary press" which operated continuously. Fruit was automatically cut in half and placed flat side down on a perforated plate, with a top plunger pressing the fruit halves until most of the juice was extracted[19, pg. 11-13]. All of these methods required manual intervention and generally resulted in high peel oil content in the juice.

In the early 1930s, a rotating reamer-based method began to be adopted in Florida, having been developed in California[19, pg. 11-13]. While still requiring manual assistance, the rotating reamer significantly reduced the peel oil content in the juice, resulting in a superior quality juice. The origin of this technology is unclear. Manual table-top reamers had been available for some time. What was innovative was incorporating the reamer idea into a machine suitable for manufacturing. It is possible an early form of this device is described in the 1932 patent by Henry C. Stephens at the Natural Foods Products Company in California[46]. Another Californian who invented a mechanical juicer in the 1920s was Frank Bireley. Bireley started an orange juice company in 1923 which was very successful and grew throughout the 1930s[47]. Although he patented citrus juice extractor designs later in the 1950s[7], there is no record of his earlier design nor the type of juicing technology used at his company in the 1930s[36, 49, 50].

In 1930, Norval Merritt Faulds, the principal of Clearwater High School in Clearwater, FL, patented a new design for a mechanical juice extractor which became known as the Faulds extractor[19, pg 14-15]. It utilized two adjacent rotating drums, with female cups in one drum to hold fruit halves, and male dies in the adjacent drum. As the drums rotated, the male dies pressed against the fruit halves, extracting the juice. This extractor was introduced to the citrus industry in 1931 and received favorable press[51, 52]. A company called Automatic Citrus Juice Extractor Inc. was formed to market the invention. Faulds made several patented improvements between 1931 and 1933, but the company dissolved in 1933[53, 54, 55]. However, the design continued to be improved and manufactured by Bronson C. Skinner of Dunedin, FL. Skinner, who is discussed in the next chapter, was long associated with manufacturing citrus handling equipment. He, along with a partner named J. J. R. Bristow and an employee named Charles Walker, made further improvements during the 1930s and established a company called Rotary Juice Press Inc. in 1939 which marketed the very successful Rotary Juice Press Extractor. This fully automated citrus extractor design became very important as orange juice concentrate gained popularity in the late 1940s[56, 20, 57, 58, 59].

There were other competing designs. One that gained some popularity in Florida and Texas was called the Polk Juice Extractor invented

---

[7]The Bireley Citro-Mat extractor was being used in Texas and California in the late 1940s and early 1950s[48, pg. 58-60].

by Ralph Polk Sr. and Ralph Polk Jr. of Tampa, FL[19, pg. 14-15]. A patent for their design was filed in 1936[60]. It operated by quartering the fruit and pressing each quarter, held in a curved groove, using a rotating whisk-like structure to extract the juice without flexing or squeezing the peel. These inventors and others were searching for improvements in automation, speed, dependability, sanitation, and reduction in peel-associated off-flavors. Reducing unit processing costs was an important consideration in the growing canned juice market.

As practical and scientific knowledge expanded regarding the role of peel oil, oxygen and heat in off-flavor formation and color deterioration, other processing improvements were made to de-aerate and de-oil the juice before packaging. Additionally, the use of flash-pasteurization, which quickly heated the juice prior to canning followed by sealing and cooling, surpassed methods such as retort pasteurization, where the can is heated after sealing. Flash-pasteurizing gave much better heat control to the process, lowering the high-temperature exposure time for the juice. Lower pasteurization temperatures resulted in better-tasting juice. Furthermore, the importance of using good quality fruit rather than processing any available fruit was increasingly recognized.

The canned juice market increased substantially in volume throughout the 1930s as consumers enjoyed the improved products. In Florida, canned grapefruit juice production grew very rapidly from 1.5 million gallons in the 1930/31 season to 23.2 million gallons by the 1938/39 season[19, pg. 23]. Canned orange juice, either blended with grapefruit juice or by itself, also grew, although it remained well below grapefruit juice volume in Florida. In the 1930/31 season, only 0.23 million gallons of orange juice were reported to have been canned. By 1938/39, it had reached 3.0 million gallons[21, pg. 55]. During the 1935/36 season, only 1.3% of the Florida orange crop was used by processors but by 1939/40, it had increased to 15.6%[19, pg. 25],[35].

Citrus Oils and Extracts

By the turn of the 20th century, there was a well-developed citrus essential oil industry with the dominant production in citrus growing areas of Italy and to a lesser extent elsewhere around the Mediterranean and in the Caribbean. Lemon oil was particularly valuable for flavoring purposes, followed by orange. The process of oil collection from the fruit peels was largely manual, using scraping or squeezing techniques to collect the oils from the oil sacs located on the outer surface of the peels. It was a painstakingly slow process to collect industrial quantities. Whole families, including child labor, were commonly employed and production was generally concentrated in economically-poor areas[61, 62, 63]. Nevertheless, the oil collected from these manual operations, if good quality fruit were utilized, was excellent and far superior to any other known methods of collecting oil. Oil from the small scale producers in various locales was collected and sold in bulk quantities, making its way to essential oil dealers and industrial users. Essential oil dealers, in particular, developed expertise in identifying the best sources for particular citrus oils and screening for adulterated products. Citrus oil adulteration was a constant concern as some manufacturers used unscrupulous techniques to enhance oil inventories, including blending with petroleum fractions or adding lower-priced citrus oils to higher-priced oils.

Basic citrus oils had a variety of uses. They possessed very concentrated flavor and odor impact as ingredients, and could be stored and shipped at room temperature if protected against oxygen exposure. Common flavoring uses were as ingredients to beverages, candies, baked products, desserts and even medicines. Beverages and beverage syrups were perhaps the biggest category with lemon and orange flavored drinks popular. Two early examples of citrus-oil containing beverages in the US were *Golden Orangeade*[15] and *Orange Crush*[64, 65]. Less obviously, cola beverages also contained citrus oils. Beverage syrups were a concentrated mixture of sugar, flavoring ingredients that often included citrus oils, and food-acids like citric acid. They were intended to be mixed with water (carbonated or still) prior to consumption. These syrups were produced both for direct sale to consumers as well as for soda-fountains or bottlers. There were many other fragrance and perfume applications for citrus essential oils too. In addition to peel oils, dried or candied peels were also manufactured and exported. These peel products contained residual levels of the natural peel oils and consequently could be used as flavoring ingredients for certain products.

The largest users of essential oils were in Europe. There, companies had developed which specialized in handling natural flavor and fragrance ingredients, including citrus oils. These companies would later develop into the modern international flavor and fragrance industry. One of the largest was Schimmel & Co. headquartered near Leipzig, Germany. Schimmel's US subsidiary was established in NY in 1871 and called Fritzsche Brothers. Other important US companies included Dodge & Olcott, dating back to at least 1861, which imported cosmetics, essential oils, chemicals and drugs,[66] and Compagnie Morana, an essential oil dealer founded in New York in 1909[67, 68]. Certainly there were other similar companies operating in Europe and the US. In addition to sourcing and supplying raw citrus oils, the industry had developed a number of sophisticated processing techniques to make these oils more suitable for flavoring applications. Processing included concentration by vacuum distillation which removed water-insoluble terpene-hydrocarbons, and solvent extraction, most predominantly by mixtures of ethanol and water. These alcohol extracts were more water-soluble than raw citrus oils because the extraction process removed insoluble terpene and sesquiterpene hydrocarbons. Companies producing these processed citrus oils used proprietary versions of these basic processes. Other simpler processing methods also existed including dissolving small amounts of citrus oils in ethanol, or combining ethanol with dried or fresh citrus peels which also yielded a flavored extract once the peel was filtered out. Different versions of these flavoring products, covering a wide variety of product sophistication, went by names including folded oils, terpene-free oils, terpeneless oils, sesquiterpene-free oils, extracts and tinctures with little standardization in the names. In practice, citrus oil processing was done by the oil manufacturers, middlemen and the essential oil dealers. The part of the supply chain near the fruit growing regions could be especially fluid and experience rapid changes due to weather, fruit supply, and competition for resources. Gildemeister and Hoffman, associated with Schimmel & Co., published a three-volume compendium between 1900 and 1922 entitled "The Volatile Oils" describing the essential oil industry at the time[69, 70, 71]. Their first volume gives an excellent review of the history and current state of the industry and technology circa 1900, as well as information about citrus oil products available at the time.

In the early 1900s, the US imported nearly all of its citrus oils. Lemon oil was the largest, followed by orange. Import quantities for 1913 which was a typical year were 410,000 pounds of lemon oil and 80,000 pounds of orange oil[15, 16]. Pricing (in the US) was quite variable due mostly to supply issues[8], with prices ranging between $1

---

[8]World War 1 raged in Europe between 1914 and 1918 affecting Italy.

and $4 per pound for lemon oil between 1913 and 1918 and $1.32 to $3.60 per pound for sweet orange oil between 1905 and 1914[15, 72, 73]. These were valuable citrus byproducts; $1 in 1915 corresponds to approximately $17 inflation-adjusted dollars in 2000. Given the growing citrus industry in both California and Florida, there was a natural desire to commercialize citrus essential oils in both locations. However, there were barriers. First, the labor costs in the US were much higher than in traditional production areas, making manual oil recovery not economical. Instead, the focus was on finding technology to recover oil more efficiently. Second, the citrus fruit varieties grown in the US, and especially in Florida, were not well-known to existing essential oil markets. Florida produced mostly oranges and grapefruits. The oil from Florida oranges was not interchangeable with Mediterranean oranges. Grapefruit oil was essentially unknown. California was in a better situation, primarily growing lemons. Lemon peel oil from California lemons was not too different from Italian lemon oil. For these reasons, as well as the fact that the Florida citrus crop took a large production hit due to the freezes in the 1890s, oil recovery in California proceeded faster than in Florida.

R. T. Will provides a description of several citrus oil commercialization attempts in California starting around 1900[15]. Oil recovery was done in conjunction with manufacturing other fruit byproducts including marmalade, dried peel, and citric acid. Beginning with culled fruit, the oil was obtained either from the wet peel or the entire crushed fruit. Due to the absence of process technology to press the oil out of the peel without ending up with a water/oil emulsion, or to separate the oil from whole crushed fruit[9], the oil was recovered through steam distillation or solvent-extraction. In the distillation process, the oil-containing mash was boiled and the volatile portion of the oil was distilled. Upon condensation, the citrus oil was easily separated from the distilled water. In the solvent-extraction process, a water-insoluble hydrocarbon solvent was mixed with the mashed peels, dissolving the peel oil, and then the solvent was removed by distillation leaving the citrus oil behind. In both methods, the recovered citrus oils differed significantly in chemical and flavor properties from oils made by manual extraction methods, which were considered superior. The economics of these operations were very precarious and oil recovery alone could not be done

---

[9]Centrifuge technology had not yet advanced to do this commercially.

profitably. Will reported three main by-products factories having operated by 1916 in California with "about 5 other minor" plants. It is noteworthy that some of these plants were also distilling the citrus oils to make terpene distillates and "terpeneless" oils. Ethanol extractions and tinctures were also made from the oils and peels.

Meanwhile, McDermott's 1911 to 1913 study of citrus byproducts from Florida (discussed above) also considered both orange and grapefruit peel oils. McDermott studied solvent-extracted oil using petroleum ether, chloroform, carbon tetrachloride, and acetaldehyde, producing products similar to those in California described by Will. McDermott considered them too inferior to imported oils to be useful. He also studied mechanical oil expression via rollers or a screw press but found the oil yields too small. Finally, he explored distilling the oil away from ground peel by means of water or an ethanol/water mix and found his best results with water only but under reduced pressure. It produced a water-white distilled oil which he described as having good odor and flavor. The process, sometimes referred to as vacuum hydrodistillation, was not new. Because his distilled oils were colorless while the standard citrus peel oils were colored, McDermott suggested passing the oil through colored peel shavings to make it appear more like the imported product. All of these results were communicated broadly in Florida but there was no existing market for these citrus oils as they were too different from standard imported oils.

The first attempt to commercialize citrus oils in Florida seems to have begun in late 1911 with the formation of a company in Tampa called International Pure Fruit Juice & By-Products Co. The lead person was a man named Aristide W. Giampietro, who was an Italian-born physician and chemist most recently residing in Baltimore, MD[74, 75]. He may have had some past connection with the Bureau of Plant Industry of the Department of Agriculture in Washington, DC[76] which was involved in essential oil experimentation in Florida (discussed below). Giampietro formed the company in collaboration with a Tampa resident L. L. Trousdale, who was experienced in the brewing industry, along with other investors.

Giampietro had invented some techniques to preserve citrus juices and recover peel oil. The company plan was to utilize culled fruit in Florida to manufacture juices and other byproducts including peel oils, a "coffee substitute" made from orange peels, marmalade, jellies, and some extracted products from the peel and seeds that Giampietro thought had health benefits[77, 78, 76]. Giampietro's approach to extracting the peel oil was new, and he was issued two patents in 1914[79, 80]. The process used small, flexible, and sharp scraping blades that could be arranged in a semi-circle or full circle around the fruit, scraping away the outer peel and bursting open the oil cells on the peel surface. The oil was captured in sponges. Sponges were traditionally used to collect oil in Italy in some manual expression methods. Giampietro's invention was essentially a mechanically-assisted manual process for oil collection. The advantage is that Giampietro's oil was very similar to what traditional hand-expression yielded. Nevertheless, even in this case, the Florida orange oils had a somewhat different flavor profile than oranges grown elsewhere. And grapefruit oil was entirely new.

By April 1912, International Pure Fruit Juice & By-Products had a large facility in Tampa and was busy installing equipment with Giampietro running the facility and acting as spokesman[77, 78, 76]. However, it seems they were short on capital as Giampietro was publicly chiding the citizens of Tampa for not investing more in his enterprise[78]. In July 1912, he reached an agreement with new investors to move the operation to Largo, FL, combining the company with other fruit and vegetable operations to operate under a new name, Pure Fruit Products Company[81, 82]. There is no record of any commercial success with their citrus oils. Giampietro himself was no longer associated with the company by 1914, being involved in a lawsuit against the company[83]. He had a short but colorful life in Florida. In 1913, he received a number of death threats which he publicized from the "Black Hand," a mafia-style criminal organization operating in Tampa at the time[84]. In 1916, he was appointed to the Naval Consulting Board of the US Navy whose president was Thomas Edison. Giampietro was nominated in recognition of his scientific achievements including with citrus[85]. Unfortunately, he died a few months later at age 35 from pneumonia in Tampa[75].

A second, seemingly better financed attempt was made in late 1913 when a Boston, MA-based company called International Food Products set up facilities in Orlando, FL and Santa Ana, CA to process culled fruit. In Florida, they reached an agreement with the Florida Citrus Exchange for culled fruit and planned to make "marmalades, jellies, preserves, extracts, oils and other byproducts derived from citrus fruits[86]." In California, their focus was initially on lemon and citrate of lime, lemon peel, and lemon peel oil[87]. The company claimed to also have plants in Sicily and Cuba[88]. Similar to the Pure Fruit Products Company, it is unclear how successful the business was. After their first year, there is no evidence of ongoing commercial activity.

In December 1916, the Bureau of Plant Industry of the USDA published a Bulletin outlining the results of a detailed study of Florida sweet orange oil recovery using a new apparatus invented by a USDA scientist named S. C. Hood[72]. The USDA had established an experimental station in Florida around 1907 to look at essential oil production, primarily focused on camphor from the camphor tree. However, they were interested in other essential oils including spices and citrus[89]. Hood's invention was an 11 foot long rotating cylinder that acted as an automatic grater to remove the outer peel of citrus fruits that were conveyed along it. The finely-grated peel was collected and the peel oil was recovered either by vacuum steam distillation, or a mechanical press. In the latter case, an oil/water emulsion was obtained which had to be broken in a complex process involving heat, chemical additives and filtration. Nevertheless, the recovered pressed oil compared favorably in flavor, odor, color and physical properties (specific gravity, optical rotation, evaporative residue) with Italian hand-pressed oil. Importantly, Hood's oil met the US Pharmacopeia specifications for orange oil, which were based on imported oils. A detailed production study was made in Orlando, FL where the apparatus was able to peel 2 tons of oranges or 3.5 tons of grapefruits per hour, and they recovered 5 oz of pressed peel oil per 100 pounds of culled oranges. The USDA patent was made freely available and the Bulletin was obviously published to encourage commercial oil recovery. The information on Florida orange oil was supplemented by O. P. Huff, a University of Florida Master's chemistry student who published his thesis in June, 1917. He studied Florida sweet and sour oranges and lemons using Hood's method to express oils from the peels, and also studied leaf oils obtained by steam distillation, and solvent-extracted seed oils from the fruits[90]. In his introduction, he alludes to little or no commercial production of oils in Florida at that time, but recognizes the desire to commercialize these products. Interestingly, Huff addressed the problem of oil adulteration which he recognized as generally widespread, especially by turpentine addition or adding cheaper citrus oils to more expensive ones. He expected that his collection of physical and chemical data would aid in discriminating contaminated oils.

In late 1917, Warren Burns, who had been a vice-president in the

New York essential oil company Compagnie Morana, relocated to New Port Richey, FL, announcing his intention to experiment with growing citrus and flowers for the purpose of recovering valuable essential oils[91]. It doesn't appear he had any quick success in that venture, and he also became a prominent property developer and later served as mayor of New Port Richey[92]. However, he remained involved in the broader citrus industry until his death in 1941, and started a company called Florida Citrus Oils in 1929 which merged in 1931 with Bruce's Juices[93, 56, 94]. The activities of this company are unknown.

Interest in grapefruit peel oil, a new citrus oil completely unknown in Europe, was slow to develop. However, in 1918 Zoeller, based at Kansas State Agricultural College, published an academic study of grapefruit byproducts including the peel oil, bitter principles and pectin he obtained from fresh Florida grapefruits. He was motivated by the growing popularity of the fruit across America and the lack of published information. His study of the peel oil included physical and chemical properties useful for essential oil users[95].

The coffee and tea industry were regular purchasers of citrus oils. In a series of trade journal articles between 1918 and 1921 for this industry, US-produced citrus oils were described as mostly distilled and viewed as generally inferior to imported oils. While some distilled oils (especially orange) were described as good fresh, they were said to be less stable than the hand-expressed imported oils. Now it is known that hand- or mechanically-expressed oils contain natural non-volatile chemicals which impart little flavor or odor, but stabilize the chemical oxidation of the oil. When the essential oils were distilled, these important stabilizing chemicals were left behind. At that time, little was known about these non-volatile chemicals. Total US production of lemon oil at the time was described to be only around 5000 pounds and even less for orange oil, a very small fraction of annual oil imports for each oil[96, 73, 97]. A 1922 investigation of citrus byproduct manufacturers in Florida by Seth Walker reported no essential oil production at the time, although one manufacturer "intended" to produce orange oil soon[98]. A follow-up survey in 1924 in Florida reported no essential oil manufacturing that year[99].

In June 1923, a business named the Essential Oils Company of America announced it was moving its facility to Groveland, FL with the intention to collect essential oils from flowers and citrus[100]. The company relocated from Nashville, TN and had been named the American Extract and Vinegar Company[101]. In April 1924, they announced they were completing construction of their plant in Groveland and had hired two experienced chemists from Ohio. A June 1924 article describes the facility, which included 170 acres of planted flowers including roses, violets and orchids, as well as the process they used for collecting blossoms from blooming citrus trees to capture the fragrant oils from the blossoms[102]. The company was clearly intending to compete with traditional European-produced fragrance ingredients, which were much more valuable on a per-pound basis than citrus peel oils. After investing at least $250,000, in the end it was not successful. Years later it was commented that the Florida dew combined with the sun each morning would evaporate the valuable essential oils from the flowers, yielding a beautiful fragrance in the air, but destroying the commercial yield of any essential oils from the flowers[103]. However, one of the chemists brought to Florida in this project was J. J. R. Bristow who was involved in the juice extractor invention described above and would make a number of other important contributions to the citrus industry.

Throughout the 1920s in Florida, with the canned grapefruit segments business growing and considerable efforts invested in canned juices, there was a ready supply of leftover citrus peels. In June 1929, J. J. R. Bristow started a company in Tampa, FL called By-Products and Sales Co. along with Wilbur Pipkin and C. E. Lund[56, 104]. Bristow had become involved in the citrus industry after the Essential Oils of America effort failed. Pipkin was a Florida native who had worked in the citrus equipment industry[105]. He invented a machine to extract citrus peel oils from waste peels. Lund was a prominent Tampa businessman and probably provided the capital. Pipkin's invention used a rotating drum to press fresh peels against a screen, breaking the oil sacks and collecting the oil free of peel fragments. The oil produced was in every way comparable to hand-pressed oil and required no external additives as in Hood's method from 1916[106]. By March 1930, they were manufacturing orange and grapefruit oils in three grades. The highest grade was produced on the Pipkin machine. A lower grade was produced by vacuum steam distillation of citrus peels. The lowest grade was made by atmospheric pressure steam distillation of the peels. The lowest grade lacked a pleasant odor and was compared to turpentine, being used as a solvent for paints and enamels. The other two retained a pleasant citrus character. They claimed to have sold 3500 pounds of oil in their first year and were operating at three locations in

Florida: Tampa, Howey-in-the-Hills, and Lake Wales. They were also trying to commercialize the waste-peel as cattle feed and fertilizer[104]. Seth Walker in his 1958 article called the By-Products business the first successful commercialization of citrus oils in Florida[20]. They would remain in business together until 1936. Pipkin would go on to make a number of improvements in his oil-recovery machinery into the 1940s[107, pg. 22] and be inducted into the Polk County (FL) public schools Hall of Fame.

During the 1930s, Bristow and Pipkin would face competition. In 1930, The Tampa Tribune reported that California was producing about 35,000 pounds of citrus oils annually[104]. One producer was Earl Silzle of the eponymous Earl Silzle Company started around 1932 in Anaheim, CA. Silzle invented a screw-press based machine for recovering citrus oil from processed fruit peels that was also comparable to hand-expressed oil. By 1937, he was producing upwards of 40,000 pounds of oil per year[108]. It seems that Silzle may have partnered with the Florida Gold juice cannery in Lake Alfred at some point in the 1930s to recover peel oil in Florida. An anecdote was reported about Bristow and Silzle that illustrated a common problem with essential oil markets[103]. As Bristow and Silzle both optimized their processes and increased their oil production, they were soon overproducing product relative to market demand. Sitting on excess stock and afraid of driving the price down, they agreed to not call on each other's customers and hold a price floor at $3.50 per pound. The floor held for a few years but as other suppliers eventually figured out how to produce comparable oil and began to offer even small quantities to the market, both of Bristow and Silzle's customers started calling them saying they were being offered product at $3.00 per pound, then $2.50 per pound and so on until the price soon fell to $0.75 per pound. New producers were attracted by the high prices but the demand for these oils was only so large.

As the canned citrus juice and fruit market grew substantially through the 1930s, there were plenty of canneries with leftover peels and a desire for a share of the peel oil market. By the late 1930s, expressed and distilled peel oils were in routine production in Florida and California in quantities sufficient to meet market demand. Centrifuge technology had developed sufficiently to break the peel oil/water emulsion produced when peel was pressed, without the complex steps outlined earlier by Hood. These centrifuges were now in routine use and increased oil recovery yields[41]. Peel oil prices reached a natural level reflecting the cost of production with price swings mostly reflecting fruit supply issues. Peel oil sales alone could not justify the cost of culled fruit, so juice and fruit canners controlled the supply of available peel mainly driven by the economics of their canned products. Peel oil was now a byproduct of their more important operations.

For citrus byproducts in general, there was now a well-established industry located in both Florida and California producing a variety of products including essential oils, juices, canned fruit, candied peels, citric acid, pectin, marmalades and jellies. Chace, von Loesecke and Heid, three USDA scientists from California and Florida, published a good overview of the entire byproducts industry in November 1940, including the technology and best practices in use[109]. For the American consumer, the transition over the prior 40 years was striking. Outside of Florida or California in 1900, citrus products were expensive and relatively rare. But now, the former idea of a fresh orange as a special Christmas gift was long past. Fresh fruit was routinely available (in season) along with many domestically-produced, relatively inexpensive byproducts. Citrus-flavored beverages, generally incorporating citrus essential oils, were common as were citrus-scented soaps and fragrances. The average consumer's life now included regular experiences of citrus aromas and flavors.

The next significant advance would come following the invention of frozen concentrated orange juice, as described in the next chapter. The impact on the citrus industry in Florida will be extreme. However, it is important to recognize the spectacular progress already achieved in citrus oil commercialization. Ernest Guenther, an important commercial expert in the broader essential oils industry, wrote in 1948:

> We are witnessing here one of the most fascinating chapters in the history of the essential oil industry. From the drudgery of primitive hand pressing of citrus fruit as practiced not long ago... to the modern, most ingeniously constructed, high-capacity machinery employed in California and Florida, there has indeed been an enormous and quite rapid progress[62].

References

[1] James T. Hopkins. *Fifty Years of Citrus: The Florida Citrus Exchange 1909–1959*. Gainesville, FL: University of Florida Press, 1960.

[2] T. Frederick Davis. *A History of the Orange in Florida 1575 - 1900*. Copy in the UF Special Collections Library. 1937.

[3] A. F. Camp, Robert C. Evans, and L. G. MacDowell. *Citrus Industry of Florida*. Florida Department of Agriculture, Aug. 1955. URL: https://babel.hathitrust.org/cgi/pt?id=uc1.31210005341530&seq=1 (visited on 07/23/2024).

[4] John A. Attaway. *A History of Florida Citrus Freezes*. Florida Science Source, 1997. ISBN: 0-944961-03-7.

[5] H. W. Hawthorne and J. E. Turlington. *Absentee Ownership of Citrus Properties in Florida*. Bulletin 287. Gainesville, FL: University of Florida Agricultural Experiment Station, Dec. 1935.

[6] James A. Jacobs. *Cooperatives in the US Citrus Industry*. Rural Business and Cooperative Development Service Research Report 137. US Department of Agriculture, Dec. 1994.

[7] Nephtune Fogelberg and A. W. McKay. *The Citrus Industry and the California Fruit Growers Exchange System*. Circular No. 121. Farm Credit Administration, June 1940. URL: https://babel.hathitrust.org/cgi/pt?id=uc1.31210021706815&seq=17 (visited on 07/23/2024).

[8] William Wilson Cumberland. *Cooperative Marketing: Its Advantages as Exemplified in the California Fruit Growers Exchange*. Princeton University Press, 1917.

[9] Andrew William McKay and Wayne Mackenzie Stevens. *Organization and Development of a Cooperative Citrus-Fruit Marketing Agency*. Bulletin 1237. US Department of Agriculture, 1924.

[10] "Super Cooperative Markets Bulk of Fresh Fruit." In: *The Orlando Sentinel* (Mar. 31, 1968), p. G7.

[11] C. E. Stewart. "The Florida Citrus Commission and Its Work." In: *Proceedings of the Florida State Horticultural Society* Vol. 49 (1936), pp. 59–63.

[12] C. E. Stewart. "The Florida Citrus Commission and Its Work." In: *Proceedings of the Florida State Horticultural Society* Vol. 50 (1937), pp. 120–123.

[13] Barbara R. Draeger and Neil J. Hayes. "The Florida Citrus Code: The Root of Florida's Sunshine Tree." In: *Stetson Law Review* Vol. 11 (Issue 2 1982), pp. 317–330.

[14] Raymond Crist. "The Citrus Industry in Florida." In: *The American Journal of Economics and Sociology* Vol. 15 (Issue 1 Oct. 1955), pp. 1–12.

[15] R. T. Will. "Some Phases of the Citrus By-Products Industry in California." In: *The Journal of Industrial and Engineering Chemistry* Vol. 8 (Issue 1 1916), pp. 78–86.

[16] James Birtley McNair. "The Present Status of the Citrus By-Product Industry in California." Masters Thesis. University of California, Dec. 1917.

[17] F. Alex McDermott. "The Utilization of Cull Florida Citrus Fruits." In: *Journal of Industrial & Engineering Chemistry* Vol. 8 (Issue 2 Feb. 1, 1916), pp. 136–138.

[18] F. Alex McDermott and Seth S. Walker. *Utilization of Cull Citrus Fruits in Florida*. Bulletin 135. Gainesville, FL: University of Florida, Apr. 1917.

[19] D. E. Timmons. *Citrus Canning in Florida: Early History and Statistics*. Report AE Series 50-4. Gainesville, FL: Agricultural Extension Service, University of Florida, Jan. 31, 1950.

[20] Seth S. Walker. "Reminiscences of Early Work in Citrus Fruit Technology." In: *Proceedings of the Florida State Horticultural Society* Vol. 70 (1957), pp. 177–182.

[21] Jack Shoemaker. *Commerical Canning in Florida*. Bulletin 117. Florida Department of Agriculture, Aug. 1960. URL: https://ufdc.ufl.edu/UF00014580/00001/images (visited on 07/23/2024).

[22] "Grapefruit for Canning Purposes." In: *The Lakeland Evening Telegram* (Nov. 12, 1914), p. 4.

[23] E. A. Moreno. "Turning Waste Into Profit." In: *The Lakeland Evening Telegram* (Feb. 25, 1915), pp. 4, 8.

REFERENCES

[24] "Circuit Court Docket Begins March the 11th." In: *The Lakeland Evening Telegram* (Mar. 2, 1918), p. 8.

[25] "Circuit Court Docket Beginning Monday March 10th." In: *The Lakeland Evening Telegram* (Mar. 8, 1919), p. 6.

[26] "Collins Canning Company Breaks Ground For Fine Canning Factory Plant." In: *The Lakeland Evening Telegram* (Aug. 1, 1917), p. 5.

[27] "Lakeland to Have Big Canning Factory; Will be Great Asset." In: *The Lakeland Evening Telegram* (Nov. 1, 1917), p. 2.

[28] "Collins Canning Co. Now Going Full Swing Putting Up 'Southland Juice.'" In: *The Lakeland Evening Telegram* (Mar. 2, 1918), p. 5.

[29] "Directors of Southland Co. Are Optimistic." In: *The Lakeland Evening Telegram* (Jan. 25, 1922), p. 1.

[30] J. W. Sample. "Citrus Fruit By-Products." In: *Proceedings of the Florida State Horticultural Society* Vol. 33 (1920), pp. 140–141.

[31] Seth S. Walker. "Some Problems in the Preservation of Citrus Juices." In: *Proceedings of the Florida State Horticultural Society* Vol. 34 (1921), pp. 137–141.

[32] Seth S. Walker. "The Canning of Grapefruit." In: *Proceedings of the Florida State Horticultural Society* Vol. 36 (1923), pp. 84–90.

[33] Francis Burkart. "Preservation of Citrus Fruit Juices and Preserved Product." Pat. 1,958,232. United States Patent. May 8, 1934.

[34] *American Can Co. v. Bruce's Juices, Inc.* Legal Decision. Case: 187 F.2d 919 (5th Cir. 1951). United States Court of Appeals, Fifth Circuit, Mar. 30, 1951. URL: https://law.justia.com/cases/federal/appellate-courts/F2/187/919/440278/ (visited on 07/23/2024).

[35] *Florida Agricultural Statistics - Citrus Summary*. Florida Department of Agriculture, Jan. 1981.

[36] "Hollywood Plant Grows." In: *The Los Angeles Times* (June 28, 1936). Section 5, p. 3.

[37] "Advertisement for Bireley's." In: *The Oakland Tribune* (Nov. 18, 1937), p. D14.

[38] "Orange is One of the Oldest Cities in Orange County." In: *The Santa Ana Daily Register* (May 21, 1936), p. 19.

[39] Frank Kay Anderson. "Science Conquers Orange Juice Preservation." In: *The Citrus Industry* Vol. 13 (Issue 1 Jan. 1932), pp. 5, 20–22, 24.

[40] Harry W. von Loesecke. "Four Years of Citrus Products Research in Florida." In: *Proceedings of the Florida State Horticultural Society* Vol. 49 (1936), pp. 64–68.

[41] Harry W. von Loesecke. "The Chemist Looks at the Citrus Products Industry in Florida." In: *Proceedings of the Florida State Horticultural Society* Vol. 51 (1938), pp. 105–108.

[42] Tom Nordlie et al. *The 100-Year Journey of the UF/IFAS Citrus Research and Education Center.* UF/IFAS Communication Department, 2017.

[43] A. F. Camp. "Citrus Fruit Juices." In: *Proceedings of the Florida State Horticultural Society* Vol. 45 (1932), pp. 60–65.

[44] M. A. Joslyn. "The Problem of Preserving Orange Juice by Freezing." In: *Industrial and Engineering Chemistry* Vol. 24 (Issue 6 June 1, 1932), pp. 665–668.

[45] M. A. Joslyn and G . L. Marsh. "The Keeping Quality of Frozen Orange Juice." In: *Industrial and Engineering Chemistry* Vol. 26 (Issue 3 Mar. 1, 1934), pp. 295–299.

[46] H. C. Stephens. "Reamer for Citrus Fruits." Pat. 1,958,399. United States Patent. May 8, 1934.

[47] "Man Who Built Fortune From Juicer Dies." In: *Sacramento Bee* (Oct. 22, 1960), p. A4.

[48] Ernest Guenther. *The Essential Oils: History - Individual Essential Oils of the Plant Families Rutaceae and Labiatae.* Vol. 3. New York, NY: D. Van Nostrand Company, 1949.

[49] "Hollywood Firm to Build Texas Orange Juice Plant." In: *The Los Angeles Times* (Nov. 22, 1936), p. 3.

[50] The University Library at the California State University at Northridge has a collection of Bireley's records in the Stevenson (Glen W.) Collection. A search of these records in 2023 uncovered no information on their early juice extractors.

REFERENCES 37

[51] "Eyes of Citrus World Turn to Up-County Demonstration." In: *St. Petersburg Times* (June 12, 1931). Section 2, p. 8.

[52] "Fla. Company Makes New Automatic Juicer." In: *Orlando Sentinel* (July 5, 1931). Section: Farm & Grove, p. 6.

[53] N. M. Faulds. "Fruit Juice Extractor." Pat. 1,888,529. United States Patent. Nov. 22, 1932.

[54] N. M. Faulds. "Fruit Juice Extractor." Pat. 2,017,960. United States Patent. Oct. 22, 1935.

[55] N. M. Faulds. "Fruit Juice Extractor." Pat. 2,065,271. United States Patent. Dec. 22, 1936.

[56] *State of Florida Business Registration Database*. URL: https://dos.fl.gov/sunbiz/search/.

[57] B. C. Skinner and J. J. R. Bristow. "Juice Extracting Machine." Pat. 2,234,880. United States Patent. Mar. 11, 1941.

[58] Charles S. Walker, B. C. Skinner, and J. J. R. Bristow. "Means for Extracting Fruit Juice." Pat. 2,354,721. United States Patent. Aug. 1, 1944.

[59] David Walker. *Interview by Robert Kryger*. By Phone. Apr. 6, 2022.

[60] Ralph Polk and Ralph Polk Jr. "Method of Extracting Juices from Citrus Fruits and Other Similar Fruits." Pat. 2,309,328. Assignee: The Polk Development Company, Tampa, FL. United States Patent. Jan. 26, 1943.

[61] E. M. Chace. "The Manufacture of Oil of Lemon and Citrate of Lime in Sicily." In: *Journal of Industrial and Engineering Chemistry* Vol. 1 (Issue 1 Jan. 1, 1909), pp. 18–27.

[62] Ernest Guenther. "Citrus Oils and Their Method of Extraction." In: *Food Packer Magazine* (1948). (Sept.) pp. 33–35, (Oct.) pp. 31–33.

[63] Charles L. Latham. "Development of Orange-Oil Industry in Jamaica." In: *Simmon's Spice Mill* Vol. 41 (1918). (Mar.) pp. 346, 348, (Apr.) pp. 476, 478, 480.

[64] Wikipedia. *Crush (Soft Drink)*. URL: https://en.wikipedia.org/wiki/Crush_(soft_drink) (visited on 12/15/2023).

[65] *All About Crush.* URL: http://www.crushsoda.com/ (visited on 10/07/2011).

[66] Gabriel Sinki. "A Tribute to the Oldest American Flavor and Fragrance House." In: *Perfumer & Flavorist* Vol. 17 (Jan./Feb. 1992), pp. 37–39.

[67] Philip Goutell. *IFF.* URL: https://www.perfumeprojects.com/museum/marketers/IFF.shtml (visited on 12/31/2023).

[68] *International Flavors and Fragrance, Inc.* URL: https://www.encyclopedia.com/social-sciences-and-law/economics-business-and-labor/businesses-and-occupations/international-flavors-fragrances-inc (visited on 12/31/2023).

[69] E. Gildemeister and Fr. Hoffmann. *The Volatile Oils.* Trans. by Edward Kremers. 1st ed. Vol. 1. Milwaukee, WI: Pharmaceutical Review Publishing Company, 1900.

[70] E. Gildemeister and Fr. Hoffmann. *The Volatile Oils.* Trans. by Edward Kremers. 2nd ed. Vol. 2. New York, NY: John Wiley and Sons, 1916.

[71] E. Gildemeister and Fr. Hoffmann. *The Volatile Oils.* Trans. by Edward Kremers. 2nd ed. Vol. 3. New York, NY: John Wiley and Sons, 1922.

[72] S. C. Hood and G. A. Russell. *The Production of Sweet-Orange Oil and a New Machine for Peeling Citrus-Fruits.* Bulletin 399. US Department of Agriculture, Dec. 16, 2016.

[73] W. D. Meldrum. "Prices of Essential Oils and Flavoring Materials." In: *Simmon's Spice Mill* Vol. 43 (Feb. 1920), pp. 282–293.

[74] "Application Made to Governor For Charter - Has Large Capitalization." In: *Tampa Morning Tribune* (Oct. 25, 1911), p. 12.

[75] "Dr. A. W. Giampietro Dies From Pneumonia." In: *Tampa Morning Tribune* (Aug. 31, 1916), p. 5.

[76] "Saving The Vast Waste Annually in Orange 'Culls.'" In: *The Tampa Daily Times* (Apr. 20, 1912), p. 21.

[77] "Squeezes From Fruit Most Delicious Juice." In: *Tampa Morning Tribune* (Apr. 2, 1912), p. 4.

[78] "Pure Fruit Juices And Coffee From Oranges." In: *Tampa Daily Times* (Apr. 2, 1912), p. 8.

REFERENCES

[79] Aristide W. Giampietro. "Flexible Knife for the Extraction of Essential Oils and Removal of Peeling From Any Spherical Fruit." Pat. 1,116,881. United States Patent. Nov. 10, 1914.

[80] Aristide W. Giampietro. "Machine for Extracting Essential Oils and Removing Peeling from Citrus Fruits." Pat. 1,116,880. United States Patent. Nov. 10, 1914.

[81] "Fruit Juice Plant Will Move to Largo." In: *Tampa Morning Tribune* (July 27, 1912), p. 5.

[82] "Steps Taken to Utilize 'Natural Monopoly.'" In: *Tampa Morning Tribune* (Jan. 21, 1913), p. 12.

[83] "Giampietro vs. Tampa Gazozo Bottling Co." In: *Tampa Daily Times* (Mar. 4, 1914), p. 5.

[84] "Death Threats Made Against Giampietro." In: *Tampa Morning Tribune* (June 4, 1913), p. 4.

[85] "West Tampa." In: *Tampa Daily Times* (Apr. 29, 1916), p. 10.

[86] "Orlando Is To Have Important Industry." In: *Tampa Tribune* (Nov. 6, 1913), p. 5.

[87] "To Utilize Cull Lemons." In: *The Los Angles Times* (Jan. 7, 1914). Section 2, p. 10.

[88] "Waste Fruit Can Be Turned Into Fortunes." In: *The Burbank Review* (June 13, 1914), p. 2.

[89] Samuel C. Hood. "Essential Oil Farming in Florida." In: *Proceedings of the Florida State Horticultural Society* Vol. 25 (1912), pp. 216–223.

[90] O. P. Huff. "A Study of Essential Oils Occurring in the Different Organs and Products of the Citrus Group in Florida." Masters Thesis. Gainesville, FL: University of Florida, June 1917. URL: https://ufdc.ufl.edu/UF00055745/00001 (visited on 01/27/2021).

[91] "Waterworks for New Port Richey." In: *Tampa Tribune* (Nov. 11, 1917), p. B6.

[92] Jeff Miller. *History of Pasco County - New Port Richey*. URL: http://www.fivay.org/new_port_richey.html (visited on 01/02/2024).

[93] "Warren E. Burns, New Port Richey Pioneer Dies." In: *Tampa Tribune* (Feb. 8, 1941), p. 2.

[94] "Citrus Products Concerns Combine in Merger Here." In: *Tampa Tribune* (Dec. 20, 1931). Section 2, p. 4.

[95] Harper F. Zoeller. "Some Constituents of the American Grapefruit (Citrus Decumana)." In: *Journal of Industrial and Engineering Chemistry* Vol. 10 (Issue 5 May 1918), pp. 364–374.

[96] C. Beilstein. "Outlook For Lemon and Orange Oils and Vanilla Beans." In: *Simmon's Spice Mill* Vol. 41 (Aug. 1918), pp. 1015–1017.

[97] G. A. Russell. "American Essential Oils." In: *Simmons Spice Mill* Vol. 44 (Aug. 1921), pp. 1432–1435.

[98] Seth S. Walker. "The Present Status of Fruit Products Manufacture." In: *Proceedings of the Florida State Horticultural Society* Vol. 35 (1922), pp. 161–164.

[99] Milo R. Daughers. "A Survey of Citrus Products." In: *Proceedings of the Florida State Horticultural Society* Vol. 37 (1924), pp. 136–138.

[100] "Lake County - Development News Shows County Progress." In: *Tampa Morning Tribune* (June 4, 1923), p. 5.

[101] "Trade Notes." In: *American Perfumer and Essential Oil Review* Vol. 16 (Issue 10 Dec. 1921), p. 445.

[102] Harry P. Leonard. "Florida Features Essential Oil Industry." In: *American Druggist* (June 1924), p. 15.

[103] James B. Redd. "The Volatile Flavors of Orange Juice." In: ASME 1988 Citrus Engineering Conference. Lakeland, FL: American Society of Mechanical Engineers Digital Collection, Mar. 24, 1988, pp. 79–93.

[104] "New Plant Here Distilled Citrus Oils from Peels." In: *Tampa Tribune* (Mar. 2, 1930), p. B4.

[105] "Wilbur Pipkin, Developed Device For Extracting Juice." In: *St. Petersburg Times* (Feb. 26, 1985). Section: Clearwater Times Edition, p. 9.

REFERENCES

[106] Wilbur A. Pipkin. "Method of Extracting the Oily Materials from the Peels of Citrus Fruits." Pat. 1,798,555A. Assignee: Wilbur A. Pipkin. United States Patent. Mar. 31, 1931.

[107] Rudolph Hendrickson and J. W. Kesterson. *Citrus By-Products of Florida: Commercial Production Methods and Properties*. Bulletin 487. Gainesville, FL: University of Florida Agricultural Experiment Station, Dec. 1951.

[108] "Orange Peelings Produce Wealth." In: *The Anaheim Bulletin* (Aug. 20, 1937). Section 3, p. 8.

[109] E. M. Chace, H. W. von Loesecke, and J. L. Heid. *Citrus Fruit Products*. USDA Circular 577. United States Department of Agriculture, Nov. 1940.

3

The Invention of Frozen Concentrated OJ

"The secret of a success story as great as Florida has ever known."

—*The St. Petersburg Times*, 1941[1].

On November 9, 1948, the United States Patent Office issued a patent entitled "Method of Preparing Full-Flavored Fruit Juice Concentrates" to three Florida Citrus Commission (FCC) scientists working in a USDA laboratory in Winter Haven, FL: Dr. Louis MacDowell, Dr. Edwin Moore, and Cedric Atkins. The patent described a process of making orange juice concentrate with suitable flavor to be consumed as 100% orange juice when reconstituted with water. The patent was assigned to the US government, and royalty-free rights for the process were available to everyone. It was issued just as frozen orange juice demand was exploding, a new product developed in Florida only a few years prior. Over the next few decades, as the frozen orange juice concentrate (FCOJ) industry in Florida grew, the fame of the patent and these three scientists likewise grew. In fact, the story of the invention of frozen orange juice concentrate by government scientists in Florida, and the subsequent commercial success of the product, has achieved near legendary status. MacDowell was inducted into the Citrus Hall of Fame in 1975, and Moore and Atkins followed in 1983 in recognition of their patent and other work for the industry. All three were also inducted into the

Florida Agriculture Hall of Fame in 1986, in a ceremony which particularly highlighted their invention of FCOJ. MacDowell, in celebration of his retirement in 1968, received a mock check for $141,968,321 representing theoretical royalties he could have received from all of the FCOJ sold in Florida since the invention[2]. Even to the present, the popular press has regularly attributed the invention of FCOJ to them[3][4, pg. 7, 37, 124–126][5, pg. 117-118][6]. Academic-oriented literature has incorporated similar ideas[7, pg. 37-41][8].

The orange juice industry became an important part of the self-identity of Florida and the invention by non-commercial scientists fit well with the subsequent Department of Citrus's campaign to position Florida orange juice as a natural and healthy product of Florida's citrus growers. Department of Citrus advertising had to be generic in nature, and highlighting the contributions associated with any commercial entities would be difficult. The incredible commercial success of the product, perhaps surprisingly, also worked to reinforce the invention narrative as companies in the late 1940s and 50s were struggling to supply enough FCOJ to satisfy consumer demand. Everyone was enjoying the benefits of the success, including the fruit growers, processors, juice sellers, and scientists, and there was little economic reason to dispute who was responsible. The straightforward invention narrative soon became entrenched in the State. That these three scientists deserve recognition can't be disputed, but their role in the invention of this product is curious. None of the three had any special training or background in citrus. Just three years after being hired, they filed their famous patent. By this time, commercial manufacturers had been producing citrus concentrates in Florida for nearly 20 years. Scientific inventions rarely occur in an isolated fashion, and in the case of frozen orange juice concentrate, the FCC work took place subsequent to and simultaneous with other commercial researchers seeking to develop a successful consumer product. A careful study of the history of this invention illustrates the complex interchange of ideas between industry and non-commercial researchers that enabled this successful development, benefiting both the citrus industry, the State of Florida and consumers worldwide. It also illustrates the sort of environment where technical innovations flourish and public and private investments spawn new industries. And not least, it is a fascinating tale of human endeavor which proved absolutely critical to the later growth of the citrus flavor industry in Florida.

Juice Concentrates Prior to 1935

Prior to 1900, two main forms of fruit juice concentration were well known. One involved the simple boiling of juices in a heated vessel, similar to the process of making maple syrup, whereby water was removed and the sugar solids in the juice concentrated. The process was simple and effective, but high temperatures induced cooked off-flavors and discoloration to the concentrated juice. Some fruit juices tolerated this better than others. An improvement was to carry out the cooking process under some type of reduced atmospheric pressure using a vacuum pump. The vacuum lowered the boiling temperature of the fruit juice, consequently reducing the exposure to damaging heat. In the mid 1800s, the invention of milk condensates using a similar under-vacuum boiling process led to the widespread availability of milk evaporators[9]. One huge practical advantage of heat-concentrated milk was that it could be canned and stored at room temperature with a long shelf-life, being pasteurized by the heated concentration process. Concentrated fruit juices were also pasteurized if sufficient heat was applied and could also be stored for long periods without microbial spoilage if placed in sealed containers. However, fruit juices pasteurized and sealed in this way could still undergo color and flavor changes which could be very detrimental, especially if stored at room temperatures.

A variation on this process involved adding external sugar to the juice, either before or after heating, to reduce the amount of water that needed to be removed or increase the effective concentration of the mixture. This was similar to the process of making marmalade or jam and was particularly useful in the preparation of citrus concentrates for use in soft-drink mixtures or baking products where additional sugar in the final product was desirable. Concentrated lemon or lime juices, made with or without added sugar, were examples of early heat-based citrus concentrates. Due to the high citric acid content in these fruit juices, the concentrates were stable when stored at room temperature and could be used as flavoring additives or sources of citric acid. Orange juice concentrate was much more sensitive to heat-generated off-flavors than lemon or lime. A different type of "citrus concentrate" could be made with little or no juice by combining sugar, citric acid, and peel oils. R. T. Will gives some information on the very limited commercial production of these byproducts in California before 1915, including import data into the US for concentrated citrus juices in 1912/1913[10]. A 1913 newspaper article announcing a new venture to make lemon juice concentrate in California suggests there was little if any commercial manufacturing at that time[11]. McNair, writing in 1916, reported no commercial production of juice concentrates in California at that time[12]. In Florida, there is no evidence of any commercial citrus concentrate production up to this time.

The second known process was freeze concentration, whereby a fruit juice is partially frozen and the unfrozen liquid, reduced in sugar content by the chemistry of the freezing process, is decanted. The remaining frozen juice is thereby concentrated in sugar. Sequential thawing and partial re-freezing can be used to further concentrate the fruit juice. A time-consuming process, it was employed in some winter climates where barrelled fruit juice could be partially frozen outdoors and manually decanted. Unlike heat concentration, the resulting juice concentrate developed few off-flavors and underwent no heat discoloration. But the juice also was not pasteurized in the process. Due to the difficulties and cost, the process was not widely practiced on a commercial scale for fruit juice products.

Part of the research project carried out by F. Alex McDermott between 1911 to 1913 (see discussion pg. 12) investigated citrus concentrates[13]. Given a general lack of refrigeration at the time, a particular point of interest was in producing shelf-stable products. It was known that concentrated lemon juice was stable at room temperature, but lemons contained much more citric acid than oranges or grapefruits, which inhibited microbial growth. McDermott explored some approaches to make both orange and grapefruit juice concentrates as these were the most common fruits in Florida. He reported successfully concentrating these juices to 20% of their initial volume by heating to 104–122°F for an hour under a vacuum of 27.5 to 28" of Hg. He described his concentrate as having no major change in the juice color or objectionable flavor off-notes. Under these conditions, he observed that essentially all of the volatile flavor character of the juice was stripped in the process. Several problems were noted including that the resulting concentrated juice was not fully pasteurized and consequently could not be reliably stored at room temperature. Also, the presence of pulp in the starting juice caused significant problems and clarified juice worked much better for concentration.

It is important for modern readers who are familiar with good-tasting fruit juice concentrates to understand that what was deemed an acceptable flavor at the time would likely be intolerable to us. No one expected processed juices to taste like fresh juice - the standards of the time were very different; it merely had to be drinkable. In any case, compared to simply buying fresh fruit and making fresh orange or grapefruit juice there seemed to be few commercial advantages for a concentrate under these conditions. McDermott himself expressed little enthusiasm for his concentrate results.

Commercializing juice concentrate in Florida started slowly. Beyond a cryptic story recorded by Timmons and discussed below about a Winter Haven veterinarian making frozen orange juice concentrate in 1920, there is little evidence of citrus juice concentrates being produced in Florida before 1922. In contrast, several companies were producing these products by the early 1920s in California, including the California Crushed Fruit Company and the California Fruit Juice Company[14, 15]. In 1922, Walker reported on one unnamed company in Florida planning to make orange, grapefruit, and lime concentrate, but it must not have been successful[16]. Timmons reports an effort in 1924 by M. M. Slayton and Orville Hawkins to make a citrus concentrate without providing any details. At this time, Slayton was working for Fruit Products Company of Florida, a cannery in Winter Haven, FL[17, pg. 8, 12]. Walker reports on what he thinks was the first commercial production of a citrus concentrate in Florida in 1925. The effort took place at the Eagle Lake Cannery when C. E. Rodgers Company, a Detroit MI manufacturer of milk evaporators, set up their equipment to manufacture a citrus concentrate. Walker described the concentrate as tasting "quite good but being rather dark in color[18, pg. 181]." In a 1926 newspaper article describing the current state of the Florida citrus industry by the Florida Citrus Exchange president C. C. Commander, he specifically addresses the new development of citrus concentrates:

> still newer ... is the successful work of a local firm which has developed a citrus juice concentrate. This product loses none of the quality of the fresh fruit and, when diluted, preserves the appearance, taste and odor of the fresh fruit juice. This concentrate can be bottled or canned. In this form it is readily adaptable to economic handling, transportation and distribution[19].

It is not clear what local firm he is describing, but by the fall of 1926, a large grapefruit concentrate plant was being planned in Bartow, FL by the Hill Bros. company[20, 21]. Timmons further states that the company Bruce's Juices was making citrus concentrates in 1927[17, pg. 5] and newspaper accounts describe an orange concentrate plant being under construction in Sanford, FL, in the fall of 1927[22]. The product from this latter plant was to be distributed by Canada Dry Ginger Ale company under the name *Sumoro Orange*. Commander, obviously a cheerleader for the citrus industry, was overly optimistic in his characterization of the flavor of this citrus concentrate. They were not intended to be consumed as reconstituted 100% juice, but rather as ingredients in mixed beverages and soft-drinks and in various desserts and baked goods. Carbonated soft-drinks were prepared by combining carbonated water with flavored sugar syrups either for immediate consumption or to be bottled. Citrus versions of these products dated back at least to the early 1900s, consisting of sugar, citric acid, water, and flavors usually derived from citrus peel oils. Two early examples were Golden Orangeade[10] and Orange Crush[23, 24]. Replacing some portion of the sugar in these products with concentrated citrus juice yielded a more juice-like citrus beverage with natural cloudiness and pulp. The quality requirements for these concentrates as ingredients were much easier to achieve than for concentrate intended for a 100% juice product. In a soft-drink, this concentrate would be diluted with sugar and outside flavoring ingredients, either natural or artificial. Whatever the intended market, capital requirements for simple concentrating equipment were low, so there were few barriers to entry for entrepreneurs with access to fruit and a sales strategy for the concentrate.

Commander's 1926 article also highlighted the nutritional benefits of citrus juices and soft-drinks containing real citrus juices compared to other soft-drinks[19]. The importance of Vitamin C was well known at this time for the prevention of scurvy and the promotion of good health in general. Interestingly, the British Navy reported in 1929 on a test of foods which could be used to replace limes for sailors on their warships[25]. They tested products like tomato juice, germinated peas, dried orange juice, and orange juice concentrate of "American manufacture." The peas worked well to prevent scurvy, but the sailors "declared such food not fit for pigs." The report stated the orange juice concentrate was much preferred and kept the sailors healthy. It was also very compact in volume and stored well on ice for long-duration sea voyages. The concentrate was not produced purely from orange juice but was blended with up to 16% sugar during manufacturing.

There was considerable business instability in canned citrus and concentrate production at this time. Fruit availability and pricing were unpredictable, depending strongly on each season's crop as well as competition with the higher-return fresh fruit market. Weather and growing conditions, of course, were unpredictable. Likewise, the effects on consumer demand of the 1929 stock market crash and economic depression that followed were a shock. A business example illustrates the risks. In the summer of 1929, a new citrus canning plant was announced in Clearwater, FL, named the Dilpako Canning and Packing Company. The new company was organized by A. N. Dillard, a local citrus grower, and various partners from Detroit. Initially, they announced their intention to can grapefruit segments and orange and grapefruit juices[26]. A year later, they had completed a number of facility upgrades and were packing the above products along with fresh boxed fruit and were installing equipment to make orange and grapefruit juice concentrate for the Atlanta soft-drink company Nu Grape among others[27]. Later that season in March 1931, the Clearwater Sun reported that Dilpako shipped the "first solid carload of concentrated citrus juices in barrels ever shipped from the state[28][17, pg. 8]." Unfortunately, the firm failed that same year[29, 30]. A 1947 article attributed the failure to "the depression, high manufacturing costs, and inadequate quality[31]."

Despite the challenges, by the mid-1930s a number of concentrate producers existed in Florida and California taking advantage of excess fruit to produce citrus concentrates for manufacturing beverages. Regional juice-containing citrus soft-drinks were numerous around the country, and the brands sometimes manufactured the juice concentrate in-house. A 1936 article lists some of the following citrus beverage brands: Bireley, Cal-Ade, Dari-O, Dair-E, Green Spot, Lash, Mission, Valen'ju, and Virginia Dare[32]. The article lists the basic process used to make these beverages, starting with the beverage base:

> ...the orange juice is usually extracted on hand reamers, since machine pressing extracts too much oil from the rind. The extracted juice is screened, and color, sugar, and citric acid or lemon juice are added. This base is then deaerated ... After deaeration the product is flash pasteurized, then cooled ... and filled into special enamel-lined sanitary tin cans. The cans are immediately placed under a shower of cold water in order to cool the juice to cold-storage tempera-

tures... Some juices are vacuum concentrated after pasteurization to give a higher juice content or to permit greater dilution.

These juice-containing beverage bases were then shipped to locations for dilution and distribution or bottling (or it was done in-house). Bireley, based in Hollywood, CA, is particularly interesting. The company started in 1923 selling fresh orange juice when Frank Bireley invented a juicing machine. By the 1930s, they had juice plants in California and Texas and were manufacturing their own orange juice concentrate for a beverage known as Bireley's Orangeade. The company was very successful and apparently quite innovative and would later (1943) be acquired by General Foods[33].

Freeze Concentration and Frozen OJ

Although freeze concentration was a well-known process, it was not widely practiced, especially in a warm climate like Florida. Timmons quotes an early citrus pioneer named Ralph Polk Sr. claiming a Winter Haven, FL doctor (Dr. J. E. Crump) made commercial frozen citrus concentrate in an ice cream freezer in 1920[17, pg. 8]. From the historical record, it is not clear whether this concentrate was produced by standard heat-based techniques and then frozen for storage or serving, or whether the concentrate was produced by freeze concentration. It could have also been some kind of ice-cream blend. Polk states a larger effort to produce frozen citrus concentrate took place in Tampa in 1928 at a commercial freezer by Clyde Perry and "Mr. Judd," but the juice did not last upon storage more than 1 month so the project was abandoned[17, pg. 8]. There is a similar ambiguity regarding what exactly this product was.

The idea of freezing juice for storage was an obvious approach for preserving fresh juices with better flavor compared to a heat-treated, pasteurized canned juice. Commercial freezers had been around for some time by the late 1920s, and home refrigerators were becoming more common. In the mid 1920s, Clarence Birdseye had successfully pioneered freshly-frozen foods starting with seafood. In 1929, he sold his company, including a number of innovative patents, to a company which would become General Foods[34, 35]. Eager to expand the technology, General Foods tested a number of frozen products including orange juice in 1930, but found the frozen juice failed in test marketing to consumers[33, 36]. Around the same time, The Vero Beach Press Journal reported the production of 10 railroad carloads of frozen orange juice by the Tampa Union Terminal Company for shipment to Chicago[37]. This was a new product which was intended to be distributed "house-to-house in the same manner as milk is distributed." Whether these two descriptions were of the same test or unrelated, it is not clear. Similarly motivated, two large dairy companies, Borden Inc. and a subsidiary of National Dairy Products Corporation named National Juice Company, both conducted tests during the 1930/31 citrus season[1] in a commercial frozen warehouse in Tampa[18, 33, 31][17, pg 5]. The Florida Citrus Exchange was closely involved in the National Juice Company tests[38, pg. 121]. None of these efforts led to a successful product. Freezing the juice certainly improved the shelf-life, and the process introduced no cooked process-notes associated with pasteurization. Nor was there a color change in the juice. But there were a number of problems. First, the product required a frozen distribution chain, and once it reached consumers it took considerable time to thaw before consuming. Consumers did not like the inconvenience[39]. Second, the thawed juice still contained the natural active enzymes which caused the pulp to quickly settle to the bottom of the juice. As well, the natural yeasts and other microbes present in the starting juice largely survived the freezing process. And the juice could develop off-flavors under storage described as "stale and disagreeable[40, 41]" or "hay like[31]."

Despite these early commercial failures, some researchers remained excited about the prospects for frozen juice in contrast to heat-treated juice. M. A. Joslyn, working at the Fruit Products Laboratory at the University of California in Berkeley, studied the problem extensively and identified residual oxygen prior to freezing as an important component associated with off-flavors[40, 41]. He reported that off-flavors would begin forming after 2 months in frozen storage and become readily apparent by 6 months. Another problem was the pulp instability after thawing and that it occurred more quickly the longer the juice was stored frozen. This instability resulted from natural enzyme activity in the juice. Around the same time, George Sperti, director of the Basic Research Laboratory at the University of Cincinnati, in conjunction

---

[1] Walker states in his 1957 article that this took place in the 1931/32 season. This is likely an error[18].

with General Foods Corporation was applying ultraviolet light exposure to deactivate the problematic enzymes in orange juice[39]. And some interest remained in the related problem of freeze concentration. Chace and Poore working for the USDA in California reported on freeze concentration experiments in 1931[42]. Professor Arthur Stahl at the UF Citrus Experiment Station conducted a number of experiments in the mid-to-late 1930s on freeze concentration[17, 43, pg 8][5, pg. 117]. But it was clear that these products were not yet commercially ready.

B. C. Skinner and J. J. R. Bristow

Up until the early 1930s in both Florida and California, citrus concentrates were routinely produced in "vacuum pans," boiled in sealed metal vessels under reduced atmospheric pressure. Heat was applied either directly to the vessel walls or by means of internal pipes. Typical vacuums were on the order of 1 to 2" of Hg. The reduced pressure lowered the temperature at which the juice boiled, which reduced heat-induced off-flavors. As better vacuum pump technology became available, lowering the vacuum more seemed attractive, but in practice it didn't help much. In a vacuum pan, the juice exerted an effective pressure on itself when the liquid was more than a few inches deep. Even with a "perfect" vacuum, only the surface of the juice would have a really low boiling point, while the liquid underneath would still require a higher temperature to boil. Mixing the juice helped marginally. Complicating the process, the hotter you heated the vacuum pan, the faster the evaporation occurred. And since the flavor off-notes and color deterioration were both time and temperature dependent, a compromise had to be sought between higher applied temperatures and longer process times. In practice, the dominant locations of juice deterioration occurred at "hotspots" near the hottest surfaces in the evaporation vessels. A related problem involved pasteurization. If the juice concentrate was never heated hot enough to be pasteurized, it would require the addition of a chemical antimicrobial like sodium benzoate or sulfur dioxide for room temperature storage or long-term refrigerated storage. On the other hand, if the concentrate was heated hot enough to be completely pasteurized, there was the danger of heat-generated off-flavors. Each manufacturer had to choose their compromises based on their target customers.

Into this environment, a business partnership arose in Dunedin, FL between two technically-minded citrus businessmen that would change this technology. How and why their partnership formed is unknown, but they would go on to make a number of revolutionary improvements in citrus processing, including the rotary juice press (see pg. 21). Bronson C. Skinner was an entrepreneurial-minded engineer who had been working in citrus all his life. His father, Lee Bronson Skinner, moved from Wisconsin to Dunedin, FL, in 1883 and invested in citrus groves. By the early 1900s, he had invented a number of machines to wash, scrub, and sort the fruit that came from his groves. By 1909, he formed a company called Skinner Machinery Company to manufacture and sell this equipment to other grove owners. In 1911, his son Bronson (B. C.) took over management of the company[44]. B. C. was quite an adept engineer. He was born in 1889, graduated from Rollins College in Winter Park, FL, then continued for a graduate degree in mechanical engineering from Stevens Institute of Technology[45]. Between 1920 and 1930, he was awarded 13 patents on equipment associated with citrus fruit handling. His company supplied citrus packing houses around the state and was apparently quite successful. By the 1930s, B. C. Skinner was a recognized leader in the citrus industry in Florida and was relatively well-off financially.

Bristow's father, Louis L. Bristow, resided in Kentucky but came to Lakeland, FL in 1884 and created one of the first orange groves in Lakeland[46]. He did not permanently relocate to Florida but traveled back and forth from Kentucky. Unfortunately, his grove was destroyed in the severe freezes in the mid 1890s. His son, James Jefferson Ricker Bristow, was born in Kentucky in 1891 and graduated with a B.S. in chemical engineering from the Massachusetts Institute of Technology in 1914. In 1919, he started working at the Procter & Gamble Company researching new processes for soapmaking[47, 48]. It was at P&G he learned about chemical processing using the high-vacuum technology of the day as well as distillation. There also, he had quite a memorable experience with how large companies can stifle new technology in the interest of protecting their assets[48]. He resigned from P&G and relocated to Florida joining the Essential Oils Company of America in 1924 which lasted only a short time. In 1926, he was involved in a fresh orange juice plant in Tampa affiliated with Borden Inc.[49], and was further involved with some of the frozen juice experiments in the early 1930s[50, 47, 37]. In 1929, he had formed a company in Tampa named By-Products and Sales Company to market byproducts from the growing processed citrus industry, including peels and peel oil[51] (Bristow's earlier career is discussed in the prior chapter).

Bristow claimed much later that he became interested in concentrating citrus juices around 1930[46]. Given his location near Clearwater, he certainly could have been involved with the Dilpako concentrate project in 1929–1931 (described above); surely he was aware of it. In any case, in 1934–1935, he began experimenting with B. C. Skinner to derive a better quality citrus concentrate process. Over the next few years, using Skinner's machinery business as a base and probably Skinner's funding, they developed a juice evaporator based upon high vacuum ($< 0.35"$ Hg) evaporation using heated vertical metal tubes. Juice was sprayed on the inner surface near the top of the tubes and slid down the walls in thin films, boiling under high vacuum as it descended. Heat was applied to the exterior of the vertical metal tubes by means of flowing water. Because the juice film on the walls was thin, the juice would boil at very low temperatures; there was no thick pool of juice exerting pressure on itself like in a vacuum pan. Skinner and Bristow found they could easily achieve 10:1 concentration of juice in one pass through the device with applied heat at only 120°F[47]. In fact, it was easy to go "too far" and end up with orange "candy" as a solid that no longer flowed. This new concentration technology was revolutionary. It significantly reduced the time and temperature exposure of the concentrate to heat and consequently minimized cooked off-flavors and discoloration. While the juice still lost its volatile flavors in the process, some of these could be easily restored by adding back peel oil to the concentrate itself. The improvement over existing products was substantial. Bristow himself credited Skinner with the vertical-tube idea, and the evaporator design was later referred to as the "Skinner Falling-Film Evaporator." Over time, they would reduce the required applied heat to 80°F.[48, 52, 47, 53].

Skinner and Bristow recognized their product was not pasteurized and shelf-life was a concern. With extensive testing, they found that the high-sugar content of the 10:1 concentrated juice (likely above 65° Brix) stored at refrigerated temperatures below 45°F seemed to "keep indefinitely[48]."[2] In developing this new process technology and ob-

---

[2]Brix is a traditional measure of sugar content in fruit juices. Single-strength orange juice is around 10–12° Brix. Modern concentrate is often produced at 65° Brix and stored frozen, but will keep for extended periods under refrigeration just as Skinner and Bristow observed.

serving the improved concentrate quality as well as the ability to store the product for long periods, they recognized they had a marketable idea. In 1936, they formed Citrus Concentrates Inc. in Dunedin, FL to commercialize the product[54]. Scaling up from their single vertical tube, they designed and built a multi-tube commercial scale evaporator and began to can 10:1 orange juice concentrate for sale, shipped to points of sale under refrigeration. As with many new products, it took a few years to achieve much success. A use for this new product had to be developed beyond the lower-quality concentrates then in use mostly in soft-drinks. It is noteworthy that Skinner and Bristow did not patent their evaporator design, even though they patented other citrus handling equipment and processes around this time. For whatever reason, apparently they did not see a commercial value in patenting the design.

There is general agreement that despite earlier positive press on concentrates (see pg. 47), it was only with this new product produced by Bristow and Skinner had the citrus industry achieved a concentrate that approximated the flavor of real fresh juice when reconstituted[17, pg. 8]. Process off-flavors were substantially reduced, and resulting concentrate color was good. Although lacking the fresh juice notes stripped by the process, reconstituted juice made from the new concentrate had the proper sugar/acid balance and sweetness, the natural color, and all of the vitamins and minerals. And it tasted good. However, it was not yet a replacement for freshly-squeezed juice. Those missing natural flavor volatiles were too important.

Bristow and Skinner had other activities throughout the latter half of the 1930s in conjunction with their concentrate activities. Bristow remained active with his company By-Products and Sales Co. Skinner announced in 1936 that he was setting up a Citrus Fruit Laboratory[55] naming Dr. Rodney Harvey as the director, a former professor from the University of Minnesota. Harvey was well-known and had invented a process to speed the ripening of fruit via ethylene gas and another process to artificially color fruit rinds. Bristow was also named as affiliated with this laboratory. And Skinner and Bristow were both working on improving and marketing their automatic juicing equipment. It is unknown how important the concentrate business was to them at this time. But they were conducting long-term stability studies of canned concentrate they packed in 1936 along with the other activities of Citrus Concentrates Inc. Later in 1941, they would highlight the quality of their 5-year-old laboratory samples[1].

Amongst other problems, the Florida citrus industry was bedeviled by boom and bust cycles since the crop size each year was quite variable due to weather conditions but whenever a period of profitability arose, more trees could easily be planted. The overall trend was increasing crop sizes always threatening to overtake consumer demand. Citrus was also seasonal, being harvested during roughly a nine month period with shorter windows for specific varieties. Nor could fresh citrus be stored season-to-season to smooth out supply fluctuations. Only canned juice could be stored all year round, but this was expensive and the product tasted much worse than fresh juice in any case. Around 1937 or 1938, Bristow credits his friend Nelson Poynter with suggesting that their concentrate technology could potentially solve this problem[1, 53]. In years with excess fruit, the fruit could be juiced, concentrated and stored in bulk for seasons when fruit availability was down. Nelson Poynter was the publisher of the St. Petersburg Times, the major newspaper serving Pinellas County. In Bristow's description, Poynter's idea was not immediately accepted but over time Bristow and Skinner became enthused about the possibility. Of course, the whole idea depended on the flavor quality of the concentrated juice as well as the ability to store it long term.

Lend Lease and Citrus Concentrates Inc.

As World War II broke out in Europe in 1939, the US government created the Lend Lease Program to deliver critical aid to our allies. Concentrated orange juice was identified as a very efficient foodstuff which was compact, could be transported without refrigeration, and would deliver Vitamin C and healthy calories in a reasonably easy-to-prepare fashion. This was an immediate business opportunity for all US producers of citrus concentrates, but the size of the increased demand was daunting. Fortunately, there were government funds available for manufacturers to increase the supply of critical materials for the Lend Lease Program. Anyone who was even marginally involved in citrus juice and concentration could see the opportunities.

With Nelson Poytner's help, Citrus Concentrates secured a $1.1M loan to build a large new concentrate facility in Dunedin, FL, with $1.5M in guaranteed orders[46, 1]. The news was announced on the front page of the St. Petersburg Times on Dec. 13, 1941, coincidentally just days after the Pearl Harbor attack. Up to this time, Citrus Concentrates had shipped about 52,000 gallons of orange concentrate in gallon-sized cans. By the war's end in 1945, they will have shipped 28 million cans of concentrate[44]. However, Bristow described the quality of concentrate they produced for the Lend Lease Program as not as good as their best product[48]. The US government wanted an 8:1 concentration instead of 10:1 because it was easier for the final consumer to reconstitute with water for drinking. And the product had to be sterilized in the cans so it could be shipped and stored without refrigeration. This made the flavor worse, but for the Europeans receiving this aid any edible product was welcome. In the same front-page article in the St. Petersburg Times, Nelson Poynter's idea that this new concentrate could help stabilize citrus prices was prominently highlighted. As was the idea that European consumers, once introduced to orange juice and following the end of the war, could become a source of new customers for Florida's citrus juices. Meanwhile, for the rest of the war, Citrus Concentrates worked at maximum effort to deliver all this product.

In addition to Citrus Concentrates, other concentrate manufacturers in Florida and California also supplied the Lend Lease Program. In addition to concentrate, canned single-strength juice and other canned products were purchased for military and Lend Lease uses. By late 1942, all citrus canning and processing operations (in Florida at least) were requisitioned for government use[38, pg. 194]. At least two other Florida citrus canners started large concentrate operations during the war with government-related financing (see below). However, with the war's end in 1945, the Lend Lease contracts for juice concentrate were canceled. New markets would need to be developed for all of this capacity quickly after the war.

Already in the fall of 1944, the Florida Canners Association representing all the Florida producers of canned citrus segments, juices, and citrus concentrates were looking towards their future markets. The Association created a Florida Division of the "Joint Problems Board on Citrus Research" to work in collaboration with the Texas and California divisions to "stimulate and correlate research by federal, state and industry agencies." The president of the Problems Board was J. L. Held who was employed with Florida Citrus Canners Cooperative in Lake Wales[56], Bristow was the vice-president and Dr. L. G. MacDowell, affiliated with Florida Citrus Commission, was the secretary/treasurer. Seth Walker, who recorded some of the early industry history described earlier in this chapter, was also a member. MacDowell was quoted in newspaper reports as saying "we will concentrate on trying to find ways of improving production and processing in canning[57, 58, 59, 60]."

In May of 1945, Citrus Concentrates Inc. in conjunction with a Clearwater, FL company named Knight & Middleton conducted the first commercial test of frozen concentrated orange juice prepared by combining an 8 to 10x strength concentrate with fresh juice, resulting in a blended juice concentrate about 4x stronger than normal juice (or 48° Brix)[48, 33, 61]. Knight & Middleton was a new company started by Marvin Knight, a retired NY advertising executive, and Clyde Middleton, a Palatka, FL citrus grower. Interestingly, the then Director of Advertising for the Florida Citrus Commission, John Moscrip, also had a financial interest in Knight & Middleton[62]. The choice of a 4x concentration for the final product was very important. Citrus Concentrates had long made stronger concentrates which saved storage space and shipping weight. And a higher sugar content meant the products were more stable against microbial deterioration at refrigerated temperature. However, orange juice concentrate at this high sugar content was very viscous and hard to pour and dilute for consumption. It required intensive mixing by the customer. In contrast, a 4x concentrate required frozen storage, but it could be easily poured into a container and reconstituted with water. The product could be pulled from the freezer, diluted, and served within just a couple minutes. The second critical manufacturing step was including the fresh juice. If 4x concentrate was made just by concentration, most of the flavor volatiles would be stripped by the vacuum process. By mixing in the fresh juice, the flavor volatiles lost in the juice concentration process could be partially restored. This product was produced by Citrus Concentrates and shipped to Peoples Drug Stores in the Washington, DC area to be reconstituted back into single-strength orange juice as part of a consumer test. Knight & Middleton managed the test, labeling the product "Purest Brand Pure Frozen Orange Juice, Condensed." A representative of the FCC was present in Washington, DC to observe and the test was deemed very successful and widely publicized[63]. Over 50,000 gallons of juice were sold during this test[64]. The representation of reconstituted frozen orange juice concentrate as a viable alternative to freshly made orange juice, and superior to canned orange juice, received a very public debut. The race to reap the commercial benefits was underway.

The contemporary record of who was responsible for the new product is unclear. The product seems identical to the product outlined in the 1948 patent by MacDowell, Moore, and Atkins, which was not filed until August 8, 1945, after this test was completed. However, as discussed below, the impending patent's existence had been publicly discussed as early as November 1944. Moscrip's involvement, perhaps with FCC insider-information, is interesting. The 1944/45 annual report of the Florida Citrus Exchange gave credit for the origination of the product idea to Professor A. L. Stahl at the University of Florida[65, pg. 7]. Newspaper articles at the time highlight Knight & Middleton's formulation of the new product[61, 63]. Bristow writes in his 1951 article that the idea of adding fresh juice to their concentrate when reconstituting it was something they had recommended to their customers "from the beginning[48]." A much later obituary for Bristow written in 1965 stated the idea was Skinner's who had seen the process done at hospitals which were buying citrus concentrates to serve juice more easily to their patients[53]. Researchers at the FCC, whose patent was not granted until 1948, would later receive much of the credit. Unfortunately, however the successful product was created, further efforts to commercialize it by Skinner and Bristow were unexpectedly interrupted.

During the night of Aug. 27, 1945, tragedy struck Citrus Concentrates Inc. Their Dunedin plant went up in flames and was completely destroyed[66, 67, 68, 69]. The facility was insured, and a new plant was built on the same site and was operational by the fall of 1946[70]. Once back operational, Citrus Concentrates continued packaging a frozen orange juice concentrate under the "Sun-Filled" label[44].

Florida Citrus Commission Research

The Florida Citrus Commission had been established in 1935 by the State of Florida to provide formal support and regulation to the Florida citrus industry, which up to then was dominated by concerns associated with selling fresh fruit. The FCC was well-aware of the problematic boom/bust nature of the industry and could envision the growing citrus juice industry as beneficial to the entire industry. The explosive growth of capacity as a result of the Lend Lease Program was also on their minds. In 1942, they hired Dr. Louis G. MacDowell as their first Director of Research. The choice of MacDowell is interesting. He had earned his Ph.D. in chemistry from UF in 1936 and had worked most recently out of state for Carbide & Carbon Chemicals Corporation[71]. Neither his thesis research nor recent work had any connection to citrus. How and why he was hired for this position is unknown[3]. He hired two coworkers, Dr. Ed Moore and Cedric Donald Atkins. Moore had just earned his Ph.D. in food technology from Massachusetts State College[72]. Atkins had a Bachelor's degree from Florida Southern College and was hired part-time initially[73]. They began research, certainly at the direction of the FCC, on a number of problems associated with canning citrus and citrus juices. One area of interest was citrus juice concentrates.

FCC meeting notes show Dr. MacDowell asking the Commission for $5000 in November 1943 to support research on citrus concentrates[74]. The Florida Citrus Exchange's annual report after the 1943/44 season (probably written after May 1944) states that MacDowell and A. L. Stahl at UF were working on the development of frozen citrus concentrate[38, pg. 195]. A November 1944 article in the industry trade journal *The Citrus Industry* refers to the small FCC team completing two years of research in June 1944 in collaboration with the USDA group in Winter Haven on citrus byproducts. Their work had included studies comparing tin cans vs. bottles for 100% citrus juices, shelf life studies on canned 100% juices, new processes for the canning of tangerine juice, production of dried juice powders, and pectin isolation from grapefruit peels[75]. The article also describes their work on citrus concentrates, stating "work is in progress on comparisons of orange juice concentrates made at the temperatures and pressures used in commercial plants with those made at lower temperatures and pressures." The article further describes their interest in flavor and "keeping qualities" when stored including flavor, color, and Vitamin C. Their work on concentrate in particular had to be somewhat recent at the time of the article, as results were given in the article for much of the other research described, but not for the work on concentrates. Most interesting is the comment that "some ... concentrates have been diluted with various amounts of fresh orange juice before canning" and "a public service patent is being applied for to protect this process for public use." Thus, by November 1944, the existence of the future patent was in open discussion. By way

---

[3]In fact, minutes from FCC meetings in 1941 and 1942 show MacDowell was not the first choice for the position. Dr. F. G. Singleton, Industrial Fellow in the Mellon Institute of Industrial Research in Pittsburg, PA was first offered the position, but decided against accepting it.

of counterpoint, a slightly earlier and very detailed May 1943 article by J. L. Heid who worked at the USDA described best practices then in use for the production of citrus concentrates. The article makes no mention of adding fresh juice to citrus concentrates, although it describes all aspects of concentrate production from fruit selection to canning and storage[76]. In describing the current uses of citrus concentrates by consumers, Heid does mention that fresh juice was being used as an ingredient with or without concentrates in citrus soft-drink blends.

In a 1945 research paper by Moore and his FCC colleagues, as well as J. L. Heid now at the Florida Citrus Canners Cooperative but previously at the USDA, the FCC research on concentrate was described in more detail. During the 1944/45 season, they compared 3 to 4x concentrated orange juice with 5 to 8x concentrate when reconstituted back to single-strength with and without fresh juice, made detailed studies comparing concentrates produced at temperatures between 40 and 120°F, compared concentrates produced from various orange varieties, and explored the effects of pasteurizing either the starting juice before concentration or the diluting fresh juice[77]. They stated they started testing the 3 to 4x concentrate produced with fresh cutback juice a year earlier, presumably in 1944 sometime.

In any case, the US Patent entitled "Method for Preparing Full-Flavored Fruit Juice Concentrates" by MacDowell, Moore, and Atkins was filed on August 8, 1945 and officially granted on November 9, 1948[78]. Although the three men were employees of the Florida Citrus Commission and the work had been financed by the FCC, it was done at USDA facilities in Winter Haven, FL[71]. An October 1945 newspaper article in the Miami News highlights the enthusiasm for the new 4+1 concentrate product that included fresh juice, quoting A. S. Herlong, the chairman of the FCC: " [the new product] is of high quality and meeting with good consumer acceptance wherever it has been introduced....and before long the housewife will be able to buy the juice just as she today buys frozen vegetables and fruits in her favorite grocery store." The article highlights that the new product was developed by the FCC's research department. As a sign of how quickly the product was being commercialized, the article states that already for the upcoming 1945/46 citrus season, at least three manufacturers in Florida would be making it[64][4]. The following year, in a 1946 article written by the staff responsible for building a new concentrate plant for Vacuum Foods which will later become the Minute Maid company, the authors specifically attribute the idea of adding fresh juice to concentrate to MacDowell[79].

Dr. A. L. Stahl, who was a University of Florida professor and also working in collaboration with the FCC, was apparently primarily focused on developing a commercial process to make juice concentrate by freeze concentration rather than heat. He described his work in a 1944 paper highlighting the advantages of freeze concentration, primarily in theoretical energy savings and a better-flavored product. Everyone acknowledged it was a better-tasting product. However, the freeze concentration process was difficult to scale up for commercial use. Stahl's work focused on trying to design a viable process and building a pilot-plant in Gainesville to test it[80]. It seems apparent that at this time, the FCC considered both concentrate production methods as potentially viable. In Stahl's 1944 paper, he has clearly identified 4x concentrate as the best concentration level, although he doesn't particularly claim credit for the assessment.

Other Early FCOJ Manufacturers

During the war years and attracted by the Lend Lease opportunities, other major concentrate operations had started in Florida. In Dade City, FL, the Pasco Packing Company, which started in 1936, had a fruit and canning plant. In 1942, they started producing juice concentrate for the US government[81, 82]. By the end of 1945, they were firmly committed to producing the new frozen concentrate product. A company executive was quoted in a 1945 newspaper article: "Any product that requires only a sixth of the canning and freight costs is going to have a future. Frozen juice will cost more than ordinary canned juice but the housewife demands it and she is going to get it[83]."

Another large facility was in Lake Wales, FL. It was owned by the Florida Citrus Canners Cooperative, which started in 1930. They ran a large canned juice and citrus segments operation and started construction on a concentrate plant in early 1942[84] which became operational

---

[4]Citrus Concentrates was not included in the list; it had burned down just a few months earlier.

in early 1943[85]. Their concentrate product also went entirely to the Lend Lease Program during the war. Around 1944, they hired J. L. Heid, who had worked at the USDA and been involved in the early FCC research[56]. Florida Citrus Canners had acquired the exclusive rights to use the *Donald Duck* name from Disney on their canned juice in 1942[86, pg 38]. In 1945 they also quickly transitioned to producing FCOJ. Coincidentally, they also suffered a fire at their plant in September 1945, but it was less devastating than the one at Citrus Concentrates the prior month[87]. Soon, *Donald Duck* branded FCOJ was being manufactured[88]. Heid and Florida Citrus Canners were working with Mojonnier Brothers, a Chicago-based equipment manufacturer with experience in dairy equipment, for the design of their juice evaporators[89]. Mojonnier's would become an early evaporator supplier and filed a patent on their design in 1945[90].

A third and very important concentrate producer began commercial production in 1946 in Plymouth, FL. Its history was quite unique. Attracted presumably by the war-time opportunities, a Boston-based company called National Research Corporation started an investigation of orange juice dehydration in 1943[91]. National Research had been started in 1940 by Richard Morse, a scientist and inventor looking to commercialize vacuum technology and processes[92]. One area of interest was freeze-drying and dehydration, and they were particularly attracted to the idea of creating a powdered orange juice mix. Ideally, a dehydrated or powdered orange juice would be the most efficient for storage and transportation. And the idea was not new. At this same time, the FCC researchers were investigating various methods to produce a powdered OJ product, and the US Army had established specifications for such a product[77]. In 1944, National Research set up a pilot plant for making dehydrated juice powder in Plymouth, FL, and developed a product suitable for sale to the US Army[91]. In the summer of 1945, they received a contract for the production of 500,000 pounds of their product, and a new company, Florida Foods Inc., was created licensing the National Research process. Florida Foods immediately offered stock to raise capital for commercial-sized equipment. They expected to commence operations in April 1946[93, 94, 95, 96]. One of the first steps of their process was to concentrate orange juice to 50° Brix before further high-vacuum drying. When the war ended later in 1945 and they lost their powdered juice contract with the army, they looked to service a new civilian market with both orange juice concentrate and their new powdered juice.

In early 1946, they changed their name to Vacuum Foods Inc[97]. Later in 1949, they would be renamed Minute Maid. Despite their initial interest in powdered juice, that product would largely fail in the consumer market. But the initial origin of their technical ideas and staff outside of Florida had two major consequences. First, they brought in a fresh perspective on product development and processing technology, including designing their own equipment, and they published extensive details[79, 91, 98]. Second, with little prior experience in citrus, they particularly benefited from the public research and marketing push that the FCC was conducting. In a few short years, after launching a clever marketing campaign featuring Bing Crosby and acquiring a large competitor, they would become the largest FCOJ producer in Florida.

Explosive Growth

The initial growth of the FCOJ business was far beyond anything that the FCC could have imagined. After the war, consumers were enthralled with this new product. According to Hopkins, the three main producers in the 1947/48 season, Citrus Concentrates (renamed Juice Industries), Florida Citrus Canners Cooperative, and Minute Maid[5], running at maximum capacity, packed 1.7 million gallons of concentrate. The next season saw 10 manufacturers producing 10 million gallons[38, pg. 222]. Similar statistics are reported by Timmons[17, pg. 18-19]. Given the newness of the product, there was still quite a bit of experimentation going on in the marketplace. In addition to the 4x FCOJ product, a 7x product was still being made and sold for more institutional use[17, pg. 18-19]. Some Florida producers had started arrangements with dairies outside of Florida to receive concentrate, reconstitute it into juice, and deliver it to consumers as milk was delivered. Timmons lists the following manufacturers of a 4x FCOJ type product in the 1948/49 season: Pasco Packing Company (Dade City), Lakeland Highlands Canning Co. (Highland City), Florida Citrus Canners Coop (Lake Wales), Juice Industries Inc. (Dunedin), Adams Packing Association (Auburndale), Wm. P. McDonald Corp. (Auburndale), Plymouth Citrus Growers Association (Plymouth), Minute Maid (Plymouth), Florence Citrus Growers Association (Florence Villa) and Sperti Citrus

---

[5]It is not clear why Pasco Packing is not included.

Inc. (Orlando). He lists the following manufacturers of 7x concentrate: Pasco Packing Company (Dade City), Florida Citrus Canners Coop (Lake Wales), Bruce's Juices Inc. (Tampa), Juice Industries Inc. (Dunedin), Plymouth Citrus Growers Association (Plymouth), Snively Citrus Concentrates Inc. (Winter Haven) and Sargent Concentrates Inc. (Lakeland)[17, pg. 18-19].

Each of these new facilities needed trained staff, complex equipment for fruit handling, juicing, concentration and packaging, frozen storage, and a host of other support services. The new industry spawned a wave of growth and prosperity around the Florida citrus industry. By 1949, FCOJ was being called "The Cinderella Product" in the popular press[38, pg. 223]. According to Hopkins, "Out of state capital began flowing into the Florida citrus industry in almost unlimited proportions as investors became entranced with citrus and most particularly with the frozen concentrate industry. Modern concentrate plants were constructed in almost every section of the citrus belt, and existing facilities were extensively remodeled and enlarged[38, p.g 223]." But rapid growth brought its own problems. By April 1949, the growth of the FCOJ business had outgrown the available fruit supply causing a supply conflict between the higher-margin fresh fruit business in Florida and the new concentrate manufacturers[38, pg. 221]. The fruit market in Florida and the citrus industry would never be the same.

One name that quickly disappears from the historical record is Citrus Concentrates. Although rebuilt following the 1945 fire, a March 1948 article in the St. Petersburg Times reported that a local attorney named H. W. Holland had acquired voting control of the Citrus Concentrates plant in Dunedin. By this time, the corporate name had changed to Juice Industries Inc. What motivated the ownership change is not stated. However, B. C. Skinner and his son Bruce Skinner are still listed as corporate officers[99]. In May 1948, another article announced a large pending contract between Juice Industries and Clinton Industries to make frozen concentrate. Clinton Industries was based in Clinton, IA, and planned to market the product under their *Snow Crop* frozen food brand. The article indicated that Bristow made the announcement, indicating that he was still involved[100]. Shortly afterward in 1948, Clinton Industries purchased the Juice Industries plant[101, 46]. The *Snow Crop*" brand of orange juice concentrate and all their citrus assets were later purchased by Minute Maid in 1954[102].

Conclusion

The commercial success of frozen concentrated orange juice obviously brought a great deal of benefit to Florida's citrus growers, the FCOJ manufacturers, and millions of consumers who could now enjoy Florida orange juice all year round. Assessing responsibility for the invention is more complex. However, recognizing the key contributors is important, and even more so is understanding the conditions and investments in time, effort, and resources that enabled the innovation.

Louis MacDowell, Ed Moore, and Cedric Atkins each spent their careers as research scientists serving the Florida citrus industry long after their 1948 patent. They made many important contributions and have been rightly recognized by the industry. For the Florida Citrus Commission, which sponsored their research and employed the scientists, the invention of FCOJ was a very important success story. The FCC was founded in 1935 on the controversial idea of forcing certain regulations on citrus growers for the beneficial interest of the entire market, including a system of self-taxation. Following the overwhelming commercial success of the FCOJ product, the FCC was in a much stronger position to capitalize on their involvement and strengthen their organization. And as the overall size of the citrus industry grew, so did the budget and power of the FCC.

However, it is clear that other contributors were as important to FCOJ's invention and success as the FCC scientists. The invention is probably best categorized as evolutionary and not revolutionary. It relied on combining fairly well-established or simple ideas: manufacturing suitable juice concentrate, adding freshly-squeezed juice, deaerating the product, and storing it frozen. Even the idea of adding back fresh juice to improve the flavor had been around earlier, at least according to Bristow[48]. And yet, it is well documented that the FCOJ product as successfully commercialized only came together in 1945. On occasion, some of the other contributors have been highlighted. A 1988 New York Times obituary for Richard Morse, the founder of National Research Corporation, was entitled "Richard S. Morse, 76, an Inventor Of Orange Juice Concentrate, Dies[92]." Morse was also highlighted in a Time Magazine article on the invention of FCOJ from 2017[6]. In 1965, a Tampa Tribune obituary stated J. J. R. Bristow "invented the concentrate process... which saved the citrus industry from boom and bust ruin[53]." In 1952, the United States Secretary of Agriculture Charles

Brannan granted an award for distinguished service to three Winter Haven USDA scientists along with MacDowell, Moore, and Atkins and Eunice Wiederhold Moore for developing FCOJ[6]. The honorary plaque stood for many years in the main lobby of the USDA Citrus & Subtropical Fruit Research building in Winter Haven but was relocated to the USDA facility in Fort Pierce, FL when the Winter Haven building was closed in 2012.

In some contrast, a 1954 article in the trade journal *Food Processing* attempted to assess all of the important contributors just a few years after FCOJ's incredible success. As part of an ongoing program of naming "Food Frontiersmen" responsible for innovations in new food products, the magazine's editors used an unnamed advisory board of "14 leading food technologists" to select 13 individuals who made the most significant contributions in the development of FCOJ. They named A. L. Stahl from the University of Florida for his work on freeze concentration, MacDowell, Moore, and Atkins and Eunice Wiederhold Moore from the FCC joined by J. L. Heid from the USDA (and later the Florida Citrus Canners Coop) for combining together all of the steps of the commercial FCOJ product in what they referred to as the "Winterhaven Process," Skinner and Bristow for the first commercial application of the new process and for inventing the first low-temperature evaporator and other high-speed processing techniques, Norman Hayes and R. H. Cotton from Vacuum Foods (later Minute Maid) for their development of an evaporator design, Heid and Joe Cross of Mojonnier Brothers for their development of an ammonia-based low-temperature evaporator at Florida Citrus Canners Cooperative, and Charles Kaufman and H. S. Madsen of General Foods for a detailed consumer acceptance study in 1944 of reconstituted frozen juice concentrate (made without adding any fresh juice)[103].

Several observations are noteworthy about the 1954 article. First, Eunice Wiederhold Moore received recognition and was the only woman to be named. Wiederhold, who later married Ed Moore, worked for the FCC and was included as a co-author on the 1945 research paper describing the FCC research[77] and in the 1944 *Citrus Industry* article describing their research[75]. However, Wiederhold was not included as an inventor on the subsequent patent, and her role seemed to be

---

[6]The three USDA researchers from the Winter Haven USDA Lab were Matthew K. Veldhuis, the lab director since 1944, Roger Patrick and A. Lawrence Curl.

minimized by the other inventors in later years[104]. However, she was recognized by the Agriculture Secretary in 1952. Second, it should be noted that the highlighted "Frontiersmen" include people from most of the major FCOJ producers operating in 1954. The magazine may have been influenced by commercial considerations to keep potential advertisers happy. Third, of all the named people, only Bristow and Skinner lacked a powerful organization behind them. They had sold their concentrate business in 1948, and although still active in the citrus industry, they seemed to be operating on the periphery afterwards. By far they were the most experienced in citrus of all the "Frontiersmen" in the mid 1940s, and their work on concentrate manufacturing certainly predates all of the others. Despite the drawbacks, this 1954 identification of important contributors may be the most accurate. Over time, as the number of FCOJ manufacturers increased, all of whom benefited from the public availability of the FCOJ process, the Florida Citrus Commission and subsequent Department of Citrus grew in size and power, and as the individual contributors retired and passed away, the invention story simplified. In the end, of these 13 individuals named as "Food Frontiersmen", only MacDowell, Moore, and Atkins were named to the Florida Citrus Hall of Fame.

Beyond individuals, the fact that all of the technology was well-established for making FCOJ by the start of the war was important. Years of canning juice had promoted juice-making technology and revealed the role of oil content, oxygen, enzyme activity and storage conditions on the product. Practical experimentation carried out by manufacturers and research by university and USDA staff had established an important body of knowledge. And the war itself, with the related Lend Lease Program, brought a huge investment in manufacturing technology and demand for citrus concentrates. As the war ended and the demand quickly subsided, the citrus industry as a whole could envision a future supplying orange juice on a much broader scale than ever before utilizing this concentrate capacity. It was just a question of how exactly to best formulate and commercialize this juice for consumers. And the post-war economic boom, with consumers now willing and able to indulge in luxuries that had been in limited supply during the war, certainly was fortuitous. Finally, the role of the public service patent is interesting. Had a commercial organization attempted to patent the process and subsequently sought to protect their invention, it could have slowed down the adoption rate of the product. A decision to protect an invention like this as a trade secret may have had a similar outcome. By choosing to file a public service patent and share the information widely before the patent was filed, the FCC created an environment for very rapid adoption and subsequent wide-spread innovation in adapting, modifying and improving the FCOJ product by all of the manufacturers. That innovation certainly benefited the Florida citrus industry and all consumers of FCOJ products. The new FCOJ industry, in turn, would foster many new innovations including a greatly enlarged citrus flavor industry.

References

[1] "U.S. Puts Up $1,500,000 for New Citrus Concentrates Plant." In: *St. Petersburg Times* (Dec. 13, 1941), pp. 1, 7.

[2] Roma Hocking. "He Made $142 Million - Somebody Else Spends It." In: *Orlando Sentinel* (Aug. 31, 1975). Section: Polk Sentinel, p. 2.

[3] John Conner. "The Industry That Laid A Golden Egg." In: *Collier's Weekly* (Aug. 12, 1950), pp. 26–27, 67–68.

[4] John McPhee. *Oranges.* Farrar, Straus and Giroux, 1966.

[5] Thomas B. Mack. *Citrifacts II: A Portion of Florida Citrus History.* Lakeland, FL: Associated Publications Corporation, 1998.

[6] Emelyn Rude. "The Surprising Link Between World War II and Frozen Orange Juice." In: *Time Magazine (Time.com)* (Aug. 31, 2017). URL: https://time.com/4922457/wwii-orange-juice-history/ (visited on 12/18/2022).

[7] Alissa Anne Hamilton. "Fabricated Fresh: What Industry and the FDA Failed to Tell You About Processed Orange Juice." Doctoral Thesis. Yale University, May 2006.

[8] Shane Hamilton. "Cold Capitalism: The Political Ecology of Frozen Concentrated Orange Juice." In: *Agricultural History* Vol. 77 (Issue 4 2003), pp. 557–581.

[9] Gail Borden Jr. "Improvement in the Concentration of Milk." Pat. 15,553A. United States Patent. Aug. 19, 1856.

[10] R. T. Will. "Some Phases of the Citrus By-Products Industry in California." In: *The Journal of Industrial and Engineering Chemistry* Vol. 8 (Issue 1 1916), pp. 78–86.

[11] "Concentrated Fruit Juice." In: *The Burbank Review* (July 19, 1913), p. 8.

[12] James Birtley McNair. "The Present Status of the Citrus By-Product Industry in California." Masters Thesis. University of California, Dec. 1917.

[13] F. Alex McDermott. "The Utilization of Cull Florida Citrus Fruits." In: *Journal of Industrial & Engineering Chemistry* Vol. 8 (Issue 2 Feb. 1, 1916), pp. 136–138.

REFERENCES

[14] "Is Introducing A New Crushed Fruit Product." In: *The Whittier News* (Jan. 12, 1922), p. 1.

[15] "Citrus Juice Industry for City." In: *The Orange County Plain Dealer* (May 22, 1922), p. 1.

[16] Seth S. Walker. "The Present Status of Fruit Products Manufacture." In: *Proceedings of the Florida State Horticultural Society* Vol. 35 (1922), pp. 161–164.

[17] D. E. Timmons. *Citrus Canning in Florida: Early History and Statistics.* Report AE Series 50-4. Gainesville, FL: Agricultural Extension Service, University of Florida, Jan. 31, 1950.

[18] Seth S. Walker. "Reminiscences of Early Work in Citrus Fruit Technology." In: *Proceedings of the Florida State Horticultural Society* Vol. 70 (1957), pp. 177–182.

[19] C. C. Commander. "The Citrus Industry of Florida." In: *Tampa Tribune* (Apr. 25, 1926), pp. E2, E4.

[20] "Ferry to Link This City to Farming Lands." In: *The St. Petersburg Times* (Aug. 10, 1926). Section 2, p. 9.

[21] "Florida Canning Industry is Forging to the Front." In: *St. Petersburg Times* (Sept. 12, 1926). Section 7, p. 12.

[22] "$30,000 Orange Concentrate Plant at Sanford to Open Novemoer [sic] 15." In: *Orando Sentinel* (Aug. 9, 1927), p. 9.

[23] *All About Crush.* URL: http://www.crushsoda.com/ (visited on 10/07/2011).

[24] Wikipedia. *Crush (Soft Drink).* URL: https://en.wikipedia.org/wiki/Crush_(soft_drink) (visited on 12/15/2023).

[25] "Concentrated Orange Juice Urged for Use on Warships." In: *The Orlando Sentinel* (May 3, 1929), p. 7.

[26] "Citrus Plant at Clearwater." In: *St. Petersburg Times* (Aug. 16, 1929), p. 3.

[27] "Dilpako Plant to Employ 300 During Season." In: *St. Petersburg Times* (Sept. 28, 1930). Section 2, p. 6.

[28] "Citrus Juices." In: *Fort Lauderdale News* (Mar. 17, 1931), p. 4.

[29] "Hill Brothers Lease Dilpako Packing Plant." In: *St. Petersburg Times* (Sept. 26, 1931). Section 2, p. 4.

[30] "Creditors Sue Packing Plant." In: *St. Petersburg Times* (Nov. 2, 1931), p. 5.

[31] L. V. Burton. "High Vacuum Technics Utilized for Drying Orange Juice." In: *Food Industries* (May 1947), pp. 107–113.

[32] M. J. Mack et al. "Vitamin-C Content of Dairy Orange Beverages." In: *Twenty-Fifth Annual Report of the International Association of Milk Sanitarians*. Atlantic City, NJ: International Association of Milk Sanitarians, Oct. 1936, pp. 267–274.

[33] Thomas A. Rector. "Frozen Concentrated Orange Juice - Its Research Background." In: *Refrigeration Engineering* Vol. 58 (Issue 4 Apr. 1950), pp. 349–353.

[34] Wikipedia. *Clarence Birdseye*. URL: https://en.wikipedia.org/wiki/Clarence_Birdseye (visited on 12/15/2023).

[35] Wikipedia. *General Foods*. URL: https://en.wikipedia.org/w/index.php?title=General_Foods&oldid=991024461 (visited on 11/27/2020).

[36] Thomas A. Rector. "Research Background of Frozen Concentrated Orange Juice." In: *Chemical and Engineering News* Vol. 28 (Issue 4 Jan. 23, 1950), pp. 242–245.

[37] "Frozen Orange Juice Provides New Market for Citrus In North." In: *Vero Beach Press Journal* (June 13, 1930). Section 2, p. 7.

[38] James T. Hopkins. *Fifty Years of Citrus: The Florida Citrus Exchange 1909–1959*. Gainesville, FL: University of Florida Press, 1960.

[39] Frank Kay Anderson. "Science Conquers Orange Juice Preservation." In: *The Citrus Industry* Vol. 13 (Issue 1 Jan. 1932), pp. 5, 20–22, 24.

[40] M. A. Joslyn. "The Problem of Preserving Orange Juice by Freezing." In: *Industrial and Engineering Chemistry* Vol. 24 (Issue 6 June 1, 1932), pp. 665–668.

[41] M. A. Joslyn and G. L. Marsh. "The Keeping Quality of Frozen Orange Juice." In: *Industrial and Engineering Chemistry* Vol. 26 (Issue 3 Mar. 1, 1934), pp. 295–299.

[42] E. M. Chace and H. D. Poore. "Quick-Freezing Citrus Fruit Juices and Other Fruit Products." In: *Industrial and Engineering Chemistry* Vol. 23 (Issue 10 Oct. 1931), pp. 1109–1112.

REFERENCES

[43] James B. Redd. "Processing - Processed O.J., Definition of Quality, Purity and the Effects of Processing on These Characteristics - Part II." In: *Citrus Industry* (Oct. 1983), pp. 15–18.

[44] Dunedin Historical Museum. *Dunedin's Citrus History.* URL: https://dunedinhistoricalmuseum.wordpress.com/2015/06/24/dunedins-citrus-history/ (visited on 01/19/2021).

[45] "Who's Who in Florida Citrus and Vegetables." In: *Orlando Sentinel Starr* (Jan. 14, 1951). Section 4, p. 12.

[46] Dick Bothwell. "Juice Drinking Breaks are Serious Business." In: *St. Petersburg Times* (Feb. 5, 1958), p. D14.

[47] "Necrology - James Jefferson Ricker Bristow." In: *Proceedings of the Florida State Horticultural Society* Vol. 78 (1965), p. 450.

[48] J. J. R. Bristow. "Technical Developments in Concentrate." In: *Proceedings of the Florida State Horticultural Society* Vol. 64 (1951), pp. 157–158.

[49] James B. Redd. "Processing - Processed O.J., Definition of Quality, Purity and the Effects of Processing on These Characteristics - Part III." In: *Citrus Industry* (Nov. 1983), pp. 12–17.

[50] Charles M. Hendrix Jr. *A History of Juice Enhancement.* Unpublished. 1986.

[51] "New Plant Here Distilled Citrus Oils from Peels." In: *Tampa Tribune* (Mar. 2, 1930), p. B4.

[52] V. C. Praschan. "Chemical Engineering In The Frozen Food Industry." In: *Chemial Engineering Progress* (June 1951), pp. 325–330.

[53] "James J. R. Bristow, 73, Dies: Invented Concentrate Process." In: *St. Petersburg Times* (Jan. 29, 1965), pp. B1, B13.

[54] "Dunedin Concern Will Can Orange Concentrate." In: *Tampa Tribune* (Oct. 9, 1936), p. 4.

[55] "Citrus Fruit Laboratory to be Established." In: *Tampa Tribune* (July 12, 1936), p. 8.

[56] Thomas W. Hagen. "Cracker In The Capital." In: *The Miami Daily News* (Apr. 2, 1944), p. B5.

[57] "Citrus Researchers Form Organization." In: *Tampa Daily Times* (Oct. 27, 1944), p. 1.

[58] "Canners Seek Subsidy From U.S. on Citrus." In: *Tampa Tribune* (Oct. 28, 1944), p. 2.

[59] "Citrus Experts Begin Series of Conferences." In: *Tampa Tribune* (Jan. 17, 1945), p. 2.

[60] "Citrus Men to Form National Organization." In: *St. Petersburg Times* (Jan. 21, 1945), p. 25.

[61] "Retired Ad Executive, Palatka Grower Develop Frozen Orange Juice Formula." In: *St. Petersburg Times* (Jan. 27, 1945), p. 7.

[62] "Butts Named Ad Director of Florida Citrus Group." In: *Tampa Tribune* (Sept. 7, 1945), p. 4.

[63] "Clearwater Firm to Enlarge Frozen Juice Output." In: *St. Petersburg Times* (Aug. 5, 1945), p. 3.

[64] "Frozen Orange Juice Gaining in Popularity." In: *The Miami Herald* (Oct. 20, 1945), p. 2.

[65] *Annual Report of the Florida Citrus Exchange 1944-45 Season*. 1945. URL: https://original-ufdc.uflib.ufl.edu/UF00075941/00017 (visited on 12/17/2023).

[66] Ralph Reed. "Citrus Concentrates Will Rebuild Plant After $1,000,000 Fire Loss." In: *The St. Petersburg Times* (Aug. 28, 1945), p. 1.

[67] Walter Fuller. "Concentrates Plant Vital to State Citrus Industry." In: *The St. Petersburg Times* (Aug. 28, 1945). Section 2, p. 9.

[68] Dorothy Edgecombe. "Dunedin Plant to Use Workers in Rebuilding." In: *The St. Petersburg Times* (Aug. 28, 1945). Section 2, p. 9.

[69] Vinnie Luisi. "History Notes: The Great Fire at the Dunedin Concentrate Plant." In: *TBN Weekly* (Mar. 27, 2020). URL: https://www.tbnweekly.com/north_county/article_4c112708-704e-11ea-ab55-a7a6521541d5.html (visited on 01/19/2021).

[70] "Building to Go On." In: *Tampa Daily Times* (May 10, 1946), p. 14.

[71] Florida Citrus Hall of Fame. *Dr. Louis G. MacDowell*. URL: https://floridacitrushalloffame.com/inductees/dr-louis-g-macdowell/ (visited on 12/17/2023).

REFERENCES 75

[72] Florida Citrus Hall of Fame. *Dr. Edwin L. Moore.* URL: `https://floridacitrushalloffame.com/inductees/dr-edwin-l-moore/` (visited on 12/17/2023).

[73] Florida Citrus Hall of Fame. *Cedric Donald Atkins.* URL: `https://floridacitrushalloffame.com/inductees/cedric-donald-c-d-atkins/` (visited on 12/17/2023).

[74] *Golden Anniversary - Florida Citrus Commission - 1935 - 1985 - Fifty Years of Service.* Florida Department of Citrus, 1986.

[75] "A Second Year of Citrus Research on Byproducts." In: *The Citrus Industry* (Nov. 1944), pp. 6–8.

[76] J. L. Heid. "Concentrating Citrus Juices By the Vacuum Method." In: *Food Industries* (May 1943), pp. 62–66, 110–11.

[77] Edwin L. Moore et al. "The Concentrating and Drying of Citrus Juices." In: *Proceedings of the Institute of Food Technologists* (1945), pp. 160–168.

[78] Louis G. MacDowell, Edwin L. Moore, and Cedric D. Atkins. "Method of Preparing Full-Flavored Fruit Juice Concentrates." Pat. 2,453,109A. United States Patent. Nov. 9, 1948.

[79] Norman V. Hayes, Robert H. Cotton, and Roy R. Wallace. "Problems in the Dehydration of Orange Juice." In: *Proceedings of the Florida State Horticultural Society* Vol. 59 (1946), pp. 26–31.

[80] A. L. Stahl. "Concentration of Citrus Juices By Freezing." In: *Proceedings of the Florida State Horticultural Society* Vol. 57 (1944), pp. 43–45.

[81] "Who's Who in Citrus: L. C. Edwards." In: *The Sentinel-Star* (Nov. 24, 1940). Section: Mailaway Section - Annual Citrus Edition, p. 1.

[82] "Orange Concentrate Plant to Open." In: *Tampa Tribune* (May 22, 1943), p. 7.

[83] J. A. Murray. "Big Dade City Citrus Plant Expands Post-War Output." In: *Tampa Tribune* (Nov. 19, 1945), p. A11.

[84] "Lake Wales to Have Big Plant for Fruit Juice." In: *Tampa Tribune* (Feb. 12, 1942), pp. 1, 3.

[85] Jack Gurnett. "Huge Citrus Concentrate Plant Opens at Lake Wales." In: *Orlando Sentinel Starr* (Jan. 24, 1943), p. 18.

[86] Susan Webb. "Citrus World, Inc. 1980 - 2015. An Examination of Adaptation in a Long-Enduring U.S. Agricultural Marketing Cooperative." Masters Thesis. University of Missouri - Columbia, 2016.

[87] J. A. Murray. "Citrus Co-Op Has Big Expansion Plans." In: *Tampa Tribune* (Sept. 26, 1945), p. A2.

[88] "Concern Signs to Deliver Orange Juice Like Milk." In: *Tampa Tribune* (Dec. 12, 1945), p. 2.

[89] J. L. Heid and C. G. Beisel. "Improved Citrus Concentrate Depends on Advanced Technique." In: *Food Industries* Vol. 20 (1948), pp. 516–519.

[90] J. A. Cross. "Evaporation Method and Apparatus." Pat. 2,570,210. United States Patent. Oct. 9, 1951.

[91] H. W. Schwarz and F. E. Penn. "Production of Orange Juice Concentrate and Powder." In: *Industrial and Engineering Chemistry* Vol. 40 (Issue 5 May 1948), pp. 938–944.

[92] Wolfgang Saxon. "Richard S. Morse, 75, an Inventor of Orange Juice Concentrate, Dies." In: *The New York Times* (July 4, 1988), p. 24.

[93] "$2,500,000 For Citrus Plant Sought." In: *Tampa Tribune* (July 4, 1945), p. 2.

[94] "Orange Powder by Ton." In: *Orlando Reporter Star* (July 15, 1945), pp. 1, 2.

[95] "Citrus Crop Insurance to Start on Trial Basis This Season." In: *St. Petersburg Times* (July 22, 1945), p. 31.

[96] "Florida Foods Driving Ahead." In: *Orlando Reporter Star* (Aug. 28, 1945), p. 3.

[97] "New Citrus Firm Changes Name." In: *Tampa Daily Times* (Mar. 29, 1946), p. 19.

[98] Hugh W. Schwarz. "Comparison of Low-Temperature Evaporators." In: *Food Technology* (Nov. 1951), pp. 476–479.

[99] "Holland Acquires Control of Concentrates Plant." In: *St. Petersburg Times* (Mar. 27, 1948). Section 2, p. 17.

[100] "Juice Industries Receives Big Order for Frozen Orange Juice Concentrate." In: *St. Petersburg Times* (May 30, 1948), p. 48.

REFERENCES

[101] "McDonald Sells Out to Snow Crop." In: *Tampa Morning Tribune* (July 26, 1949), p. 1.

[102] Jack Gurnett. "Minute Maid Buy Brings Mixed Views." In: *Orlando Sentinel* (Dec. 1, 1954), pp. 1, 2.

[103] "Food Frontiersmen of Frozen Orange Juice Concentrate." In: *Food Processing* Vol. 15 (Issue 12 Dec. 1954), pp. 6–10.

[104] Gaynell Terrell. "Citrus Pioneers Concentrated on Breakthrough." In: *Tampa Tribune* (Feb. 26, 1989), pp. E1, E14.

4

Developments with the Growth of FCOJ

> *"The concentrate boom is the boomiest boom since the Brazilian rubber boom."*
>
> —Citrus Scientist William Grierson, quoted in 1965 by John McPhee, *Oranges*[1].

The Florida orange juice industry had developed an extremely successful new product, frozen concentrated orange juice (FCOJ), that efficiently delivered a remarkable facsimile to home-made freshly squeezed orange juice to the consumer. The product offered many conveniences compared to home-made juice. It was no longer necessary to procure fresh fruit, which was available only during certain growing seasons and was difficult to store after purchase, nor was the consumer required to juice the fruit and deal with the clean-up and peel waste. Instead, the product stored safely frozen until desired and could be mixed easily in the usual 3 parts water plus 1 part FCOJ without prior thawing and consumed chilled immediately. When mixed, the product had an appearance and taste that matched consumers' expectations for orange juice and it provided the same nutritious mix of vitamins and minerals. For the manufacturer, there were also many benefits. Although the fruit was only available in season, the manufacturer could process fruit and store the finished product frozen year-round for sale. Storage and transportation of the FCOJ product were also easier compared to canned juice or fresh fruit due to the reduced weight. Finally, the same equipment used for orange juice manufacturing could be used for other citrus juices including the next most popular juice, grapefruit juice, which allowed for a somewhat extended fruit processing season, more efficient equipment usage and more products to sell.

The rapid growth in FCOJ production in Florida was staggering. In the 1950/51 season, just a few years after the product's introduction, FCOJ production was 30.7 million gallons[1]. By the 1958/59 season, production was 79.9 million gallons, and it continued to grow throughout the 1960s reaching 124.9 million gallons in 1969/70[2, 3]. Not only FCOJ, but canned single-strength citrus juice also saw increased demand. In the 1939/40 season, Florida packed 4.7 million cases of grapefruit juice, 2.9 million cases of orange juice and 1.4 million cases of blended juice[2]. By the 1958/59 season, these quantities were up 215%, 460%, and 30%, respectively[2]. In order to support this demand, Florida needed a lot more citrus fruit and the growers responded. Orange production in Florida was 28.2 million boxes in the 1940/41 season, 66.2 million boxes in 1950/51, 82.7 million boxes in 1960/61, and 142.3 million boxes in 1970/71. Florida orange production overtook California's in the 1945/46 season and would greatly surpass it for the rest of the century. In the 1960/61 season, for example, California orange production was only 24.7 M boxes[2, 3, 4]. In addition to orange concentrate, both grapefruit and tangerine concentrates were produced in much lower but growing quantities.

The successful new product attracted new juice manufacturers to Florida. In the 1948/49 season, there were about 10 processors making orange juice concentrate in Florida[5, pg. 222], but the number grew quickly as out-of-state investors rushed in. By the 1953/54 season, the FCC was monitoring concentrate production at 23 plants using 37 brand names[6]. Some were successful, and others less so. Inevitably, certain manufacturers came to dominate the market either through organic growth or acquisitions. Rector lists the three largest OJ brands in 1950 being *Minute Maid*, from the recently renamed Vacuum Foods company, *Snow Crop*, which purchased the Dunedin, FL plant of Citrus Concentrates/Juice Industries in 1948, and *Birdseye*, owned by General Foods. General Foods was a leader in frozen foods and had been inter-

---

[1] measured in 42°Brix gallons.
[2] 1 case = 24 No. 2 cans or 3.75 gallons.

ested in orange juice since the early 1930s. General Foods purchased the California orange juice company Bireley's in 1943 and marketed FCOJ produced by the Florida Citrus Canners Coop in Lake Wales under their brand. They also opened a small experimental juice processing facility in Lakeland, FL in 1947[7]. Minute Maid acquired the Snow Crop business in 1954[8] in a major acquisition, cementing their position as the largest Florida FCOJ producer. Another important national company that came into Florida was Libby, McNeill & Libby. Libby purchased a concentrate plant in Ocala, FL in 1950 to enter the FCOJ business. At this time, Libby was an 86 years old company and had 40 plants in the US and Canada making canned foods and beverages[9, 10]. They would invest heavily in R&D to improve their FCOJ product over the next few decades.

Given the recent development of the FCOJ process and the rapid market growth, there were a lot of unknowns that manufacturers would only discover with time and experience. Meanwhile, these companies had to design, order and commission equipment and processes and train new employees. In the midst of busy production schedules, problems were identified, and potential solutions sought. It would be some time before equipment and processes became standardized. Meanwhile, processing plants operated with considerable independent experimentation and innovation, while researchers at the USDA, University of Florida, or the Florida Citrus Commission (FCC) addressed the largest common problems. Some of the major practical problems that plants faced were fruit procurement, the improvement juice quality, sanitation and waste handling. Additionally, each manufacturer had to make specific decisions on exactly what type of FCOJ product they would produce, given their access to fruit and their processing capabilities. The broad category of FCOJ included a variety of different product formulations. The optimum product for the new consumer market was not yet determined.

Practical Challenges of FCOJ Growth

Citrus growers in Florida had long cultivated fruit for the fresh fruit market and selected cultivars to maximize fresh fruit sales. Varieties maturing in November and early December, for example, were ideal for Christmas marketing. The earliest maturing orange cultivars in Florida typically ripened in October, while the late-maturing Valencias weren't harvested until April or later. The best looking fruit commanded the highest prices as fresh fruit, so excess fruit or packing-house eliminations were traditionally used for canned juice production. The eliminations included fruits deficient in size or appearance. Some imperfections had no effect on juice quality, while others did. As the FCOJ market exploded in size, citrus began to be planted specifically to satisfy this market. One important goal for processors was to grow cultivars selected both for juice quality and to provide mature fruit throughout as much of the growing season as possible. For a processing plant, it was inefficient to have all fruit maturing at the same time. Very quickly, orange juice processors came to dominate fresh fruit customers for Florida's fruit. In 1935/36, over 97% of oranges grown in Florida were sold as fresh fruit. By 1949/50, the allocation to fresh fruit fell to 40% and down to 28% by 1955/56[2]. In this changing environment, there was ongoing tension between the grower and processor, each seeking their advantage in the market. Growers had to make long-term commitments to tree selection and care. Processors had immediate needs for particular fruit as well as long-term concerns about future fruit availability. And both parties had to deal with uncontrollable events like weather, diseases, and the like.

Process technology was another concern for juice manufacturers. In the early 1950s there were several different juice extractor designs, but the two most common in Florida were the Rotary Juice Press Extractor and the Food Machinery Corporation (FMC) In-Line Extractor[11]. Each extractor technology required careful tuning to produce its optimal juice, and the different extractor designs differed in juice yield, pulp content, and peel contamination. Equipment manufacturers were continually improving the equipment, and over time the best designs became standardized. But this standardization took decades. Also, rather new was the high-vacuum evaporator technology. The earliest concentrate manufacturers utilized custom-built evaporators, and with the associated vacuum systems, juice pumps, heat transfer zones, and control systems, they were very complex and expensive machines[12]. Rapid design improvements were made in the first decade as equipment builders moved into the market. But due to the large expense, plants hesitated to replace working evaporators. Thus, as juice plants grew capacity over time, it was common to be running several different evaporator designs of various ages. Early evaporator manufacturers included Mojonnier Brothers, Buflo-Vak, and Kelly Co.[13]. All of these evaporators had lengthy startup and shutdown procedures. Once in operation, they required carefully trained operators to keep the process running properly. And each machine possessed its quirks, which were sometimes reflected in the concentrate produced. In addition to extractors and evaporators, fruit handling equipment, blending and storage tanks, and freezer storage all had to be designed and built. Lacking any well-tested model facilities, each plant made the best decisions they could given the time pressures, available capital, facility location, and other constraints they operated under.

Sanitation and pasteurization were additional challenges for juice processors. Fresh citrus fruits harbor naturally occurring microscopic flora, including yeasts and molds on the fruit surface. During the squeezing process, some of these are invariably transferred to the juice and can grow under suitable conditions, limiting the shelf-life of the juice when stored. When a consumer carefully selects sound fruit and washes the peel prior to juicing, the microbial count is low. The lower the microbial count at the start, the longer it takes for juice to spoil in refrigerated storage. In the FCOJ manufacturing process, both the cutback juice and the juice sent for concentration would contain some microscopic flora. But the contamination could be exacerbated by microbes growing within the processing equipment itself, especially on the warm, wet surfaces of the equipment and pipes. The low-temperature evaporators had a particularly large impact because they operated at warm temperatures which encouraged microbial growth, and they were often difficult to clean. At very high levels, microbes would affect the juice flavor. Unlike for canned juice, where high-temperature pasteurization was required for a shelf-stable product at room temperature, pasteurization was not required for the FCOJ product as long as it was stored frozen. Frozen storage inhibited any further microbial growth. And the high natural citric acid levels in citrus juice killed most known pathogens. However, many natural microbes survived freezing and would reactivate once the juice was thawed, shortening the product shelf-life for the consumer. For the manufacturer, keeping the microbial count in their products low was an important part of producing good quality juice with appropriate shelf-life. In addition to effective fruit screening, cleaning, and equipment sanitation, juice manufacturers had the option to pasteurize either the fresh cutback juice or the juice being concentrated, or both, to reduce the microbial count. However, the high-temperature pasteurization conditions used for canned juice were avoided because of the flavor impact. Instead, more gentle conditions were favored as the FCOJ didn't need to be microbe-free. Since pathogens were a minor concern, processors could experiment with a variety of pasteurization conditions in conjunction with their sanitation protocols to provide the best-tasting FCOJ with an acceptable microbial content. The pasteurization process was also used to deactivate natural juice enzymes that affected the cloudiness of the juice (discussed below).

Measuring the microbial content in the production facility and finished products was difficult and time-consuming as the microbes themselves are invisible to the naked eye. The industry developed testing methods based on plate-counting[14]. By taking samples of juice, carefully diluting it, and applying the various dilutions to agar plates, the microbes could be grown under ideal conditions, and the colonies visually counted. The process took approximately 48 hours for each test and required considerable care and expertise to perform. Furthermore, each agar plate provided an evaluation of the microbial count at a single instant in time but 48 hours after sampling. Before a plant knew they had a problem, two days had elapsed. Developing routine sanitation procedures to prevent microbial problems was an important early effort across the industry. Selecting fruit carefully before juicing to avoid damaged fruit and washing the fruit thoroughly was an important step. So was designing processes to minimize the time juice was handled at warm temperatures. And equipment had to be designed to avoid supporting microbial growth and regularly cleaned. Cleaning, in particular, seems obvious but it took considerable time and shut down manufacturing. Plants wanted to do it only when necessary. Furthermore, the industry and equipment were so new and customized, juice processors had few standards to rely on. Each plant had to determine what worked for their facilities and products.

Finally, the processing plants were producing large quantities of leftover peels and waste process water. Fortunately, a valuable use for the excess peel as cattle feed was quickly identified[15] (see below). Waste process water, on the other hand, remained a big problem. This process water contained both dissolved juice as well as residual citrus oils. The water could ferment and develop strong decay odors. At first, it was just discharged, but soon the quantities overwhelmed nearby fields and streams. Juice processing plants then had to develop wastewater treatment plans, under State mandated guidelines.

Non-Flavor Properties of FCOJ

An important characteristic of manufactured FCOJ was the pulp content. All mechanically-pressed juice required some form of filtering or screening process to remove pieces of fruit segments and juice-cell membranes, with the smallest pieces referred to as pulp. In orange juice, the pulp distribution is quite complex. Larger pieces tend to sink to the bottom while other pulp will float on the top surface. The suspended pulp gives the juice its opaque color and impacts the mouthfeel, which consumers associate with the overall taste. Just as the pulp content of home-made juice can be modified by how vigorously the fruit is squeezed, the pressing and filtering process at a juice processor could be "tuned" for a desired distribution of pulp. The smallest pulp particles are held in suspension by the action of large pectin molecules in a very complex system of interactions. Keeping these particles in suspension is important, but naturally occurring enzymes, produced when the fruit is squeezed, slowly deactivate these pectin networks, causing the pulp to settle to the bottom of the container. This effect can leave juice looking like a clear, colorless sugar syrup. Stirring the juice before serving temporarily redistributes the pulp, but it quickly resettles. The proper suspension of the pulp in citrus juice is referred to as cloud stability, and FCOJ is subject to cloud failure when reconstituted unless the naturally occurring enzymes are deactivated during processing. Another related problem that early manufacturers discovered was gel formation, which changed the appearance, viscosity, and thawing behavior of concentrate in storage. It too was related to enzyme activity. The most economical way to deactivate the pectin enzymes was by heating the juice. But the low temperatures used in the high-vacuum evaporators were insufficient. Instead, FCOJ manufacturers had to consider a pasteurization-like heating step for both the fresh cutback juice and the juice for concentration. Typically, they attempted to deactivate the enzymes and pasteurize the juice in one heating step, choosing a pasteurization time and temperature that was a compromise between competing microbial, enzyme, and flavor impacts.

Even with similar pulp levels, the color intensity of juice from oranges was known to vary widely. For a given variety of orange, more mature oranges were more strongly colored than less mature fruit. But importantly, juice from certain fruit varieties was naturally more deeply colored. In Florida, Hamlin oranges, which mature earlier in the season, produce a less intensely-colored orange juice than Valencia oranges, which mature later. Manufacturers had to balance producing more product over a wider manufacturing window using a range of orange cultivars with producing a more uniform product during a narrower time window. Given the overall shortage of fruit as FCOJ demand exploded, color uniformity was largely neglected at first. It became more important as concentrates came to be stored from season to season. In addition, using up to 10% tangerine fruits in orange juice came to be accepted for improving the color, as Florida tangerines were generally deeply colored.

Flavor Challenges in FCOJ

The new FCOJ product was clearly a compromise, with manufacturers keenly aware that FCOJ produced by combining fresh cutback juice with concentrated orange juice necessarily resulted in a less flavorful product compared to the starting juice. In practice, the manufacturing process could produce a broad spectrum of juice flavor quality, ranging from quite good to rather poor.

The overall flavor impact of citrus juice results from a complex combination of sensory stimuli resulting from the taste and smell of the juice, as well as the tactile perception of the juice in the mouth, often referred to as "mouthfeel." Taste is mostly perceived on the tongue, from receptor cells sensitive to sweet, acidic, and bitter compounds present in the juice. For fruit juices, sweet and acidic flavors dominate, resulting from natural sugars and organic acids. A juice with too little sugar tastes weak; too little acid makes the juice insipid, while too much acid makes it tart. Humans are particularly sensitive to the sugar-to-acid ratio in fruits. Fruit naturally changes its sugar and acid content throughout the maturing process, with sugar increasing and acid decreasing over time. Based on taste experience, consumers recognize the typical values of sugar and acid in ripe citrus fruits. Lemon juice is easily distinguished from orange juice, even when a strong cold prevents one from smelling either. Juice manufacturers had long used simple tests for sugar and acid content in fruit to monitor fruit maturity. Both measurements were easy to make quickly, so the data were routinely available.

Of secondary importance to juice taste is bitterness. A number of bitter compounds are naturally present in citrus juices at low levels, blending well with the sugar and acid. These bitter compounds are present at much higher levels in the peel and account for the bitter, astringent and generally unpleasant flavor of raw citrus peels. Among citrus fruits, grapefruit are well-known to be more bitter than oranges, which strongly influences preference among certain consumer groups (e. g. children vs. elderly). Even within a fruit variety like orange, different cultivars have different levels of bitterness, and among all varieties immature fruit are more bitter than mature fruit. Chemical methods to measure and quantify these bitter compounds were not available when the FCOJ industry began. Only much later were the most important of these compounds identified and testing methods developed. At first, juice manufacturers had to rely on basic taste tests. Another type of bitter taste occurs when too much peel oil is present in the juice. People are used to a certain amount of peel oil in their juice, as it is introduced naturally by most juicing techniques. Juice without any peel oil seems "flat," lacking its characteristic odor. On the other hand, if too much oil is present, it causes an unpleasant bitter-like taste and sometimes even a burning sensation on the lips or in the mouth. The industry had long experience with monitoring oil content in canned orange juice, and a simple analytical test, called the Scott oil test, was available for measuring oil content.

Juice mouthfeel is primarily associated with viscosity, resulting both from the amount of dissolved sugars as well as the quantity and nature of the suspended pulp. To a lesser extent, acid and bitter compounds also impact consumers' perception of the juice mouthfeel. Adjusting the pulp content of the juice was the primary variable that a manufacturer could control, along with deactivating the enzymes that cause cloud instability in the juice.

But by far the most complex part of the juice flavor results from aroma chemicals that give the juice its odor. The odor of juice is caused by hundreds of low molecular weight organic compounds that evaporate from the juice into the surrounding air. These very dilute chemicals are carried into the nasal cavity when air is inhaled during drinking (the orthonasal perception) and are transported into the nasal cavity up from the throat when swallowing (the retronasal perception). Inside the nasal cavity is a small patch of olfactory sensory neurons known as the olfactory epithelium where specialized neurons respond to various aroma molecules. The perception of odors is constructed in the human brain from the way odor-active molecules interact with these sensory neurons. There are literally millions of different combinations of interactions that lead to the huge range of different smells that humans perceive. The nasal-based odor system is much more complex and discriminating than the taste receptors in the mouth. Tuned by evolution, humans perceive some odors to be associated with good, healthy foods and others to signal danger (e. g. odors of decomposition). The olfactory neurons are also very sensitive. Many common aroma molecules are easily perceived at part-per-million levels in air. Others can be detected at much lower part-per-billion levels. Taken together, the hundreds of individual odor-active juice chemicals are called the juice volatiles, and humans experience the combined odor impact as the juice aroma. Humans generally perceive the aroma and taste of foods together in one experience as the overall flavor. The vast number of individual aroma chemicals and their very dilute concentrations make them very difficult to measure with instruments. In practice, human testing was the only available method for the first few decades of the FCOJ industry.

For juice manufacturers, producing the best-tasting juice required carefully managing the raw materials and processes to optimize the levels and proportions of the important flavor and aroma molecules and to avoid introducing any off-flavors into the product. Given that the vacuum concentration process removed nearly all of the juice aroma, restoring some portion of this odor was critical. The addition of the fresh cutback juice restored some of it.

The starting point was the selection of undamaged, good-quality, mature fruit as the raw material. Damaged, moldy, or rotten fruit had to be avoided as these could introduce off-flavors (and microbial contamination) into the juice. In practice, this required human visual screening of large quantities of incoming fruit and could only be done so well. Fruit was then evaluated based on the sugar and acid content. Manufacturers knew certain sugar and acid levels were preferred, but it was not always possible to achieve these targets given the available fruit. Even in ideally mature fruit, there is year-to-year variation in both quantities. Different cultivars of oranges were known to be sweeter or more sour compared to others, with various types of oranges maturing at different times during the citrus season. Thus, manufacturers had to deal with a constantly changing mix of oranges. The largest and most exacting manufacturers soon developed storage facilities to hold juice with different properties to produce a better, more standardized juice by blending lots throughout the manufacturing season. In fact, fruit could be selected and specifically processed to make the cutback juice separately from the juice destined for concentration, taking advantage of the juice with the best aroma for use as cutback. Juice concentrate, once frozen, could be stored for long periods of time. This meant that juice concentrate could be stored segregated by sugar/acid ratio, cultivar or any other attribute (including color or flavor) to blend with cutback juice in designated recipes according to any specification the manufacturer was willing to entertain, provided the inventory and storage costs were supportable.

At times, there was an incentive for juice manufacturers to utilize immature or lower-quality fruit. This might come about because of limited fruit availability or in the interest of reducing raw material costs. Or, in the case of a freeze, growers might harvest freeze-damaged fruit to recover some return on their crop instead of losing it. Fresh fruit marketers had long battled the incentive for an individual grower to market immature fruit early in the season, getting a jump on their competitors while prices were high. If the fruit looked good, the buyer would often not discover the inferior taste until it was too late. Unfortunately, the entire market suffered from future depressed demand due to disappointed customers. Fruit exchanges and later (in Florida) the FCC had established minimum maturity standards for fresh fruit to prevent this. These same maturity standards were soon applied to citrus juices. By as early as 1940, the FCC had required Florida orange juice to meet maturity standards, including a minimum sugar/acid ratio[16]. These standards helped to minimize the production of low-quality juices.

One easy way to improve juice flavor was to add sugar, yielding a less than 100% juice product. This was common practice by the earliest citrus juice canners. As canned juice took off in the 1930s, both 100% juice and sugar-added canned juice were available. Likewise, when the FCOJ market developed after 1945, both sugar-added and 100% juice FCOJ products were introduced. The sugar-added products were easier to manufacture. Over time, consumer preference for 100% juice and citrus grower pressure to sell fruit strongly favored the juice products with no added sugar. Product labeling regulations became increasingly strong to clearly distinguish sugar-added juice from 100% juice products.

The juice extraction process also had important effects on the juice flavor. In addition to juice quality, manufacturers were also concerned with processing speed, juice yield, sanitation, and reliability. Juice yield, in particular, was very important. Several designs were available from the canned juice industry and rapid improvements were made as the FCOJ industry grew. However, a common feature of the juicing process was that squeezing harder increased the juice yield but at the expense of introducing more bitter compounds into the juice. And all of the mechanical pressing methods resulted in too much peel oil. Excess peel oil in juice that was to be concentrated was not a problem as the vacuum concentration process stripped out the oil. However, the fresh cutback juice usually needed to be de-oiled, which was done either by centrifuge or flash-evaporation under vacuum. But other bitter flavors were a larger problem and could not be removed from the juice once present. Rather, extractor performance and juice needed to be regularly monitored and tasted. Consequently, manufacturers were constantly balancing their competing interests to produce their product.

Restoring the juice aroma lost by the concentration process was a challenge. Mixing in 10% cutback juice with the concentrate restored only a fraction of the natural juice volatiles. Yet more cutback juice couldn't easily be used in FCOJ. That would require concentrating the other ingredients more to end up at the same blended 42°Brix strength that consumers preferred. Juice concentration had a limit beyond which the concentrate could be practically handled as a liquid. Additionally, the aroma profile of the cutback juice could vary considerably in both strength and quality, depending on the fruit and process used. Ideally, juice processors would utilize oranges with the best aroma profile for cutback juice, but the practical availability of fruit limited their flexibility. The very first manufacturers produced their concentrate, cutback juice, and peel oil from the same lots of oranges, combining them into the final FCOJ product in one step. But over time, they would get more creative.

In addition to cutback, manufacturers could improve the FCOJ aroma by adding fresh peel oil to the blended product. This oil acted to replace the volatile oils lost during vacuum concentration. Although the peel oil didn't exactly match the lost volatile profile, it was reasonably close. It was also an easy addition, as the fruit processor almost always had excess peel oil on hand. And peel oil addition to juice or FCOJ was not considered a foreign ingredient but a natural part of citrus juice, so no label disclosure was required. Another reason to add peel oil to concentrate was soon found. Processors discovered that concentrate, when stored frozen for an extended time, could develop a "cardboard" off-flavor if the oil content was too low[17, 18]. Adding peel oil prior to storage was found to mitigate this problem.

With the technology available at the time, it was impossible to understand the complex role of all of the interconnected volatile chemicals giving the juice its aroma. But the impact could be assessed by tasting. Complicating matters was the fact that different lots of oranges had different aroma profiles, and these profiles were constantly changing throughout the season with maturity and changing mixes of cultivars. The juice from certain oranges smelled "fresher," "juicier," or "sweeter" compared to others. As an example, mature Valencia oranges, which are only available late in the citrus growing season, were generally found to have better aroma compared to many other orange cultivars. There was also season-to-season variation in the aroma profile even of the same cultivar at the same level of maturity. Large variations were also seen in the flavor of peel oils. In juice, some oils tasted much better, while others were inferior. And consumers could detect these differences. Since there was no inherent reason that FCOJ ingredients needed to be from the same fruit lot, manufacturers quickly learned that a better FCOJ product could be produced by careful selection and blending of their raw materials. And manufacturers experimented extensively in the interest of producing their products with the best flavor and least cost possible.

Another difficult problem with juice manufacturing was the accidental incorporation of aroma off-notes. Just as small amounts of bitter compounds can ruin the flavor of juice, the presence of these aroma compounds can also ruin the juice even if all the other aroma chemicals are perfect. A common example is fermentation odors from fruit that sits too long after picking before being processed. Small amounts of rotten fruit can also introduce unpleasant odors. Another important problem was associated with microbial growth in the vacuum evaporators used to concentrate juice. The warm equipment temperatures encouraged microbial growth. These microbes could generate unpleasant odors which would be incorporated into the juice concentrate. Determining how often to stop processing and clean equipment was a manufacturing challenge. Moreover, cleaning chemicals and other processing supplies (gaskets, lubricating oils, etc.) could accidentally introduce unpleasant odors into the juice. Finally, the pasteurization process was another common source of off-odors. It was not unusual for localized hot-spots to be much hotter than the average temperature, introducing unexpected cooked odors into the juice. For most of these odor contaminants, they could only be detected by human testing after the contamination occurred. Employees had to be trained and processes developed to monitor and mitigate these problems. It was not unusual for a strange off-note to appear and later disappear without an obvious cause. Over time and with experience, many of the sources of off-odors were identified, but other times they remained annoying mysteries.

An additional source of off-flavors was associated with the product under storage. As the manufacturing process became more complex, and both cutback juice and juice concentrates started to be stored prior to final blending, storage induced off-notes in these ingredients as well as the finished packaged product became an important concern. Whether stored chilled or frozen, certain off-odors or flavors could develop over time. The industry had some experience from canned, single-strength juices. For example, oxygen content was well-known problem, and canned juices, and later FCOJ products, were routinely deaerated to minimize oxygen content. Initially, shelf-life concerns with FCOJ were minimal because chemical changes were known to happen more slowly in frozen juice compared to room-temperature canned juice. However, flavor changes in frozen FCOJ were soon observed and the slower chemistry meant it took longer to track down the sources of these changes. There was considerable uncertainty at first whether peel oil caused off-flavors under storage or not, and what level was optimum. Understanding the flavor change of FCOJ under storage was a very complex problem. Not only could off-notes develop, but the beneficial aroma compounds could chemically change or be absorbed by the packaging. As long as the FCOJ was consumed soon after manufacturing, the storage problems were minimal. But as manufacturers sought to store the concentrates from one season to the next and FCOJ distribution chains became longer, these storage issues became more important and an active area of ongoing research.

Despite the flavor and other manufacturing challenges, the FCOJ product was a huge success because consumers found that the convenience, flavor, and year-around availability offset the possibly better-taste but inconvenience of handling fresh fruit. And the ability for Florida manufacturers to produce it at affordable prices and in large quantities grew the market. Over time, competitive pressure drove the industry to seek continual improvement. Over the next few decades, orange juice in the US would continue to get better and better.

Florida and USDA Regulations

Florida FCOJ manufacturers were subject to specific regulations issued by the Florida Citrus Commission and the US Department of Agriculture (USDA), as well as broader rules applicable to all food manufacturers in the US. The USDA issued federal standards for canned orange juice in 1949, defining US Grade A ("Fancy") and US Grade C ("Standard") product requirements[19], which were updates of earlier canned juice grade standards from 1946[20]. Compliance with these standards was voluntary unless the manufacturer claimed or advertised a particular grade. The specifications included limits on the Brix, acid, and oil content of the juice, as well as requirements for typical color and flavor. The canned juice grades did not apply to concentrated OJ. The USDA also had established standards for shelf-stable canned concentrated orange juice during the war years before the commercialization of FCOJ. New revised grade standards for FCOJ were issued in 1953[21]. Grades for both sugar-added and 100% juice FCOJ products were specified. These federal grade standards remained voluntary until a USDA standard of identity for orange juice was developed in the 1960s.

The State of Florida's citrus regulations were revised and reorganized in 1949, creating the Florida Citrus Code[22]. The Code reaffirmed minimum maturity requirements for all fruit grown in Florida and mandated that all fruit be inspected and graded according to either USDA or FCC standards. Fruit used for canned or concentrated juice had to meet the same standards. Overall, Florida collaborated closely with the USDA, mandating the use of USDA trained inspectors for all in-state fruit inspections. State of Florida requirements were similar to or more restrictive than federal standards, but were mandatory rather than voluntary.

Industrial Innovation and Entrepreneurs

The rapid growth of the Florida FCOJ industry, the relative ease of entry for new entrepreneurs, and the largely unexplored variations possible around the basic FCOJ concept spawned a great deal of experimentation and innovation. While much of the focus for both manufacturers and the research community was on the practical problems of producing enough FCOJ, there were others exploring fundamentally different ideas.

One interesting entrepreneur was Anthony Rossi, an Italian immigrant to the US, who came to Florida in the 1940s. After trying a number of small ventures, by 1947 he owned a citrus packing house in Palmetto, FL, selling fresh fruit in the Northeast and fresh orange juice locally. In 1949, he renamed his company Fruit Industries Inc., moved to nearby Bradenton, and became more focused on orange juice. Although he was also manufacturing FCOJ, he was most interested in commercializing fresh orange juice on a large scale. He started shipping orange juice to New York City by trucks packed with ice, using pit-stops to replenish the ice along the several-day journey. Soon he was using the name *Tropicana* as a trademark for his product. In 1954, he developed a process to package and sell flash-pasteurized fresh juice in special waxed-cardboard gable-top cartons. Despite running counter to the successful FCOJ boom, his effort selling more-expensive, fresh juice was successful. By 1957, he had purchased a ship, named the S. S. Tropicana, to ship fresh orange juice directly from Florida to New York City and renamed his company Tropicana. Although Tropicana would operate mostly in the shadow of much larger concentrate producers for a number of decades, it would come to lead Florida's production of orange juice by the end of the century[23, 24, 25, 26]. Tropicana's important role in Florida is described more fully in later chapters.

Another area of interest to a few FCOJ producers was freeze concentration. The idea had been around for decades and was explored in the early 1940s by the FCC around the time FCOJ was invented. Compared to heat concentration under vacuum, freeze concentration had several disadvantages. It required multiple sequential partial-freezing steps to achieve concentration to 42°Brix, the now-standard consumer product. Separating the ice crystals from the juice concentrate was difficult, and the process required more initial capital investment for equipment. However, the method had one distinct advantage in that it produced a better-tasting product. No heat-induced off-flavors were introduced, nor were any of the juice volatiles lost during a vacuum concentration process. In freeze concentration, the aroma volatiles largely remained with the concentrate, yielding a product that matched the aroma of the original juice much better. Given the commercial success of the standard FCOJ product, the FCC largely lost interest in freeze concentration, but not everyone did.

By 1950, an Ohio company named Commonwealth Engineering Corporation had developed a process to sequentially concentrate orange juice using freezing. The process was named "Step Freeze" and a Florida company called Step Freeze Corporation of Florida Inc. was set up to attempt to commercialize the technology. In June 1950, they opened an experimental freeze concentration plant in Orlando, FL[27]. In the next year, their processing plant was in operation using four sequential freeze stages to reach 42°Brix concentrate[28]. Unfortunately, the venture proved largely unsuccessful. Whether the new process was not yet perfected, or simply too expensive, is unclear, but no further manufacturers in Florida implemented the Step Freeze technology at this time, and the Orlando facility quietly closed. Step Freeze Corporation of Florida was dissolved in 1956[24]. Commonwealth sold the technology, which had potential application to other juices and even beer, to Union Carbide. In the late 1950s, Minute Maid collaborated with Union Carbide to make improvements to the process and later built their own freeze concentration plant[29, 30]. However, they too would conclude it was too expensive.

Another particularly fascinating out-of-state entrepreneur who invested considerable effort in freeze concentration was George Sperti. Sperti had graduated from the University of Cincinnati in 1923, and by the early 1930s was the director of the University's Basic Research Laboratory. In 1932, he had studied the application of UV radiation to orange juice for deactivating enzymes/pasteurization[31] among many other activities. In 1935, he was hired as the first director of the Institutum Divi Thomae Foundation, a brand new education and research institute created by the Archdiocese of Cincinnati. The Archbishop at the time was concerned about the lack of Catholics employed in science and conceived the institute to complement other educational activities of the Archdiocese[32, 33, 34]. Sperti was both a successful researcher and entrepreneur, having starting a company in 1933 to manufacture UV light bulbs. Over the next 15 years, he was named to the Pontifical Academy of Sciences and his small team of researchers and students conducted research on a number of topics including applications of UV light, cancer treatments, and pharmaceuticals. One noteworthy invention from the laboratory was the medicine Preparation H, initially designed to enhance cell growth for burn treatment[35]. In 1951, the Institutum Divi Thomae Foundation was formally separated from the

Archdiocese of Cincinnati, but the Foundation remained in operation independently with George Sperti as the Director.

Sperti must have maintained an interest in orange juice from his earlier work, as he created the company Sperti Citrus in Orlando, Florida in November 1945, and was among the early producers of frozen orange juice concentrate[36, 37, 38, 39, 24]. But by 1950, he had turned his attention away from standard FCOJ. He filed a patent on a very innovative method to combine freeze concentration with vacuum-heat concentration to make a superior orange juice concentrate. His method used a single pass of freeze concentration to produce 30°Brix concentrate which contained most of the aroma volatiles. Then, he took the remaining ice crystals (having few odor volatiles but still containing some of the original sugar from the orange juice), melted them, and concentrated the liquid to 57°Brix by standard vacuum concentration. Finally, the two streams were combined to make 42°Brix juice concentrate. The obvious advantage was the preservation of most of the original fresh juice volatiles and the reduced heat-contact of the product[40].

Sperti Citrus worked with Charlie Walker, one of the early colleagues of J. J. R. Bristow and B. C. Skinner who commercialized the rotary juice press (see pg. 21), to design and build a facility. By this time, Walker owned his own company, Gulf Machinery Corp., building processing equipment. Walker would file a patent on the process in 1955, assigning rights to the Institutum Divi Thomae Foundation[41]. While this work was going on, Sperti began selling fresh juice instead of concentrate, implementing a new pasteurization process using UV light. Sperti had worked on this in the 1930s and evidently had some ideas to improve it. He filed a patent on this process in 1954[42]. A company called Golden Gift was set up in DeLand, FL to make this product. By 1954, along with Fruit Industries Inc. (Tropicana), it was one of the largest suppliers of non-concentrated orange juice[43].

By late 1956, Sperti was ready to market his new freeze-concentrated orange juice. He set up a company called Hi-Ester Corporation in DeLand, FL for that purpose and began advertising the superior nature of his orange juice concentrate[44, 45]. The "Ester" in the company name referred to the natural juice volatiles in orange juice, sometimes called "esters" by scientists at the time. Whatever the merits of the new product, Hi-Ester quickly ran into legal trouble with the FCC. The FCC, likely supported by most other FCOJ producers, filed a legal complaint with Hi-Ester's use of "fresh, tree-ripened orange juice" to describe their product. Hi-Ester was making reconstituted, single-strength juice from their new concentrate and selling it without disclosing that it had been concentrated[46, 47]. Despite their counter-arguments "Every word we say in our advertisement has been scientifically proven" and "...we add the same quality and amount of water removed in the freezing process[48]", the broad question of whether reconstituted juice and never-concentrated juice were the same was an industry minefield. Hi-Ester was out of business in 1958[49]. George Sperti would remain interested in citrus, patenting a few other citrus-related ideas and even suing Minute Maid and Union Carbide in the late 1960s for infringing on his freeze-concentration [50]. His research institute remained in operation until the 1980s.

Finally, Minute Maid established its dominant position as Florida's largest FCOJ producer following its 1954 acquisition of the *Snow Crop* brand and Dunedin, FL plant. Given their very successful advertising effort utilizing Bing Crosby, which began in 1949, the Minute Maid brand became synonymous with orange juice for many US consumers. True to their historical ties to the National Research Corporation and scientific research, they invested heavily in research facilities and programs to remain a technological leader in the FCOJ industry in Florida. In one fashion or another, Minute Maid researchers would either lead, or be closely involved in, nearly every major development in orange juice technology for the rest of the century.

The Impact on Citrus By-Products

The enormous quantities of citrus peels generated in the manufacturing of FCOJ and canned citrus juices presented both a significant disposal problem as well as a new resource for citrus by-products. Traditional products made from peel such as marmalades, jellies, candied peels, and pectin could not utilize all of the new peel supply. In the 1930s, canneries often disposed of their excess wet peel by giving it away to farmers or disposing of it in fields. However, in large quantities, it created an unsightly waste that fermented and attracted insects[51]. Disposal quickly became a major concern for citrus processors.

Researchers from the USDA (in California and Florida) and the UF Citrus Experiment Station explored potential new by-product uses and disseminated the latest developments. In 1940, the USDA published a detailed survey of citrus fruit products reflecting the pre-FCOJ environment[51]. In 1951, two UF Citrus Experiment Station scientists published an updated version, reflecting the new post-FCOJ situation in Florida[52]. Citrus essential oils, of course, were one byproduct, but the most significant development was a process whereby citrus peel could be pressed to recover residual sugar and then dried for use as cattle feed[15]. The recovered peel sugars were concentrated and called citrus molasses. The molasses was very bitter due to natural chemicals from the peel, and it was primarily used for animal feed and fermentation. The dried peel, known as citrus pulp, was found to be quite nutritious for cattle, and they enjoyed it. Givn that the peel constituted about 50% of the raw weight of a citrus fruit, the production of dried citrus was a large and necessary operation for citrus processors. The pulp could be sold to offset the additional processing cost and generate a profit. Another by-product of the citrus molasses operation was stripper oil. This was the distilled peel oil obtained when the pressed peel liquid was concentrated into citrus molasses. Stripper oil was approximately 95% d-limonene, the major terpene hydrocarbon in orange or grapefruit peel oil. The molasses concentration was carried out at high temperatures after treating the peel with lye, which destroyed the orange-like odor of the stripper oil. However, it could be used as a solvent or chemical feedstock, similar to turpentine which was then a much larger byproduct of the paper-making industry. Perhaps surprisingly, pectin was not found to be very economical to recover in Florida. Pectin had been produced in California for decades, most notably by Sunkist/California Citrus Fruit Exchange from lemons and oranges, but they were able to produce more than the market needed[53]. Additionally, pectin from lemons was generally superior to that from oranges and it never became a major by-product for Florida. The 1951 UF report on Florida's citrus by-products was next updated in 1965[54].

The USDA, on the other hand, updated their 1940 publication in 1956, now entitled "Chemistry and Technology of Citrus, Citrus Products and By-Products," and again in 1962 which covered Florida, California and Texas[55, 56]. In addition to the by-products discussed above, they mentioned powdered juices, which had been commercialized in small quantities after Vacuum Foods/Minute Maid dropped the product in the mid 1940s, and attempts to identify and commercialize specialty chemicals from citrus peels. These specialty chemicals included the flavonoids hesperidin and naringin, and a peel extract sometimes referred to as Vitamin P[57, 58]. These chemicals were being investigated for physiological effects and other pharmaceutical or chemical uses.

Research and development of citrus by-products was largely done at this time by fruit growers, non-commercial researchers like those at the USDA, regulatory groups like the Florida Citrus Commission, or entrepreneurs, and not by the juice plants themselves. For juice producers, the foremost priority was producing more good quality juice which entailed constant innovation at this time. This research dynamic was discussed at the time by Baier from Sunkist[53]. For the juice processors, the important byproducts were the ones they had to engage in for making juice, primarily dried peel, citrus molasses, stripper oil, and in some cases, the recovery of essential oils.

Florida Chemical Company

In 1942, as the US entered World War II, William H. Schulz, Jr. and his son H. E. "Bert" formed a venture called Florida Chemical Company in Lake Alfred, FL to capture the pressed liquid from waste peels and ferment it. Industrial ethanol for the war effort was in demand[59, 60]. Bert had just graduated from the University of Florida, with a biology degree. His father William, originally from Wisconsin, was the son of German immigrants. William had moved to Florida in 1912 for health reasons, studied horticulture and chemistry at UF, and after graduation started a fernery in Auburndale, FL. The fernery was successful, and William went on to develop other agricultural and real estate interests. By the start of the war, he was a successful businessman in Auburndale[61].

Unfortunately, William and Bert's alcohol venture was short-lived. They set up their facility next door to a waste peel processing plant, installing the necessary equipment to capture and ferment the waste sugar, and recover the alcohol. But the business struggled to achieve a profitable scale given their process yields and limited capital. Bert lost his draft-deferral, which was dependent on the business, and went into the Navy. He returned home in 1946, with the war over and industrial alcohol demand evaporating. Soon after, the company, now called the Florida Molasses Corporation, closed, having lost its supply of press liquid when the feed mill next door closed. Bert spent the next three years dismantling the factory and selling the equipment to pay off debts. His father William returned to other non-citrus activities[61]. Meanwhile, the new FCOJ industry began processing waste peel for citrus molasses and cattle feed in volume.

In 1951, Bert, then 30 and quite knowledgeable regarding the ins and outs of citrus peel waste, became interested in developing a market for stripper oil, which was available in surplus from the fruit processing plants. He struck a deal with Winter Garden Citrus Cooperative to install tanks and condensing equipment on their waste peel processing line at his expense, giving him a steady supply of the product. For the next decade, Bert slowly developed a small market for this new solvent, also referred to as limonene based on its primary chemical component. The chemical properties of limonene were similar to turpentine, which had an extensive industrial market at the time, but the turpentine supply was much larger and the market price was low. Given the relatively small production of stripper oil, and the effort to collect and sell it, Bert needed to uncover applications where the product performed better than turpentine and justified a higher price. He operated as a one-man effort as the Florida Molasses Corporation in a very seasonal business. Citrus was only processed part of the year in Florida, but the limonene could be stored year round if needed. The seasonal schedule suited Bert quite well as he was single and thoroughly enjoyed traveling during the off-season. A quiet but determined man, by 1957 Bert had developed a profitable enough business to fully support himself and got married. Most of his product was sold into industrial markets in the northeast US.

Although Florida Molasses was a small affair at first, in a short decade the limonene market that Bert helped create would develop into something much more important for citrus processors, a profitable value-added byproduct that nearly all citrus processors would exploit[62]. And this new limonene market would be critical to helping launch the Florida citrus flavor industry.

The Florida Essential Oil Industry

The explosive growth in processed oranges, and to a lesser extent grapefruit and tangerines in Florida, completely changed the situation regarding peel oil availability. There was now such a large supply of processed peel that the oil had become a pollution problem. Processors had the choice of collecting the peel oil at several points during their operation. The best quality oil was collected from the peel by pressing at the same time as the juice was collected. Alternatively, the processor could recover distilled oil from the waste peels via hydrodistillation or recover stripper oil from the citrus molasses operation. The stripper oil was exposed to lye and high heat and lost any usefulness as a flavoring product. There was also excess oil removed from juice by centrifugation or vacuum flash-evaporation, which was sometimes collected, but only in relatively small quantities. Mostly uncollected at this time was distilled oil from the juice concentrate evaporators. This oil largely ended up in the vacuum pump effluent as waste.

Processing plants in Florida used four main techniques to press the oil from the peel. One, the Pipkin Juice Extractor, squeezed the fruit to recover both the juice and the peel oil simultaneously, but in two different process streams. The other three methods recovered the juice first, then separately obtained the oil from the left-over peel (screw press, Pipkin roll, and Fraser-Brace extractor)[52]. All four processes used water to help recover the oil. But the pressed oil yields were often low, with much of it left behind in the wet peel to be collected as stripper oil or distilled oil or lost to the atmosphere when the peel was dried. The quality of the cold-pressed oils was variable, with the best lots being as good or better than imported oils, but many lots were inferior. The reasons were largely unknown at first. And for the reasons discussed above, each processing plant was primarily concerned with their juice products while essential oils remained a secondary concern at best.

In 1947, a chemist named James Walter Kesterson arrived at the UF Citrus Experiment Station. He set out to understand what was influencing peel oil quality. He would go on to play a significant role in improving and promoting Florida citrus oils. Starting during the 1947/48 citrus season, Kesterson and his colleague McDuff embarked on a season-long effort to monitor essential oil production at all the juice plants in Florida. Their goal was to identify the equipment and methods used by each plant, to collect and analyze oil samples, and to determine best practices for producing the highest quality peel oils. The project was conducted jointly with the FCC. To assess oil quality, Kesterson used the US Pharmacopeia specifications for orange oil and compared samples with physiochemical data collected by the Fritzsche Brothers essential oil/flavor company. One important parameter for citrus oils was the total aldehyde content, as higher aldehyde levels was known to correspond to better-flavored oils. Kesterson and McDuff published their initial results in 1948[63]. They continued the project in the next season, collecting many more oil samples[3], and detailed results were published in 1953[64]. While their primary interest was in orange oils, they also analyzed oils from grapefruit, tangerine, Meyer lemon[4], and Persian limes. Due to variations in equipment and processed fruit cultivars, it was challenging to draw general conclusions. However, they made several important observations: First, the extraction process impacted oil quality. Second, different orange cultivars produced oils of different qualities with Valencia oranges giving the best peel oil. And finally, minimizing the amount of contact water used when extracting the oil improved the total aldehyde level.

In 1949, Ernest Guenther, an essential oils expert with Fritzsche Brothers, greatly expanded the availability of citrus essential oil data by publishing a very detailed comparison of commercial oils from all the world's growing regions[65]. He combined information from samples analyzed by Fritzche Brothers over many years with data from other researchers. Florida and California citrus oils were well represented in his data. Guenther also gave detailed descriptions of the different commercial citrus oil collection methods used globally.

By the mid 1950s, US citrus oil production had surpassed domestic demand, and the oils began being exported. Florida's processing plants were individually deciding the extent of their oil collection processes. The best quality peel oils were sold as flavor or fragrance ingredients, primarily to out-of-state flavor and fragrance companies, as well as large end-use manufacturers in food and beverages, soaps, cleaning supplies or other industries. Peel oil prices, especially for orange, reflected the increased supply.

At this time was there was only two semi-official specifications for citrus oils: the US Pharmacopeia specifications for orange and lemon peel oil. These specifications were based on a few physiochemical properties such specific gravity and optical rotation derived from commercial samples. The specifications were created many decades prior based on imported oils and largely ignored odor or flavor, as there was no good way to quantify them. It was well-known that oils meeting the USP specifications could have poor sensory qualities, while seemingly good-quality oils might fail to meet these specifications. Companies outside the pharmaceutical industry typically set their own internal specifica-

---

[3]R. Hendrickson joined the project at some point.
[4]A lemon hybrid very different from California or Italian lemon.

tions, often using the USP specifications as a starting point. In the flavor industry, the US company Fritzsche Brothers (and their sister company Schimmel & Co. before the war) was particularly open about sharing data on what they considered authentically-produced essential oils. The data collected by Kesterson and Guenther (among others) helped establish a library of data for authentic Florida-produced oils, distinguishing them from California oils which could differ due to growing conditions, fruit cultivars and processing methods.

Finally, commercial distillation or extraction of citrus oils was minimal in Florida before 1960. The USDA reports from 1956 and 1962 suggest that no terpeneless or sesquiterpeneless oils were commercially produced in Florida or California[55, 56]. On the other hand, the flavor companies located outside of Florida were certainly using raw Florida citrus oils to produce more sophisticated flavoring ingredients for various food and beverage applications.

The California Industry

It is interesting to compare the processed citrus industry in Florida after the invention of FCOJ with that of California, the next largest citrus-growing state. California had long dominated the fresh-fruit market, taking advantage of its dry Mediterranean-like climate which yielded fruit with excellent peel color and appearance. Additionally, California had a robust by-products industry in peel oils, pectin, and canned juice. With the success of FCOJ in Florida, there was an obvious interest to produce the product in California. However, unlike Florida, the majority of California's fruit was controlled by a single entity, the California Fruit Growers Exchange, renamed Sunkist in 1952. The exchange had long manufactured citrus by-products using two production companies called the Exchange Orange Products Company and the Exchange Lemon Products Company. Sunkist initiated FCOJ production in 1949, integrating it within their other byproduct operations. Hull provides a description of their juice and byproduct production in his 1953 article[57]. Sunkist was well-run and had an large operation, but by controlling most of the fruit in the state, they limited their competition. Only a few smaller juice producers could gain a foothold. One was General Foods, which acquired the Bireley orange juice and beverage business in 1943. Enjoying a near monopoly in California, Sunkist possessed considerable resources to invest in any project they pursued. Their R&D investments were significant, and their personnel were excellent. However, they faced limited pressure to succeed. In contrast, the situation in Florida was far more competitive, with success or failure always looming for any plant. Texas, the third-largest citrus growing state, had a much smaller production volume, but supported a number of early juice processing plants[66]. The state operated between the competitive extremes of Florida and California.

The US Flavor Industry

Following World War II, the US flavor market was primarily serviced by private, family-owned companies that had evolved from earlier essential oil traders. Europe was devastated by the war and their essential oil, flavor and fragrance companies would take time to recover. One of the largest, the Schimmel & Co., which had played such an important role before the war, was largely gone. What remained of Schimmel was trapped behind the Iron Curtain. Polak Frutal Works (PFW), based in Holland, actually relocated its main headquarters to its US subsidiary just before the war[67]. Others that remained in Europe to pick up the pieces after the war included Firmenich and Givaudan.

In the US during the 1950s, the largest flavor companies included Fritzche Brothers, originally a subsidiary of Schimmel & Co., which acquired Dodge & Olcott in 1952, Van Ameringen-Haebler Inc., which had acquired Compagnie Morana around 1920, PFW, and Fries & Fries, a Cincinnati company with ties to liquor flavors dating back to the 1860s (see earlier discussion on pg. 23). The industry underwent substantial changes over the next few decades. First, the science of flavors advanced rapidly along with analytical chemistry. Tools like gas chromatography and mass spectrometry revolutionized the industry's understanding and practices. Meanwhile, improvements in synthetic flavor chemistry rapidly pushed the industry away from natural flavoring products, traditionally made from essential oils and essences, towards less expensive flavors dominated by synthetic flavor chemicals. Simultaneously, as these companies grew larger and family members aged, some were acquired by larger corporate entities. International Flavors and Fragrance, which went public in 1961, was formed from Van Ameringen-Haebler, for example. In Europe, Givaudan was acquired by the pharmaceutical-chemical company Hoffman-LaRoche in 1963. Even more corporate acquisitions took place in the 1970s. Chemical and pharmaceutical companies, in particular, viewed these specialized businesses as attractive acquisition targets with relatively high profit margins.

The larger national flavor companies, along with many regional ones, serviced the rapidly growing US food and beverage industry following the war. Consumers were enthusiastic about new products and open to technical innovations. Many new product concepts like powdered drinks (e. g. Kool-aid) and flavored breakfast cereals (e. g. Cocoa Puffs) were either introduced or gained in popularity as national brands during this time. They joined the growing market for carbonated soft-drinks and other beverages. All of these products required new flavors, often tailored to perform well in unusual environments, such as in dry, unrefrigerated powders or low-pH soft-drinks. It was the flavor specialists at the flavor companies who developed these sophisticated new flavoring ingredients, combining the latest science with their traditional artistry. Hand-in-hand with their customers, the flavor industry experienced a period of extraordinary growth.

References

[1] John McPhee. *Oranges*. Farrar, Straus and Giroux, 1966.

[2] *USDA NASS 1960 Citrus Summary*. United States Department of Agriculture, Mar. 1961. URL: https://www.nass.usda.gov/Statistics_by_State/Florida/Publications/Citrus/Citrus_Summary/index.php (visited on 12/30/2023).

[3] *USDA NASS 1970 Citrus Summary*. United States Department of Agriculture, 1971. URL: https://www.nass.usda.gov/Statistics_by_State/Florida/Publications/Citrus/Citrus_Summary/index.php (visited on 12/30/2023).

[4] *USDA NASS 1980 Citrus Summary*. United States Department of Agriculture, Jan. 1981. URL: https://www.nass.usda.gov/Statistics_by_State/Florida/Publications/Citrus/Citrus_Summary/index.php (visited on 12/30/2023).

[5] James T. Hopkins. *Fifty Years of Citrus: The Florida Citrus Exchange 1909–1959*. Gainesville, FL: University of Florida Press, 1960.

[6] E. L. Moore. *Laboratory Notebook of E. L. Moore started 4/2/1951*. Unpublished. Original in FDOC Headquarters, Bartow, FL. Apr. 2, 1951. (Visited on 02/28/2024).

[7] Thomas A. Rector. "Frozen Concentrated Orange Juice - Its Research Background." In: *Refrigeration Engineering* Vol. 58 (Issue 4 Apr. 1950), pp. 349–353.

[8] Jack Gurnett. "Minute Maid Buy Brings Mixed Views." In: *Orlando Sentinel* (Dec. 1, 1954), pp. 1, 2.

[9] "Mutual Gains Strength With Ocala Contract." In: *Tampa Morning Tribune* (Dec. 21, 1949), p. 2.

[10] William Gober Jr. "Concentrate Boom Draws Large Investors to State." In: *The Bradenton Herald* (Feb. 19, 1950), p. B8.

[11] H. W. von Loesecke. "Orange Juice." In: *The Chemistry and Technology of Fruit and Vegetable Juice Production*. Ed. by Donald K. Tressler and Maynard A. Joslyn. Westport, CT: Avi Publishing Company, 1954, pp. 411–446.

REFERENCES

[12] V. C. Praschan. "Chemical Engineering In The Frozen Food Industry." In: *Chemial Engineering Progress* (June 1951), pp. 325–330.

[13] C. S. Chen. "Citrus Evaporator Technology." In: *Transactions of the ASAE* Vol. 25 (Issue 5 1982), pp. 1457–1463.

[14] E. C. Hill and L. W. Faville. "Comparison of Plating Media Used for the Estimation of Microorganisms in Citrus Juices." In: *Proceedings of the Florida State Horticultural Society* Vol. 63 (1950), pp. 146–149.

[15] F. J. Van Antwerpen. "Utilization of Citrus Wastes." In: *Industrial and Engineering Chemistry* Vol. 33 (Issue 11 Nov. 1, 1941), pp. 1422–1426.

[16] *Florida Citrus Commission - Revised Rules and Regulations.* Jan. 19, 1940. URL: https://babel.hathitrust.org/cgi/pt?id=ufl.31262099399494&seq=3 (visited on 02/11/2024).

[17] R. W. Olsen et al. *Oxidised Flavors in Frozen Citrus Concentrates.* Citrus Station Mimeo Report 56-1. Florida Citrus Commission and Florida Citrus Experiment Station, Oct. 4, 1955.

[18] F. W. Wenzel, E. L. Moore, and R. W. Olsen. *Factors Affecting the Flavor of Frozen Concentrated Orange Juice.* Citrus Station Mimeo Report 58-2. Lake Alfred, FL: Florida Citrus Commission and Florida Citrus Experiment Station, Sept. 26, 1957. URL: https://ufdc.ufl.edu/UF00072393/00001/1j?search=f.w.%2B=wenzel (visited on 07/23/2024).

[19] "United States Standards for Canned Orange Juice." In: *Code of Federal Regulations* Title 7 Section 52.488 (1949).

[20] "United States Standards for Canned Orange Juice." In: *Federal Register* Volume 11 (Issue 218 Nov. 7, 1946), pp. 13244–13245.

[21] "United States Standards for Grades of Canned Concentrated Orange Juice." In: *Federal Register* Volume 18 (Issue 221 Nov. 11, 1953), pp. 7155–7159.

[22] *The Florida Citrus Code of 1949.* Legislative Summary. Florida Department of Agriculture, June 1, 1949.

[23] Sanna Barlow Rossi. *Anthony T. Rossi, Christian and Entrepreneur: The Story of the Founder of Tropicana.* Intervarsity Press, 1986.

[24] *State of Florida Business Registration Database.* URL: https://dos.fl.gov/sunbiz/search/.

[25] David O. Hamrick. "Problems Related to the Production and Distribution of Cartoned Orange Juice." In: *Proceedings of the 1956 Citrus Engineering Conference.* Citrus Engineering Conference. Winter Haven, FL: American Society of Mechanical Engineers Digital Collection, Mar. 27, 1956, pp. 1–15.

[26] Florida Citrus Hall of Fame. *Anthony T. Rossi.* URL: https://floridacitrushalloffame.com/inductees/anthony-t-rossi/ (visited on 01/19/2021).

[27] "Citrus Experiment Plant Opens Here." In: *Orlando Evening Star* (June 20, 1950), p. 5.

[28] Frank K. Lawler. "Engineering Advances FREEZE-Concentration." In: *Food Engineering* (Oct. 1951), pp. 68–71, 210–212.

[29] Maynard A. Joslyn. "Concentration by Freezing." In: *Fruit and Vegetable Juice Processing Technology.* Ed. by Donald K. Tressler. Westport, CT: Avi Publishing Company, 1961, pp. 314–333.

[30] J. G. Muller. "Freeze Concentration of Food Liquids: Theory, Practice, and Economics." In: *Food Technology* Vol. 21 (Issue 49 Jan. 1967), pp. 49–61.

[31] Frank Kay Anderson. "Science Conquers Orange Juice Preservation." In: *The Citrus Industry* Vol. 13 (Issue 1 Jan. 1932), pp. 5, 20–22, 24.

[32] University of Villanova. *Dr. George Speri Sperti.* URL: https://www1.villanova.edu/villanova/president/university_events/mendelmedal/pastrecipients/george_sperti.html (visited on 01/19/2021).

[33] Wikipedia. *Institutum Divi Thomae.* URL: https://en.wikipedia.org/wiki/Institutum_Divi_Thomae (visited on 01/29/2024).

[34] Brian Alexander. "The Milkman Cometh." In: *Cincinnati Magazine* (Sept. 26, 2013). URL: https://www.cincinnatimagazine.com/features/the-milkman-cometh/ (visited on 02/24/2024).

[35] Deborah Rieselman. "Secrets of Sperti Ointment Revealed: The Whole Story." In: *University of Cincinnati Magazine* (Aug. 20, 2011). URL: http://magazine.uc.edu/famousalumni/inventors/sperti.html (visited on 02/24/2024).

REFERENCES

[36] "Rotarians Hear Dr. Hoffman." In: *The Stuart News* (Apr. 25, 1946), p. 1.

[37] "H.S. Parker Heads Sperti Foods, Inc." In: *Palm Beach Post* (Aug. 20, 1946), p. 2.

[38] "First County Concentrate Plant Begun in Plant City." In: *Tampa Morning Tribune* (Nov. 4, 1949), pp. 1, 11.

[39] D. E. Timmons. *Citrus Canning in Florida: Early History and Statistics*. Report AE Series 50-4. Gainesville, FL: Agricultural Extension Service, University of Florida, Jan. 31, 1950.

[40] George Sperti. "Concentration of Orange Juice." Pat. 2,588,337. Assignee: Institutum Divi Thomae Foundation. United States Patent. Mar. 11, 1952.

[41] Charles S. Walker. "Continuous Process and Apparatus for Making Concentrated Liquids." Pat. 3,156,571. Assignee: Institutum Divi Thomae Foundation. United States Patent. Nov. 10, 1964.

[42] George S. Sperti. "Preservation of Fruit Juices." Pat. 2,824,014. Assignee: Institutum Divi Thomae Foundation. United States Patent. Feb. 18, 1958.

[43] James J. Nagle. "New Type Squeeze For Orange Juice." In: *The New York Times* (Nov. 28, 1954). Section: Business, pp. 1, 8.

[44] "Advertisement for the Hi-Ester Corporation." In: *The Orlando Sentinel* (Mar. 24, 1957), p. G19.

[45] Sid Porter. "Concentrate Field Gets New Firm." In: *The Orlando Sentinel* (Mar. 24, 1957), p. G11.

[46] "Citrus Firm Accused of 'False' Ads." In: *Tampa Morning Tribune* (June 29, 1957), p. A16.

[47] "FCC Files Complaints on Hi-Ester Firm Ads." In: *The Orlando Sentinel* (June 29, 1957), p. A3.

[48] "Hi-Ester Firm Official Says Ad Claims Proved." In: *The Orlando Sentinel* (June 19, 1957), p. B5.

[49] "Creditor Asks Court For Hi-Ester Receiver." In: *The Orlando Sentinel* (Mar. 14, 1958), p. A6.

[50] *Sperti Products Inc. v. Coca-Cola Company.* Legal Decision. Case: 272 F. Supp. 441. US District Court, D. Delaware, Aug. 17, 1967. URL: https://www.casemine.com/judgement/us/5914c82bad d7b049347e85d3 (visited on 02/25/2024).

[51] E. M. Chace, H. W. von Loesecke, and J. L. Heid. *Citrus Fruit Products*. USDA Circular 577. United States Department of Agriculture, Nov. 1940.

[52] Rudolph Hendrickson and J. W. Kesterson. *Citrus By-Products of Florida: Commercial Production Methods and Properties*. Bulletin 487. Gainesville, FL: University of Florida Agricultural Experiment Station, Dec. 1951.

[53] William C. Baier. "Citrus By-Products and Derivatives - An Introductory Survey." In: *Food Technology* Vol. 9 (Issue 2 Feb. 1955), pp. 78–80.

[54] R. Hendrickson and J. W. Kesterson. *By-Products of Florida Citrus. Composition, Technology, and Utilization*. Bulletin 698. University of Florida Agricultural Experiment Station, Oct. 1965.

[55] Agricultural Research Service. *Chemistry and Technology of Citrus, Citrus Products, and Byproducts*. Agricultural Handbook No. 98. Washington, D.C.: United States Department of Agriculture, Nov. 1956.

[56] Agricultural Research Service. *Chemistry and Technology of Citrus, Citrus Products, and Byproducts*. Agricultural Handbook No. 98. Washington, D.C.: United States Department of Agriculture, Sept. 1962.

[57] William Q. Hull, C. W. Lindsay, and William C. Baier. "Chemicals From Oranges." In: *Industrial and Engineering Chemistry* Vol. 45 (Issue 5 May 1, 1953), pp. 876–890.

[58] R. Hendrickson and J. W. Kesterson. *Vitamin P in Citrus Products*. Citrus Station Mimeo Report 56-10. Lake Alfred, FL: Florida Citrus Commission and Florida Citrus Experiment Station, Oct. 5, 1955. URL: https://ufdc.ufl.edu/UF00072378/00001/citation (visited on 07/23/2024).

[59] "Citrus To Be Used To Make War Explosive." In: *Tampa Tribune* (Oct. 8, 1942), p. 3.

REFERENCES

[60] R. M. French Jr. "Around Florida - Canning Plant To Convert Citrus By-Products Into Alcohol and Molasses for War Purposes." In: *Miami Herald* (Oct. 9, 1942), p. 1.

[61] Henry Elbert Schulz. *Bert's Story - The Life & Heritage of Henry Elbert Schulz*. Lakeland, FL: Genie Publishing, 2000. ISBN: 1-889137-13-8.

[62] Caroll Teeter. "A Wonderous By-Product of Citrus." In: *Citrus Industry* (July 1996), pp. 14–18.

[63] J. W. Kesterson, O. R. McDuff, and Harold Mowry. *Florida Citrus Oils: Commercial Production Methods and Properties of Essential Oils (Season- 1947-48)*. Bulletin 452. Gainesville, FL: University of Florida Agricultural Experiment Station, Nov. 1948.

[64] J. W. Kesterson and R. Hendrickson. *Essential Oils from Florida Citrus*. Bulletin 521. Gainesville, FL: University of Florida Agricultural Experiment Station, July 1953. URL: https://ufdc.ufl.edu//UF0026864/00001 (visited on 09/16/2020).

[65] Ernest Guenther. *The Essential Oils: History - Individual Essential Oils of the Plant Families Rutaceae and Labiatae*. Vol. 3. New York, NY: D. Van Nostrand Company, 1949.

[66] Will H. Shearon Jr. and E. M. Burdick. "Citrus Fruit Processing." In: *Industrial & Engineering Chemistry* Vol. 40 (Issue 3 1948), pp. 370–378.

[67] *Polak's Frutal Works, Inc. v. United States of America*. Legal Decision. Case: 281 F. 2d 261 (2d Cir. 1960). US Court of Appeals, 2nd Circuit, July 21, 1960. URL: https://law.justia.com/cases/federal/appellate-courts/F2/281/261/60504/ (visited on 03/16/2024).

5
Essence Recovery

"...the biggest thing that's happened in the industry since concentrate came along..."

—Tom Millsaps, *Tampa Tribune*, 1967[1].

For the American consumer, the food and beverage market was an increasing array of interesting choices at affordable prices. The act of exploring new products itself influenced consumers and altered their expectations. Food manufacturers sought to influence consumer selection with their marketing efforts and new product introductions. Orange juice suppliers responded to this competitive landscape by seeking to differentiate their products based on flavor, price, and other qualities.

Orange juice, being a 100% juice product, benefited from consumers' perception of citrus as healthy, nutritious, and free of artificial ingredients. Consumers associated orange juice with a familiar yet premium flavor experience. And, regulatory constraints on 100% juice products, developed with industry cooperation, strictly limited the ingredients that could be used to enhance the flavor, unlike many competing citrus-flavored products. Maintaining and even enhancing orange juice's reputation for excellent flavor was crucial for the entire citrus industry. Yet, for Florida FCOJ, most of the fresh-juice flavor was lost during the juice concentration process. Key flavor volatiles were removed from the concentrate along with the water and exhausted into the air by the processor's vacuum pumps. Only a small portion were restored by adding fresh cutback juice to the concentrate during manufacturing. Finding a commercially-viable solution to this problem would take years and involve numerous contributors. However, the outcome was an improved orange juice product and the emergence of a new citrus flavor industry in Florida.

What is Missing?

The earliest concentrate-based products were bedeviled by off-flavors associated with the concentration process. With Bristow and Skinner's development of a high-vacuum, low-temperature citrus juice concentration process in the late 1930s[2] and later independent work by the USDA[3, 4], the process-induced off-flavor problems were essentially solved. However, the concentrated product was stripped of all its fresh flavor volatiles, leaving a noticeably inferior flavor. The cutback process restored some of these lost volatiles, but without any detailed understanding of what was being lost or added. Improving upon this would require more knowledge about these lost flavor volatiles and, more generally, about the science of citrus flavors.

There had been both academic and commercial interest to identify the important juice flavor compounds, as well as to understand their role in juice shelf stability. Citrus peel oils were obviously playing a role, and these oils had long been commercial items of trade to the flavor and fragrance industry. Much research had been done on those products, albeit using the limited analytical technology available at the time. The earliest work was summarized in 1922 by Gildemeister and Hoffman [5]. At the University of Florida, O. P. Huff published a 1917 thesis studying the preparation and chemical properties of some Florida citrus essential oils[6]. In 1925, Hall and Wilson, working for the California Fruit Growers Exchange (Sunkist), reported the results of an extensive study of the volatile flavor components in Valencia orange juice. They isolated a volatile mixture directly from the juice that was "distinctly different" in odor character from peel oil. With considerable effort, they analyzed these flavor volatiles and found components like acetaldehyde and ethyl acetate which were not found in peel oil[7]. Today, these chemicals are known to be quite important to fresh juice flavor. In 1932, the USDA in Winter Haven, FL began a long-term research effort, under the leadership of Harry von Loesecke, to support the utilization of citrus fruits not suitable for the fresh market. His team investigated many citrus products then in production (or under consideration) including canned and frozen single-strength citrus juices, citrus concentrates and the peel oils themselves[8, 9]. At this time, there were well-known problems with off-note flavors developing in canned single-strength orange and grapefruit juices under storage. Understanding the sources of these off-flavors was important to the industry, and the flavor volatiles themselves were thought to play an important role. There were also USDA facilities in California supporting the citrus industry there. This combined USDA effort would form a core of technical expertise for the nascent processed citrus industry. It is not clear if the USDA experimented themselves with aroma recovery, as they reported no successful results, but they would likely have been aware of others' efforts. In 1940, on the topic of the lost essence in citrus concentrates, the Florida-based USDA team commented, "Returning the volatile compounds that come over at the beginning of the evaporation does not seem to improve the flavor of the concentrates[10]."

As orange juice concentrate began to achieve commercial success after 1945, and despite considerable knowledge concerning the lost volatiles, aroma recovery was largely a minor concern. In retrospect, there were several interrelated problems specific to citrus that would take years to solve. First, the flavor volatiles of citrus were very complex compared to other fruits like apple. The lost compounds included compounds like acetaldehyde, which boil away at much lower temperatures than water, but also other compounds which were much less volatile than water. The complex mixture of important aroma chemicals included aldehydes, esters, alcohols, and terpenes. The latter compounds, in particular, being essentially insoluble in water, exhibited unusual behavior when evaporated. In addition, the citrus flavor profile lacked one or two "character compounds," such as methyl anthranilate in grape, that dominate the aroma perception. In those cases, it is easy to focus recovery and restoration efforts on those specific character compounds. Rather, in citrus, the flavor is the result of a complex interplay of many different compounds where relative ratios are critical to the overall sensory impression. The chemical complexity of the lost essence meant any aroma capture equipment would need to be likewise sophisticated.

Second, the heat sensitivity associated with citrus concentrates required very high vacuum environments for the early evaporators. And precisely under high vacuum, the collection of the flavor volatiles is most difficult. This was especially true in production-scale equipment where the very low-temperature, high-efficiency condensers that could possibly trap the essence were very expensive to build and operate. The high-vacuum conditions also made any essence concentration process much more difficult, as chemical fractionation techniques work better at higher system pressures. And in all cases, the condensation process and fractionation impacted the relative ratios of the aroma compounds, which was so important to the overall flavor profile.

Finally, there was considerable confusion at the time regarding the role of the volatile aroma and peel oil in the development of off-flavors in citrus juices under storage. Problems associated with the peel oil content had been well-known in canned orange and grapefruit juices since the 1920s. Similar problems were observed when adding oil to juice concentrates, although deterioration when frozen happened more slowly than for canned juices. Thus, determining whether a juice was better after aroma addition was a complex question involving product shelf-life and storage conditions. The chemistry of terpene oxidation, largely responsible for these problems, would take some time to be understood.

Meanwhile, the cutback process, known universally as the "Florida Process," was patented in 1948. It provided a very efficient solution and certainly enabled the orange juice concentrate business to succeed. In fact, just managing the very rapid product growth was about all industry could do for a few years. For all these reasons, the most important early discoveries with aroma capture were done for non-citrus juice products.

Early Success in Apple, Pineapple and Grape

Early experiments in the commercial capture and use of apple volatiles from the concentration of apple juice were reported by Carpenter & Smith in 1934[11]. These authors, based at the New York State Agricultural Experimental Station in Geneva, NY, were interested in the use of apple juice concentrate for carbonated beverages. Referring to the lost apple aroma from the juice concentration process as "esters," based on the then-current knowledge regarding the dominance of esters in natural apple flavor, the authors successfully captured some of these volatiles and returned them to apple juice concentrate, improving the resulting flavor of the product. Interestingly, the equipment being used by the authors was recently commercialized by the Pfaudler Company of Rochester, NY, under the name "Fruit Juice Concentrator with Ester Impregnating Unit." The Pfaudler process consisted of two stages. In the first stage, apple juice was concentrated by boiling under moderate vacuum. In the second stage, chilled concentrate was used to scrub the remaining vapor from the first stage after it passed through a condenser designed to remove the water. The chilled concentrate in the second stage would capture some of the flavor volatiles from the vapor. The design was patented in 1932 by U. G. Todd (it was filed in 1926) motivated in part by the Prohibition-era desire to dealcoholize beer but not lose the important flavor volatiles, which are also dominated by esters[12]. With Prohibition having ended in 1933, clearly new markets were needed!

Apple juice has a key advantage over citrus in that the juice is far less heat-sensitive, allowing it to be concentrated at higher temperatures without developing objectionable off-flavors. The higher concentration temperatures mean less vacuum is needed, which implies less complex effort to condense the volatiles. Nevertheless, the volatiles must still be separated from the water removed during concentration, and these early efforts were not terribly efficient. Many important flavoring compounds were still being lost. With most apple juice sold fresh at farmside stands at the time, apple juice concentrate was very much a niche product. Production equipment for concentrate was relatively inexpensive, and commercial barriers to entry low. Producers could have easily experimented in-house with volatile recovery, and undoubtedly some did. A simple system of sequential chilled condensers would have captured some important apple aroma compounds, and there was little motivation for commercial innovators to disclose their methods. By the late 1930s, apple essence was being collected and used commercially at least in a limited way[3].

Extensive efforts to improve the commercial apple aroma collection process were undertaken by H. P. Milleville, R. K. Eskew, and colleagues working at the Eastern Regional Research Laboratory of the USDA in Philadelphia, PA, starting in the early 1940s. In 1945, Milleville submitted a patent for a new essence recovery system[13] that attempted to strip the volatiles from pre-heated apple juice under vacuum, leaving the heated juice to be subsequently concentrated via standard commercial techniques with the volatiles already gone. The stripped vapor containing water and most of the flavor volatiles was directed to a fractionating column to more efficiently separate out the desired aroma from the dominant water vapor. The invention was assigned to the USDA and extensively publicized in 1946[14].

Milleville updated his patent in 1949[15]. He was no longer working at the USDA and assigned the patent rights to a commercial interest. Meanwhile, Eskew carried on the work at the USDA and published in 1951 a complete description of a commercial process for manufacturing 42°Brix apple juice concentrate based upon the very successful 3+1 concentrated orange juice product but using concentrated apple essence added back to the apple juice concentrate in place of the cutback juice used in orange[16]. Eskew *et al.* deemed their concentrated essence "150-fold" based upon the theoretical concentration factor of the volatiles compared to the starting juice and specifically contrasted the advantages of concentrated aroma use over the so-called "Florida Process" of single-strength juice addition to the concentrate. An important observation made in this work was that apple juice could be rapidly heated to 99°C and flash-boiled under moderate vacuum to quickly strip the volatiles away from the concentrate as the juice fell in a vacuum chamber. The rapid evaporation cooled the concentrate quickly, and a vapor/liquid separator was used to direct the essence-containing vapor to a fractionating column while the somewhat cooled juice, slightly concentrated, could be directed to standard evaporator equipment. Even though apple juice concentrate was traditionally produced at temperatures $\leq 60°C$ to minimize the development of cooked off-flavors, higher heat was found to be acceptable if the time was limited to seconds. The higher heat improved the efficiency of vaporizing, concentrating, and condensing the important flavor volatiles.

By 1952, the Hawaiian Pineapple Company was building a large commercial plant in Honolulu for the production of concentrated pineapple juice, equipped with a system for the recovery of "volatile esters" utilizing a 44-ft fractionating column. Deemed "one of the largest canneries in the world devoted to a single fruit," the project was enormous. The recovered pineapple essence was stored and recombined with the pineapple concentrate prior to canning[17]. Some additional details are given by Milleville in a 1954 article[18]. Interestingly enough, a key person employed by the refrigeration contractor associated with this plant was E. J. Kelly[17]. E. J. Kelly would soon start an engineering company that was quite involved in building citrus processing equipment in Florida and California as well as in early efforts to collect orange essence.

H. P. Milleville, now working in private industry, wrote a 1954 review article on volatile flavor recovery in fruit and vegetable juices[18]. He stated that aroma recovery was in commercial use then for apple, grape, and pineapple juices, but efforts for citrus were unsuccessful so far. He also discussed the change of nomenclature that had occurred, bearing unfortunate connotations. Early literature had referred to the lost fruit flavor volatiles from the juice concentration process as "esters" and the recovery as "ester recovery" or an "ester trap." Recognizing the chemical diversity of fruit flavor volatiles, the newer term was "essence recovery," motivated by the fact that the recovered volatiles reproduced the characteristic fruity odor or the "essence" of the processed fruit. Unfortunately, Milleville comments, "essence" was a common term in the food flavor industry where it was associated with "alcoholic solutions of ethereal synthetics or to a lesser extent with alcoholic solutions of natural flavorings." The connotation that recovered essence from juice was somehow not a natural product or not a part of the juice or even liable to synthetic modification would influence later regulatory consideration of these essences in orange juice.

Early Efforts in Citrus

There is scant evidence reported in the literature of citrus essence capture experimentation prior to the late 1940s. However, some experimental work must have been done as J. L. Heid of the USDA commented in 1943, "Efforts to return fractions of condensates to citrus juice concentrates have usually resulted in off-flavors which offset any improvement which might otherwise have been obtained...[3]." Heid himself described the routine early use of rapid single-pass heating of juice, prior to concentration, for the purpose of microbial reduction and juice cloud stabilization in orange juice. When carried out under vacuum, a small portion of the juice would be volatilized in this process. It would have been relatively easy to condense these vapors and consider their use for flavor restoration. However, absent any form of concentration, this condensate would be very weak in flavor. Commercial juice concentrators evidently found little benefit if they tried it at all. More sophisticated experiments were quite difficult in citrus. The essence is actually two-phase, with the oil- and water-phase each possessing different flavor characters and responding differently to fractionation methods. At the time, none of this was understood. It seems likely that any negative essence experimentation results were simply left unpublished. The 1948 USDA patent on the cutback juice process stated the common understanding at the time: "It is possible to improve the flavor of apple and grape juice concentrates by the reincorporation of the flavoring compounds; but in the case of other fruit juices, particularly citrus juices, the results have been unsatisfactory[19]."

In 1949, Kaufman and Campbell, working for General Foods Corporation, reported on extensive experimentation being carried out there on frozen orange juice concentrate, including volatile recovery and incorporation into the concentrate[20]. By this time, General Foods was one of the largest producers of frozen orange juice concentrate and a national leader in frozen foods under the *Birdseye* label. The authors described experiments capturing the first "10% of distillate from vacuum concentration by means of low-temperature condensation" and then blending this essence with orange juice concentrate either "as is" or further concentrated ten-fold. Both variants were compared with the "Florida Process" and found to be unfavorable. Thomas Rector, a General Foods Vice-President, provided some additional commentary in a 1950 article[21, 22], which otherwise glowingly described the successful new FCOJ product for General Foods. He commented, "Unfortunately, the volatile flavors turned out to be very unstable and, to date, no one has succeeded in removing these flavors from the juice and restoring them to anything like their original acceptability." Interestingly, Rector stated that a California company called Bireley's, which was acquired by General Foods in 1943, had built essence capture equipment including some sort of essence concentration process and experimented with including it in OJ concentrate. Frank Bireley started the company in 1923 and initially produced orange juice but by the 1930s was also manufacturing concentrate as a base for a successful beverage called "Bireley's Orangeade." Rector does not specifically indicate when this essence-capture work was done, but seems to indicate it was before the General Foods acquisition and he comments that the results were not considered successful.

The USDA work by Eskew *et al.* on apple certainly gained the attention of USDA colleagues in Florida. Veldhuis and Morgan from the Winter Haven, FL USDA facility, the same laboratory credited with the "Florida Process," reported in 1952 on experiments capturing orange essence using Eskew's pilot-plant equipment[23]. The initial results were discussed at a local industry conference in Florida, followed up by a peer-reviewed publication in 1953[24]. They were successful in capturing essence they described as "150-fold" using terminology from Eskew's apple work, but indicated that the use of the aroma in orange juice concentrate was somewhat disappointing: "Orange essence, when added in normal amounts to orange concentrate becomes organoleptically undetectable in the reconstituted juice after about six months of storage at 0°F. A residual effect noted was a heightening of the peel oil taste of the reconstituted juice[23]." The later paper gave more details and indicated that the authors tested the captured essence with various combinations of peel oil additionally added to the FCOJ. The results hinted at some of the problems associated with determining whether the flavor was better or not:

> A comparison of reconstituted concentrate with added essence and without essence showed that the presence of essence did contribute to orange aroma. There was some difference of opinion in comparing desirability of products with cold-pressed peel oil only and those with both essence and peel oil. Some individuals expect and look for a fairly strong peel oil taste, while other prefer milder oily taste and tend to favor the essence. The consensus of the laboratory taste panel was that essence, when freshly added, complemented the taste of cold-pressed peel oil and made it approach the fresh natural flavor of oranges, but not as closely as when cutback juice was used[24].

As taste panels in Florida – both in research and industrial settings – were often dominated by persons well-acquainted with "Florida Process" orange juice, the panels could easily skew towards the familiar. In any case, the 1953 paper also concluded that the essence stability in juice was poor, but not because of off-flavor development but just due to loss of impact over time.

In 1952, Rice, Keller, and Beavens from the USDA laboratory in Pasadena, CA reported on extensive studies of aroma recovery and volatile restoration in California Valencia orange juice concentrate[25]. This work was done in 1950. The authors used a pilot-plant scale low-temperature recirculating evaporator running at 12–14 mm Hg vacuum very similar to commercial evaporators of the time. A chilled-water condenser captured most of the evaporated water, while the remaining vapor passed through a dry-ice secondary condenser prior to entering the vacuum pump. The condensed water from the first condenser was concentrated in a continuous fractionating column to concentrations of 20x, 80x, or 110x which produced an orange water-phase essence with $\sim 0.1\%$ entrained volatile oils. The authors point out that the dry-ice condenser captured a small amount of oil/water emulsion which possessed an "intense" aroma of fresh orange. They combined this oil emulsion with the distilled essence for their flavor studies.

The observation of the captured oil-phase essence was very important as this oil-phase product would become extremely important in future years. Prior authors had identified only the water-phase essence, similar to what is seen in most other fruits like apple and pineapple. These authors further characterized this oil-phase essence as arising both from peel oil present in the juice during concentration, but also finding some present even when extreme care was taken to juice the oranges only after the peel was completely removed, minimizing any possibility for peel oil to end up in the juice. Rice et al. then reported the flavor impact of using various combinations of this captured essence, peel oil, and a whole-fruit puree in place of cutback juice for volatile restoration to FCOJ. They explained their motivation in terms of the advantages that a flavoring substitute for cutback juice could provide. Several of their conclusions are noteworthy: First, they found that the captured essence, peel oil, and fruit puree all did a good job in restoring the lost aroma of the concentrate. However, they found that the results with peel oil were quite dependent on the sample of peel oil - with certain samples being much better than others. They found the results with the oil-phase essence to be similar to those with the good peel oil. The authors found the use of peel oil and fruit puree to be most noteworthy (probably because of the ease of sourcing these ingredients compared to the complicated essence collection equipment) and based upon extensive taste tests with multiple fortified lots and large taste panels (including industry representatives) they concluded "the flavor and aroma were described as being very good" and the fortified concentrates showed no significant changes in flavor after storage at $0°F$ for 8 months.

About the same time, G. J. Keller, one of the USDA scientists in Pasadena, filed a patent for a very innovative design for an essence unit[26]. Unlike the conventional fractionating column and condenser combination which was used in the work described above, the Keller design specifically focused on capturing the lost oil-phase essence by means of a vapor-scrubbing process using chilled calcium chloride solutions in a recirculating falling-film design. The process was specifically optimized to capture the water-insoluble oils removed in the juice concentration process. Keller's design lost the water-soluble components of the essence, but he clearly believed the oil-soluble essence was the most important for flavor restoration to the juice concentrate. No evidence was found that this design was implemented outside of pilot-plant trials by Keller himself, although his reasoning regarding the difficulty of condensing very small quantities of entrained flavor oils in the condensate vapor and the application of a vapor-scrubber approach seemed to influence later designs.

Meanwhile, research on essence collection was also clearly underway at the citrus plants themselves in Florida. E. J. Kelly, who had been involved in the construction of the 1952 pineapple concentrate plant in Hawaii, had formed an equipment company E. J. Kelly and Associates in Los Angeles, California and turned his attention to citrus products. In 1955 he was constructing evaporators for the Florida Citrus Canners Cooperative in Lake Wales, FL[27], and the following year for Treesweet in Ft. Pierce[28, 29, 30]. By 1958 he had teamed up with the Libby, McNeill & Libby company, who had a plant in Ocala, FL. Kelly filed a patent on October 13, 1958 entitled "Apparatus for Producing Flavor Constituents" describing an essence unit operating in conjunction with conventional low-temperature, high-vacuum orange juice evaporators[31]. The system was clearly production-scale and quite complex, utilizing a fractionating column, multiple condensers at various temperatures, and vapor scrubbers. He filed later continuation patents in 1960 and 1962 which were assigned to Libby, McNeill & Libby[32, 33] detailing further modifications and improvements.

Kelly's efforts with essence were well-regarded within the company. By 1959, Libby was supplying numerous samples of their essence to R. W. Wolford, who worked at the Citrus Experiment Station (CES) for the Florida Citrus Commission (FCC), for analysis and study[34]. Libby likely aimed to ensure that Florida citrus regulators were comfortable with essence collection and use. The initiative at Libby was closely associated with Howard Trumm who worked at Libby throughout the 1950s and by 1961 was the Laboratory Manager of the Citrus Division. Trumm and his senior colleague Robert Schaffner, VP for Research and Quality Standards, testified in 1961 before the FDA on the topic of essence use in orange juice concentrate[35, pg. 3146ff, pg. 3292ff] (These hearings are described in more detail below). Schaffner indicated that Libby was collecting orange essence on commercial evaporators in their facility under regular operating conditions and had conducted extensive blind taste panel tests in 1959 of FCOJ with and without essence compared to a cutback-containing control. The tests were conducted at three Libby plants using mostly company employees, meaning most of the testers would have been outside of Florida and therefore perhaps not so familiar with the "typical" Florida FCOJ product. Schaffner reported that the essence-containing FCOJ rated very well[35, pg. 3294-3310].[1] In a 1961 national campaign directed at the public, Libby claimed, "A new orange juice concentrate developed after five years of intensive research is on its way to market under the *Libby* label. The new product has more of the aroma and flavor of freshly-squeezed orange juice than was ever before possible in commercially-packed concentrate, says Libby research and marketing officials[37]."

As evidenced by the Kelly patents, the essence collection work at Libby was extensive, involving a complex design and improvements throughout the 1958–1962 time frame. The technological approach seemed to be an extension of the Eskew apple-essence design and was likely influenced by Kelly's experience with the Hawaiian Pineapple Company's pineapple concentrate essence design. In fact, the Libby company was also involved in pineapple concentrate in Hawaii and Howard Trumm had worked there with Libby earlier in his career[38]. The fractionating column utilized in the essence unit was a 22 plate 36" bubble cap column[39] which was standard distillation technology but of rather large size. Yet, the patents disclosed an interesting perspective on their approach as they considered the oil-phase essence removed in the concentration process a defect. In US Patent 3,223,534 filed on November 7, 1962 and assigned to Libby, Kelly stated:

> Prior workers in this art appeared to be confused and looked for an oily material as a source of flavor. The present invention obtains the flavoring and aromatic constituents in a non-oily, water-soluble, and miscible form ... Contrary to the teaching of the prior art, it has been found that the oily contaminants (present with the flavor and aromatic con-

---

[1]Hamilton's claim that this is the first documented use of orange essence in FCOJ is probably a misinterpretation of Schaffner's testimony[36, pg. 20, 119].

stituents in citrus products) impart unpleasant taste and odor characteristics...[33]

Kelly's patent particularly focused on the water-phase essence and proposed using the ester content of the aroma, which was dominated by ethyl acetate, as a measure of aroma strength or fold. Commenting on the water-phase aroma that Libby was collecting at the time, an industry expert with extensive experience with orange essences and unaffiliated with Libby recalled in 1988 that "some of the essences were quite good and others were less than desirable. The results were most erratic. No one could understand why[39]."

Around 1957, experimental work on essence collection was also being done at Winter Garden Citrus Cooperative. The efforts were led by Charlie Hendrix, in charge of Quality Chemistry and Research, and an outside technical consultant James Redd. These two attempted to collect essence from Thermal Recompression Mojonnier production evaporators[39], which were standard equipment at the time and operated at low temperatures and high vacuum. The details of the essence collection equipment are unknown, but the results were quite unsatisfactory according to Redd[39]. One constant difficulty with low-temperature commercial evaporators at the time was biological growth. Operating at low temperatures in the range of 18–50°C to minimize cooked off-flavors, the warm interior coated with juice provided an excellent substrate to grow yeast and molds which were naturally present in the juice. These microorganisms produced their own volatile odorants which were generally unpleasant, including diacetyl which has a dairy/butter-like odor. Cleaning the evaporators was a difficult manual job, and citrus plants ran regular diacetyl and plate-count measurements of the concentrate to monitor microbial growth and schedule cleanings. Any essence collection process would capture and concentrate the odorants associated with this biological activity, which were far more concentrated in the essence than in the concentrate. After a series of disappointing experiments with bad-smelling essence, Redd and Hendrix identified microbial growth as a major problem after disassembling an evaporator in the summer of 1958 and observing the biological growth inside[39]. But from a practical perspective, this was not easy to solve. It would have been difficult to motivate plant management to modify equipment cleaning schedules for an experimental new product.

The problem of off-flavor concentration by essence collection equipment would have been an ongoing issue for all experimenters and was not limited to the sanitation of the evaporators. Any sort of microbiological growth generates volatile molecules, many of which are readily associated by human experience with decay and deterioration. When processing citrus, it is important that moldy or damaged fruit be efficiently removed prior to processing, or they can introduce these off-flavors into the juice. Even good fruit, if bruised in harvesting or transport and left in warm temperatures, will slowly generate fermentation flavors due to naturally present yeasts. Additional microbial growth during processing, especially under the warm, wet conditions inside an evaporator, compounds the problem. Other odor active compounds present in the processing environment at very low levels, such as in the process waters used for fruit washing, may also be concentrated in the essence capture process. Since these off-notes were mostly stripped from the concentrated juice, their negative impact on operations was less apparent in FCOJ than in the essence. Until essence experimenters became experienced with "good essence," it was hard to identify all of the negative contributing factors.

James Redd was early to recognize another important feature of essence collection which was its role as a pollution control device[39, 40]. All of the commercial evaporators required very high vacuums. Generally, this vacuum was provided by means of multiple-stage steam ejector systems, which required substantial water and produced a water discharge. Any flavor volatiles that were released by the juice concentration process and not internally condensed were captured in the vacuum system exhaust water or released in the exhaust vapor. For citrus, the volatile oils condensed in the vacuum pump exhaust were readily apparent as they didn't mix and dilute, but floated to the top. Additional volatile oils were released by the citrus plants when leftover fruit peels were dried for cattle feed. When the citrus concentrate industry was small, this was less of a problem, but as the industry grew in size, pollution control became increasingly important to regulators.

General Foods also had a program investigating essence collection in FCOJ in the late 1950s. Ellis Byer and Alfred Lang developed an essence collection apparatus which they submitted for a patent initially on December 16, 1959, and subsequently modified on December 3, 1962[41]. Perhaps influenced by the earlier work of G. J. Keller and in contrast with the Libby efforts, Byer and Lang focused on the oil-phase essence, considering the water-phase essence as commercially "impractical." They utilized a series of condensers and a reboiling step with the essence, but absent any specific fractionating column, to capture a two-phase essence with the oil-phase top layer described as a "minor subfraction" which was found to offer "the desirable flavor enhancement to the juice concentrate." On January 1, 1961 the two submitted another patent describing the use of this essence in FCOJ[42] with a particular focus on making sure the mixture was oxygen-free for shelf-life stability.

The largest FCOJ manufacturer in Florida, Minute Maid, had maintained a state-of-the-art R&D laboratory in Plymouth, FL, since 1953[43]. On September 18, 1961, one of their employees, Jewell Allen Brent, submitted a patent application describing the use of essence collected from a conventional Mojonnier evaporator in making FCOJ. The patent didn't describe the essence equipment in detail but outlined a conventional vacuum flash evaporation step for the concentrate, followed by essence concentration by "selectively condensing the water vapors and the essence in suitable condensers[44]." On the same day, a patent application for an essence unit was submitted by Jewell Brent, Clarence Du Bois, and Carl Huffman, all employees of Minute Maid. This particular application was abandoned, and the details are unavailable, but a revised application was later filed on June 2, 1964[45]. Nevertheless, the Minute Maid Chief of Quality Control, Charles Brokaw, testified in 1961 before the FDA that "we think this practice of adding the orange essence is extremely important, and we want to avoid any obstacles which might arise to prevent us from adding the orange essence.... the process is now in commercial use, and from my knowledge of the technical activities in the industry at this time, I feel that it will be in widespread use in not too many years[35, pg. 2407]." When asked during the hearing, "Could you tell me without revealing any practice which is considered by you a trade secret of your organization how these volatile constituents are captured and then after that, how you get them back into the juice?", Brokaw responded, "No, I am afraid that I could not outline for you any such piece of equipment or process to do that, other than to say that in general, it involves a process of volatilizing the constituents on a controlled basis and condensing and capturing those constituents[35, pg. 2603]." Coca-Cola, which purchased Minute Maid in 1960, has always had a reputation for corporate secrecy. Minute Maid, under Coke, would have worked hard to protect their internal research from competitors. But it is clear they were working on essence collection too. An industry insider with knowledge of construction activities for Gulf Machinery Corporation, a major equipment builder for the Florida citrus industry, reported that during the early 1960s, essence units and related parts were constructed by Gulf Machinery for a number of clients including "Minute Maid, Libby McNiel [sic], and Birdseye[46]."

Other manufacturers were certainly keeping tabs on their colleagues' efforts, if not conducting their own experiments. One area of growing interest was the potential advantage of producing high Brix concentrate. Orange juice could be concentrated up to around 70° Brix and still remain a flowable liquid. While difficult for consumers to use at this high concentration, it was potentially very useful for industrial use, saving transportation costs. But when single-strength cutback juice was added back to concentrate, it diluted the mixture, limiting the overall concentration. It was quickly recognized that this problem could be solved by using concentrated essence in place of cutback juice. Meanwhile, concerns were being raised by industry participants and regulators about how essence might "fit" into the industry and its regulatory framework. And on the horizon, unbeknownst to everyone, big changes were coming to the citrus evaporator technology then in use. The decade of the 1960s would prove decisive for this new essence technology.

Regulatory Issues

An important regulatory issue arose early in the commercialization of essence collection. Fruit essences contained the natural alcohol present in the raw fruit, concentrated by the collection process. The amount of alcohol was highly dependent on the type and ripeness of the fruit and the concentrating power of the essence equipment, but was typically above 0.5%, the lower limit above which the US government considers a potable alcoholic solution to be a beverage. To the IRS, the government body responsible for the regulation and taxation of alcoholic beverages, essence equipment looked like distillation and essence like a distilled fruit wine. Regulations following the repeal of Prohibition required an expensive federal excise tax to be collected for every gallon of alcoholic beverage produced. And the ownership and operation of distillation equipment was highly regulated. For fruit juice concentrate processors, the potential regulatory burdens and taxes associated with essence collection were extremely troublesome. The IRS recognized the special circumstances and issued new regulations in 1949 concerning

"Volatile Fruit Flavor Concentrates[47]." "Concentrate" in this title referred to essence. Under these regulations, any essence equipment needed to be registered with the IRS and extensive record-keeping was required. Juice concentrate plants could collect essence and add it back to their juice with no tax assessed on this essence. For any essence intended to be moved offsite or sold, excise tax would be due as for an alcoholic beverage with two exceptions: either the alcohol was < 6% in the essence or, if between 6 and 15%, the essence had to be "denatured" by adding ingredients making it undrinkable (and unusable in 100% juice). Language in the regulation also prohibited processing of fermented fruits. All of these requirements were codified in Title 26 Part 198 of the Code of Federal Regulations.

Aside from the registration and record-keeping requirements, these regulations allowed the juice concentrate companies to collect and use essence in their own products with minimal constraint. For apple essence in particular, where essence collection technology was most advanced, the alcohol content was typically under 6%. The same regulations were quite suitable at first for citrus too, as the alcohol was low in the earliest essences and all use was internal. Later in the 1960s, these constraints would prove more difficult to manage and important changes would be made.

A second regulatory concern was more critical at the time for citrus. The orange juice industry had long sought to distinguish their juice product from other orange-flavored beverages such as sodas or juice drinks that may contain real orange juice, but are blended with additional ingredients. Consumer willingness to pay a higher price for juice depended on the distinction. But the definition of what exactly is orange juice is fraught with complexity. For example, what fruit varieties exactly qualify as "orange"? Can orange juice contain liquified peel? If the orange color and pulpy cloud settles out, does the remaining clear, water-white syrup still qualify as "orange juice"? In the case of the orange juice concentrate, the manufacturer removes much of the water from the product and ships it to a consumer who adds different water back to reconstitute the product. Is the product still "juice"? These distinctions rely on legal and regulatory frameworks which oftentimes have to balance conflicting points of view. For FCOJ, it was clearly recognized by the USDA as "orange juice" in the 1940s and USDA standards of grade were developed early to define quality and promote fair commercial practice. Additionally, consumer product labeling regulations helped support the distinction between FCOJ and other orange-flavored drinks.

But additional complexities continued to arise for the industry periodically. For example, by the 1950s certain processors discovered that the crushed orange peels, after the juice was pressed out, could be washed with processing water to extract out the remaining juice. This so-called "pulp-wash," when concentrated, was essentially identical to orange juice concentrate. It was clearly 100% derived from the orange and seemed chemically identical to orange juice. And yet, there was considerable industry controversy whether pulp-wash should be considered juice. Under certain conditions, the extraction process yielded a more bitter juice compared to the pressed juice from the same oranges, especially if yield was maximized. Processors liked the increased yield from the same fruit, while growers preferred selling more fruit. Regulators had concerns about flavor and consumer expectations for juice. The whole industry was concerned with brand protection and uniform and fair business practices and economic impact.

To deal with these types of problems, the industry had been pressing the USDA to develop a legal standard of identity for orange juice for some time. The existing USDA standards of grade defined various quality parameters for Grade A ("US Fancy") or Grade C ("US Standard") juice, but these grade standards included only a very short legal product description, leaving many questions of identity unanswered. By the late 1950s, several different standards of identity had been proposed for adoption, but they were controversial and had not yet been finalized[48, 49]. With essence collection for citrus certainly possible, and perhaps beneficial and maybe even likely in the future, how should it be used and regulated? A number of complex questions were raised and needed to be resolved, including: Was citrus essence added to concentrate or restored? If a manufacturer included it with concentrate, did it need to be labeled on the consumer package? How did essence differ from peel oil legally? Is a FCOJ product without essence the same as one with it? Could you add "too much" essence to a concentrate? Could you collect essence from one batch of oranges, say high-quality Valencias, and add it to concentrate from lower-price Hamlin oranges? Could essence be easily "manipulated" by adding synthetic additives without detection? How might essence affect the consumer perception of juice?

In late 1960[2], the FDA announced an investigatory hearing on the topic "Re-Establishment of Definitions and Standard of Identity for Orange Juice and Orange Juice Products[51]." Over six months in 1961, thirty-three industry representatives, consumer organization representatives and regulators were queried under oath about issues associated with completing a standard of identity, including questions on the nature, use and consumer perception of orange essence. The hearings were fully documented by transcription into 27 volumes, providing a fascinating perspective on the orange juice industry in 1961[35][3]. More than a year after the hearings, the FDA published their findings of fact in 1963[52]. With regard to essence, the FDA concluded orange essence obtained from flash-heating or concentration of orange juice was a natural part of orange juice and could be added to FCOJ in addition to or to replace cutback juice. Any essence obtained from crushed peels after juice removal was deemed unacceptable. The resulting orange juice products' USDA Standards of Identity came into force in 1964[52]. The new standards for concentrated orange juice products specifically allowed the addition of peel oils and essences without label notification. Questions of appropriate quantity of essence or whether essence should be sourced from the same lot of oranges as the concentrate were left unaddressed. With this regulatory outcome, the industry had considerable latitude to continue innovating on essence collection and utilization.

Around the same time as these new Standards of Identity were adopted, the IRS updated and simplified their 26 CFR 198 Regulations concerning the Production of Volatile Fruit-Flavor Concentrates[53]. Registration and record-keeping requirements were eased, and a method to denature essence with alcohol between 6 and 15% was included by means of mixing with juice concentrate. This process allowed for easier shipping of essence offsite that could still be used in 100% juice production with no excise tax. Essence below 6% alcohol was still considered exempt from taxation. In 1965, the IRS further ruled that high-alcohol essence could be diluted with water to bring it below 15% or 6% as desired[54]. And in 1967, the IRS eased the requirements even more allowing all essence with $\leq 15\%$ alcohol to be exempt from excise tax[55].

---

[2]On March 1, 1960 the FDA established Standards of Identity for various orange juice products, publishing the regulations in [50]. These new regulations were stayed the next month.

[3]Hamilton provides an interesting interpretation of these hearings which in many ways contrasts with the overall perspective of this work[36].

During the same time these regulatory questions were being developed, essence research continued in the industry. Meanwhile, a new citrus evaporator design was being developed which would have an important impact.

Gulf Machinery and the TASTE Evaporator

Gulf Machinery Company was started in the 1940s by Charlie Walker to provide fruit processing equipment for citrus plants. Walker, a graduate of Clearwater High School in 1933, soon joined B. C. Skinner and J. J. R. Bristow to work on improving their automated juice extractor. Gifted mechanically, Walker was an early employee of the Rotary Juice Press Company and eventually led the company until 1951 when the company was acquired by Food Machinery Corporation (FMC). Recognizing an opportunity beyond juice extractors, Walker founded Gulf Machinery while still employed at Rotary Juice. By the late 1950s, Gulf Machinery was building low-temperature evaporators, fruit-handling equipment, and canning equipment. Walker possessed a remarkable ability to conceptualize, design, and construct intricate mechanical equipment. He was also an astute businessman with an entrepreneurial eye for new opportunities.

Walker was also aware of his limitations and actively sought out technical experts who could help him. By 1958 or 1959, he was collaborating with Ralph Cook and James Redd, both engineers with extensive experience in the citrus industry. Ralph Cook, an engineering graduate from the University of Florida, had been consulting since at least 1950. James Redd, who also had been working as a consultant in the 1950s, knew Walker from the early 1940s. Walker engaged Cook and Redd to provide engineering support on his various projects. The trio were quite friendly and often worked together.

Meanwhile, throughout the 1950s, Eskew's group from the USDA in Philadelphia continued their work to improve concentration and essence recovery technology for various juices besides apple, including grape, cherry, strawberry, and other berries. Their primary goal was to remove all of the aromatic volatiles from the juice in a vapor stripping step, resulting in a somewhat concentrated juice that could be further concentrated to meet a desired Brix specification using conventional equipment. The stripped vapor was then directed to an essence concentrator to eliminate excess water vapor and concentrate the essence. While they found that only 8% of the juice needed to be evaporated in the first step to capture essentially all the flavor volatiles for apple juice, other fruit required up to 50% of the juice be evaporated in that step[56]. To achieve this flexibility with minimal thermal impact to the juice, they experimented with a single-pass flash-evaporator. They rapidly heated the juice above its boiling point (for a given reduced pressure in the system), passed it through a needle-valve (to maintain pressure upstream, keeping the juice from boiling too soon), and then flash-boiled the juice in a reduced-pressure "vaporizor" chamber. At the bottom of the vaporizer, the somewhat concentrated juice was separated from the vapor and cooled in a chilled heat-exchanger. The entire process exposed the feed-stock juice to elevated temperatures for less than 3 seconds[57]. The vapor was subsequently directed to the essence recovery system for further concentration by means of distillation. By controlling the initial juice temperature, flow rate, and system pressure, they could regulate the amount of vapor produced in the vaporizer chamber.

James Redd himself recalls becoming aware of Eskew's recent work through a publication around 1958[39]. He likely saw the 1958 USDA report by Claffey, Eskew, and Eisenhardt [57] or perhaps a draft of Eskew's 1959 paper[56]. Both documents described the same general research. Intrigued by the rapid process, Redd arranged a visit to Philadelphia to meet Dr. Eskew. During extensive discussions about their approach, one particular problem was identified. The process worked well on clear juices, but not for pulpy juices like citrus which tended to clog the pre-heater and needle-valve, disrupting the vaporization. Redd managed to leave the meeting with a set of blueprints for the equipment. Back in Florida, Redd, along with Cook and Walker, recognized the advantages of a similar higher-temperature, rapid, single-pass evaporator for the citrus industry. They set out to design one[39].

Over the next few years, the design underwent several iterations. In the end, they utilized multiple sequential vertical evaporators with the juice sequentially pumped from one stage to the next. In each stage, the heated juice entered from the top through a nozzle forming a mist due to rapid boiling, and was propelled downward by the expanding vapor. At the bottom, the concentrated juice was separated from the vapor and the liquid was pumped back up to the top of the next stage. The hot vapor served as a heat source for the next stage, as each stage required additional heat to drive the water evaporation. The entire system operated under a moderate vacuum with an initial juice feed temperature ranging from 90–105°C, significantly hotter compared to typical high-vacuum evaporators then in use. However, the juice moved very rapidly through each stage, and it dissipated heat by evaporation throughout the process. The mist velocity in the evaporator body could reach 170 ft/second[58], ensuring that the time the juice was exposed to the highest temperatures was brief. Each stage operated at a different temperature and vacuum, with the goal to evenly remove water until the desired level of concentration was achieved. A critical feature was the design of the juice inlet nozzle at the top of each stage. The distribution nozzle produced a turbulent fog as the hot juice entered the evaporator and rapidly boiled due to the reduced pressure. This nozzle replaced the needle-valve in the Eskew design and was less prone to clogging by pulpy citrus juice.

The design came to be known as the TASTE evaporator, standing for Thermally-Accelerated Short Time Evaporator, and it offered numerous advantages for citrus concentrate production. First, the hot feed temperature pasteurized the juice as it entered the evaporator system, eliminating natural microbial contamination and greatly simplifying overall sanitation. The initial heat also deactivated the enzymes responsible for cloud loss, requiring no additional processing step or energy. Since the juice was exposed to high heat for only a short time, heat-induced flavor off-notes in the concentrate were minimal. The use of multiple stages and the recycling of heat in the evaporated vapor was very energy efficient. Additionally, the higher system pressure, compared to low-temperature, high-vacuum evaporators, required less expensive equipment and utilities. Finally, in operation, the single-pass TASTE evaporator had minimal product hold-up, making it easier to start, stop, and clean, and the entire system was easy to control with less operator effort.

Determining the specific contributions of each member of the trio to the final design is challenging and was the subject of some dispute in later years. Cook filed for a patent on an early design in 1960[59], which caused some consternation among Walker and Redd[60]. They favored a trial-and-error approach to building the evaporators, foreseeing continuous improvement as they gained experience constructing and operating the units. In their view, patents were more likely to help their competitors than themselves. Nevertheless, Gulf Machinery served as the equipment builder for these evaporators, with Redd and Cook employed as consultants[61]. According to Redd, the first TASTE evaporator was built in 1960 for Pipkins Dairy in Lakeland, FL[39]. It had an evaporation capacity of 3000 pounds of water per hour. Additional units were designed and installed thereafter, in Florida and outside the US. The TASTE design soon displaced low-temperature evaporators in the industry, becoming the preferred choice for new plants and gradually replacing older units during upgrades. By 1980, there were 110 citrus juice evaporators operational in Florida, with 94 of them being of the TASTE design[62].

Widespread Adoption of Essence Collection

The TASTE evaporator design had several clear advantages for essence collection. Most importantly, the volatile evaporation took place at higher system pressures than in the low-temperature evaporators, so the essence could be condensed and fractionated more easily away from the water vapor. Condensation efficiency, for a given surface temperature, decreases with increasing vacuum. For the lightest boiling essence compounds, condensation was very difficult in the old-style evaporators. Under the moderate vacuum of a high-temperature evaporator, it was much easier. Second, chemical separation in a fractionation column relies on boiling point differences between the chemical components. These differences get smaller at the higher vacuum required by low-temperature evaporators. Consequently, the fractionating system also worked better on the TASTE evaporator. Third, higher juice temperatures promoted the quicker flash-evaporation of low-boiling, oil-soluble compounds which constituted the oil-phase essence. At lower temperatures, these compounds distilled away more slowly. Fourth, the division of the concentration process into multiple sequential stages meant most of the volatile components were evaporated in the first stage or two and permitted efficient energy recycling. The early-stage vapors, after being used to heat the juice in a subsequent stage, were partially fractionated in the evaporator shell, preferentially condensing much of the water vapor away from the aroma. The remaining enriched vapors could be directed into the essence unit for further concentration. Vapor from later stages, containing much less essence, could bypass the essence system. The continuous single-pass operating mode for the evaporator meant the vapor flow to the essence recovery system was uniform and continuous, providing ideal operating conditions for the fractionating column to function. And finally, the higher operating temperatures greatly reduced microbiological growth and subsequent essence off-notes.

In November of 1960, at the same time Cook filed his patent on an early form of the TASTE evaporator, he also filed a patent on an associated essence recovery system[63]. Relying on a by-now conventional condensing system and fractionation column to capture the essence, the focus of Cook's patent was to utilize the residual heat in the juice to drive the essence fractionation process, and to automatically regulate the pressure in the essence fractionating column relative to the evaporator. It was a complex design and it remains uncertain whether this version was ever built.

Redd also saw the obvious advantages and began designing essence units for TASTE evaporators. Working in a collaboration with Gulf Machinery Corp, he was often hired by citrus plants in a consulting capacity to help with equipment installation, initial operations and QC procedures as he was extremely well-versed in most aspects of citrus production. He installed his first essence unit on a 10,000 pound/hr TASTE evaporator in Venezuela in the early 1960s. Choosing a less-than-optimal selection of vapor to direct to the essence unit, and lacking enough refrigerated condensing capacity, Redd himself described the results as "unsuccessful[39]." Nevertheless, he was quickly learning. In early 1963, Redd and Walker were hired on a project to set up a new citrus concentrate plant in Brazil which became known as Suconasa. As part of the facility, Redd designed and installed an essence unit on a new 15,000 pound/hr TASTE evaporator. It began operations in June 1963, and Redd described it as his first successful commercial essence unit[39]. This plant began producing high Brix concentrate and essence (and probably peel oil) which were shipped to Canada to produce a consumer-style 3 + 1 orange juice concentrate using the essence without any cutback juice. The product was sold in Canada, which bypassed any regulatory concerns in the US at the time. But for commercial reasons the buyer still required USDA inspection, and the USDA product scores (including flavor) were very good[39, 64]. The USDA scores and commercial success of the product provided an independent measure of the value of the essence. And the simplicity of handling essence in place of cutback juice was obvious.

Redd designed and installed additional essence units for Concentradora de Puerto Rico in PR (1963 or 64), M&O in Wachula (1964),

Alcoma in Lake Wales, and Treesweet Products in Ft. Pierce (1966)[46, 39]. In each case, he adapted and improved his design for yield, ease of use, and essence quality. In the case of the M&O unit, Redd negotiated a deal to supervise the operation of the essence unit and help the plant reduce polluting wastewater, in exchange for receiving all of the essence "for free[39]." Redd was prescient in seeing value in the essence (and other citrus byproducts) aside from direct addition to on-site FCOJ. Through his involvement in the design, installation and initial operations of the essence units and his consulting services at citrus concentration plants, he developed practical experience in essence products and operations, and a variety of contacts throughout the citrus industry. Redd also discovered early that apart from the operating conditions for the evaporator and essence unit, some recovered aroma was much better in odor and flavor character than others. The fruit itself contributed significant variation to essence quality, due to maturity, cultivar, and fruit-handling conditions, among other factors. Any practical use of essence would need to take this quality variation into account.

With the regulatory status of essence in the US being resolved by 1964, Minute Maid, General Foods and Libby each continued their internal essence efforts through the 1960s. At Minute Maid, Brent, Du Bois and Huffman filed their revised essence recovery patent on June 2, 1964[45]. Their design used a flash evaporation stage to remove the aroma prior to conventional juice concentration, similar to Eskew's latest design, followed by conventional condensers and an essence fractionation column. The system ran at relatively high vacuum and was clearly designed to operate with conventional low-temperature citrus evaporators. However, to overcome the poor condensation efficiency, the authors employed chilled-water based vacuum pumps to efficiently scrub the remaining essence from the vapor in a closed system. The patent's main focus was to efficiently capture essence components that were lost in previous designs. At General Foods, Byer and Lang continued their essence work, submitting a number of related patents in the 1960s which applied their earlier technology to other fruits and coffee[65, 66, 67]. Their basic design remained unchanged from earlier work.

Amidst the commercial interest in essence, the Florida Citrus Commission developed their own program to study essence. The initial focus was on monitoring industry activity, assessing essence composition, and determining whether essence collection would provide any practical benefit to the juice industry. Later, the FCC would design their own essence collection equipment. Most of this research was carried out at the Citrus Experiment Station (CES) in Lake Alfred, FL.

As early as 1958, R. W. Wolford with the FCC was working to evaluate the chemical properties and usefulness of the orange essence collected by Libby[34]. A little later in 1964, Wolford and his collaborators constructed a pilot-plant scale essence unit at the CES[68]. That year, the group also reported on an extensive taste test study to examine various alternatives to cutback-juice addition to restore the flavor volatiles to FCOJ[69]. In addition to essence, they evaluated the addition of juice oil and juice emulsion. Juice oil and emulsion were oily flavor fractions isolated by centrifugation directly from single-strength juice. Although the work recognized the various advantages that essence would provide the manufacturer over cutback juice, the taste panel results were not very positive for the aroma-containing samples. Cutback juice, the experimental control, gave the best results in all panel evaluations. Wenzel *et al.* concluded, "There is little evidence that frozen concentrated orange juices produced using such flavor-enhancement materials as essence, essence and cold-pressed oil, juice emulsion or juice oil have better flavor than concentrates made using cutback juice and cold-pressed orange oil." The juice emulsion and oils for the study were provided by centrifuge companies active in Florida, but the source of the aroma was not mentioned. It seems likely that it was their own pilot plant essence. Compared to industry efforts going on at the time, this essence unit was quite simple. There is no way to judge the quality of the aroma that was used. In any case, the tone of the summarized taste-panel results was not very positive for essence addition.

By 1966, Wolford and his collaborators were sounding more positive regarding the collection and use of aroma in FCOJ. In December 1966, his group installed a pilot-plant scale essence unit at a commercial processing plant, Pasco Packing Company[70]. The so-called "FCC-CES essence unit" was relatively unsophisticated, lacking a fractionation column, but it employed multiple condensers which supplied some intrinsic fractionation. That same season, a larger commercial essence unit was installed at Pasco based upon the same design by the group. The equipment was described in some detail in Ref. [71]. The authors reported quite positive results with the essence collection on this equipment. At this time, Pasco was operating a traditional low-temperature, high-vacuum evaporator. It is likely that the FCC-CES design was conceived and tested only on these old-style evaporators. This design was soon abandoned and the two installed at Pasco were the only two installed commercially.

The FCC, being a state regulatory agency, had the advantage of access to all citrus facilities in Florida, and consequently they possessed more knowledge about proprietary essence collection and use than anyone else. In 1968, Wolford *et al.* reported, "During the 1967-68 season a considerable volume of orange essence was produced in the Florida Citrus Industry. At least seven processing plants in various stages of essence production accounted for approximately 1,500,000 gallons of the recovered flavor material[72]." USDA researchers in Winter Haven were even experimenting with aroma recovery from citrus fruit byproducts, other than juice, in recognition that essence had flavor uses beyond juice[4], and that there could be a future essence supply issue.[73]. With or without the FCC effort, it was clear by now that orange essence collection and addition to FCOJ was both commercially successful and was going to replace cutback juice. Tom Millsaps, a reporter for the Tampa Tribune with a regular column on citrus industry news and gossip called "Citrus Notes," wrote on December 17, 1967, "Anticipating a switchover to the new concentrate using orange essences instead of cutback juice, the powers are getting on the ball already to see if Mrs. Housewife is going to like the stuff[1]."

The FCC research effort on essence collection ended within a few years with two patent filings. In 1968, the Florida Department of Citrus (FDOC) was created as the executive and regulatory agency governed by the FCC, and the FCC research staff became employees of the FDOC. On January 26, 1971, FDOC employees C. D. Atkins and J. A. Attaway submitted two patent applications on essence technology which were later approved. One application described an essence unit utilizing a spiral fractionating column, while the second described the use of the collected two-phase essence to restore flavor to FCOJ[74, 75]. A followup filing was done on September 6, 1972[76]. Aside from the specific type of fractionating column described in the essence unit patent, both the essence unit design and the information on essence use were conventional. By this time, commercial essence units were in operation all around the world and essence was being regularly incorporated

---

[4]Flavor volatiles collected from citrus byproducts other than juice would not be allowed for use in OJ by the USDA Standard of Identity.

into FCOJ. The basic ideas had been worked out earlier by others and most new optimizations involved capital costs, ease of operation, flavor optimization, and other efficiencies.

Early Essence Use in OJ

The development of essence collection equipment obviously went hand-in-hand with experimentation on the use of the recovered volatiles in concentrate. Yet, documenting the experimentation is more difficult than the hardware beyond certain milestones, some of which were mentioned above. While it was clear that the juice concentration process drove away important flavor volatiles, understanding which aroma chemicals were important and in what concentrations and ratios was a daunting task. Even with the advent of chemical analysis tools like gas chromatography, much of the work had to be done by human tasting. Certainly, the chemical complexity of the citrus juice volatiles was a big challenge. There were three main sources of volatile flavors: the peel oil, the water-phase essence, and the oil-phase essence. All of these were complex chemical mixtures, and the latter two were particularly affected by the condensing efficiency and fractionating properties of essence collection systems. The oil-phase essence, which turned out to be very important, was present at such low levels compared to the water-phase that it was, at first, entirely missed. Later, differing opinions were seen regarding whether the water-phase or oil-phase essence was most important. Additionally, the fruit supply, which changed throughout the processing season, strongly affected the essence quality. Furthermore, the essence units were occasionally capturing off-notes that would appear and disappear without a clear explanation. Less obvious factors, such as how the essence was stored and added to concentrate, are now known to also have important effects, but this was not fully understood at the time. Oil-phase essence is particularly unstable when exposed to air and elevated temperatures, developing its own off-flavors if not handled with particular care. The role of oxygen content in concentrate, which can interact with the essence, would also need to be discovered over time. And finally, the effect of packaging and storage on the added essence in juice had to be understood throughout the entire product shelf-life.

All of the commercial FCOJ producers had developed experience selecting fruit for both cutback and concentrated orange juice as the processing season progressed. By holding inventory of different concentrates (or even cutback juices) with various brix/acid ratios or flavor profiles, the manufacturer could improve yield and produce a more standardized product. Professional blenders and taste testers guided the blending of the raw materials into the final consumer FCOJ product. To the blenders, the essence oils and aromas were simply additional ingredients that could be added to the final product, subject to other product specifications or regulatory requirements. Determining whether essence addition improved the juice involved a comparison to a taste standard, as essence didn't impact the other quality parameters used at the time such as brix/acid ratio. For most processors, the standard for comparison would be some type of cutback product. The evaluation process was complex, involving selection of concentrate and essence lots, production of multiple samples and taste testing at intervals over the product shelf life. Alternatively, a company might pursue consumer taste testing, such as Libby, McNeill & Libby did in 1959, but consumer taste testing is even more complex, expensive, and time-consuming. Research organizations, such as the USDA or CES, also faced a need to use taste testing to evaluate citrus essences, but they lacked an ongoing need for dedicated evaluators. Consequently, their flavor evaluations often relied on volunteers in the form of coworkers, other laboratory staff, and sometimes industry representatives. One common problem with taste panels, especially composed of tasters very familiar with a given product, is a bias towards familiar flavor profiles. Since the industry had produced the cutback product for more than 20 years, many industry-insiders preferred it by acclimation.

Consumers who self-identified as OJ consumers at the time were also likely to have been very familiar with FCOJ produced with cutback juice, and subject to the same possible familiarity bias. It is quite possible that this bias influenced early evaluations of FCOJ using essence in place of cutback juice. For example, the taste panel results of Wenzel *et al.* in 1964[69], which favored the control juice (cutback + concentrate) against all other flavor variants, may have been influenced in this way. Jim Redd provided another example of this effect in a 1983 paper describing his attempt to introduce essence-containing OJ concentrate into England in 1963[77]. The company Armour & Co. did consumer testing on canned OJ that Redd prepared using Brazilian concentrate with added essence. After the test results came in, the company decided against commercializing the new product. The decision greatly puzzled Redd, who had the juice privately evaluated by the USDA where it received a 94 score, which was excellent for canned juice. Given access to the test results, he found women and children preferred the product while men had rated it poorly. The adult men preferred overcooked, bitter and astringent orange juice which was the typical product then available in England. The traditional use of canned juice for mixed-drinks probably also played a role in the men's preference. In light of the very complex and changing nature of the raw flavor materials and the complex evaluation process and regulatory concerns, it is quite understandable that citrus essence acceptance took decades. Additionally, the commercial success of early adopters such as James Redd and the Brazilian Suconasa product was critically important. By offering an essence-containing FCOJ product without cutback juice, and competing successfully in Canada with consumers as the ultimate arbitrators, systemic inertia could be challenged by a small group of innovators.

Summary

The question of who deserves credit for the invention of citrus essence capture has been controversial for some time. In late 1967, Tom Millsaps, writing in his regular "Citrus Notes" column in the Tampa Tribute, identified essence as "...the biggest thing that's happened in the industry since concentrate came along..." and he credited Dr. L. G. MacDowell, the long-time Director of Scientific Research for the FCC. However, MacDowell downplayed his role, responding, "it was more of an evolution than a discovery[1]." A few weeks later, Millsaps reported receiving a letter (the author was not identified) suggesting that "congratulations should be given to the right people" and naming the CES researchers R. W. Wolford and C. D. Atkins, while further acknowledging the earlier work of E. J. Kelly and the Libby, McNeill & Libby essence team[78]. A few years later, when Attaway and Atkins of the FDOC disclosed their patents on essence collection and aroma use, James Redd was initially furious and consulted lawyers to contest the patents, in collaboration with his employer, A. E. Staley Manufacturing Company. Redd and Staley, who were successfully running a business installing and operating essence units, felt that the patents copied Redd's work from the 1960s and could impede their future business[46].

However, the FDOC, apparently, never intended to enforce the patents and Redd and Staley did not act on their internal deliberations. Meanwhile, the rest of the processing industry continued to operate whatever evaporator and essence equipment they had, while transitioning to the new TASTE evaporator design that was replacing older evaporators. Often, when installing a new evaporator, a new essence unit was also installed. Both James Redd and Ralph Cook, independently, continued to design and install essence units. In time, almost all the citrus processors in Florida and Brazil adopted the Redd or Cook design for their essence units.

Ultimately, MacDowell's opinion that the invention was evolutionary provides a good summary. Clearly, the work of Eskew and collaborators on non-citrus products at the USDA in Philadelphia was very important, as much of their design was adapted and incorporated into the citrus essence units. And yet, the particular sensitivity of citrus juices to heat, the pulpy nature of the juice, and the complex two-phase nature of the essence contributed unique problems that had to be solved. Although the USDA and the FCC/CES efforts were important, more credit belongs to the industrial research efforts because they were more practical and had a greater impact. The industrial researchers worked from the basis of an existing successful FCOJ business with a clear goal of product improvement. They focused on the practical questions of how to recover and utilize essence profitably. Existential issues of whether the essence was "good" or "bad" and its exact chemical constituency were either already known or of secondary importance to commercial success. These researchers also had access to industrial-scale evaporators so their experimental results were more directly applicable to the commercial environment. The development of the TASTE evaporator design in the early 1960s was also important, both in improving the operating environment to collect essence as well as facilitating the introduction of new evaporation equipment industry-wide. Ultimately, the success of the citrus essence unit was determined by processor choice to install them.

The success of the citrus essence collection process launched the Florida citrus flavor business. Prior to this, Florida was a producer of citrus peel oils which were used both in citrus juices and exported outside of Florida for other flavor and fragrance applications. Florida citrus oil producers had no special expertise in these other applications. That expertise resided in flavor and fragrance companies located mostly in the northeast US, or in other food and fragrance companies. However, with the advent of routine essence collection and continued growth in the FCOJ business, Florida began producing three flavoring ingredients, peel oil, water-phase essence, and oil-phase essence, from oranges as well as other citrus varieties. Florida became the center of a new and growing market niche for flavor products, the specialized flavors needed for citrus juices. And finally, the expertise needed to formulate these products had to be developed and Florida was best positioned to lead this effort.

References

[1] Tom Millsaps. "Citrus Notes." In: *The Tampa Tribune* (Dec. 17, 1967), p. D9.

[2] J. J. R. Bristow. "Technical Developments in Concentrate." In: *Proceedings of the Florida State Horticultural Society* Vol. 64 (1951), pp. 157–158.

[3] J. L. Heid. "Concentrating Citrus Juices By the Vacuum Method." In: *Food Industries* (May 1943), pp. 62–66, 110–11.

[4] "A Second Year of Citrus Research on Byproducts." In: *The Citrus Industry* (Nov. 1944), pp. 6–8.

[5] E. Gildemeister and Fr. Hoffmann. *The Volatile Oils*. Trans. by Edward Kremers. 2nd ed. Vol. 3. New York, NY: John Wiley and Sons, 1922.

[6] O. P. Huff. "A Study of Essential Oils Occurring in the Different Organs and Products of the Citrus Group in Florida." Masters Thesis. Gainesville, FL: University of Florida, June 1917. URL: https://ufdc.ufl.edu/UF00055745/00001 (visited on 01/27/2021).

[7] J. Alfred Hall and C. P. Wilson. "The Volatile Constituents of Valencia Orange Juice." In: *Journal of the American Chemical Society* Vol. 47 (Issue 10 Oct. 1, 1925), pp. 2575–2584.

[8] Harry W. von Loesecke. "Four Years of Citrus Products Research in Florida." In: *Proceedings of the Florida State Horticultural Society* Vol. 49 (1936), pp. 64–68.

[9] Harry W. von Loesecke. "The Chemist Looks at the Citrus Products Industry in Florida." In: *Proceedings of the Florida State Horticultural Society* Vol. 51 (1938), pp. 105–108.

[10] E. M. Chace, H. W. von Loesecke, and J. L. Heid. *Citrus Fruit Products*. USDA Circular 577. United States Department of Agriculture, Nov. 1940.

[11] D. C. Carpenter and E. C. Smith. "Apple Juice Concentrate." In: *Industrial and Engineering Chemistry* Vol. 26 (Issue 4 Apr. 1934), pp. 449–454.

[12] Ulysses G. Todd. "Extract and Beverage and Method for Making the Same." Pat. 1,856,979. Assignee: Pfaudler Company. United States Patent. May 3, 1932.

[13] Howard P. Milleville. "Volatile Flavor Recovery Process." Pat. 2,457,315. Assignee: Secretary of Agriculture. United States Patent. Dec. 28, 1948.

[14] Howard P. Milleville and Roderick K. Eskew. "Recovery of Volatile Apple Flavors in Essence Form." In: *Western Canner and Packer* Vol. 38 (Issue 11 1946), pp. 51–54.

[15] Howard P. Milleville. "Process for Recovering Volatile Flavors." Pat. 2,513,813. United States Patent. July 4, 1950.

[16] Roderick K. Eskew et al. "Frozen Concentrated Apple Juice." In: *Industrial & Engineering Chemistry* Vol. 43 (Issue 10 1951), pp. 2397–2403.

[17] H. D. Jefferson and Robert H. Lloyd. "The World's Largest Plant for Freezing Pineapple Juice." In: *Refrigerating Engineering* Vol. 60 (Issue 11 Nov. 1952), pp. 1167–1171.

[18] H. P. Milleville. "Volatile Flavor Recovery." In: *The Chemistry and Technology of Fruit and Vegetable Juice Production*. Ed. by Donald K. Tressler and Maynard A. Joslyn. Westport, CT: Avi Publishing Company, 1954, pp. 778–801.

[19] Louis G. MacDowell, Edwin L. Moore, and Cedric D. Atkins. "Method of Preparing Full-Flavored Fruit Juice Concentrates." Pat. 2,453,109A. United States Patent. Nov. 9, 1948.

[20] C. W. Kaufman and H. A. Campbell. "Some Fundamental Considerations in the Processing of Frozen Orange Juice Concentrate." In: *Food Technology* Vol. 3 (Issue 12 Dec. 1949), pp. 395–404.

[21] Thomas A. Rector. "Frozen Concentrated Orange Juice - Its Research Background." In: *Refrigeration Engineering* Vol. 58 (Issue 4 Apr. 1950), pp. 349–353.

[22] Thomas A. Rector. "Research Background of Frozen Concentrated Orange Juice." In: *Chemical and Engineering News* Vol. 28 (Issue 4 Jan. 23, 1950), pp. 242–245.

[23] D. A. Morgan and M. K. Veldhuis. "Recovery of Essence from Citrus Juices." In: USDA Citrus Processing Conference. Winter Haven, FL: US Department of Agriculture, 1952, pp. 16–18.

[24] Donald A. Morgan et al. "Studies on the Recovery of Essence from Florida Orange Juices." In: *Food Technology* Vol. 7 (Issue 8 Sept. 1953), pp. 332–336.

[25] Randall G. Rice, George J. Keller, and E. A. Beavens. "Flavor Fortification of California Frozen Orange Juice Concentrate." In: *Food Technology* (Jan. 1952), pp. 35–39.

[26] George J. Keller. "Method of Recovering Volatile Flavoring Oils." Pat. 2,729,564. United States Patent. Jan. 3, 1956.

[27] "Giant New Evaporator Is Installed by Citrus Co-Op." In: *Tampa Tribune* (Mar. 20, 1955), p. A19.

[28] "Concentrate Plant Site Is Cleared." In: *The Miami Herald* (Apr. 7, 1956), p. A19.

[29] "Construction Work is Begun on New $2,000,000 TreeSweet Corp. Plant." In: *Fort Pierce News-Tribune* (June 5, 1956), pp. 1–2.

[30] Anne Wilder. "Treesweet Plant Set to Open." In: *The Miami Herald* (Nov. 30, 1956), p. D1.

[31] Edgar J. Kelly. "Apparatus for Producing Flavoring Constituents." Pat. 2,992,978. United States Patent. July 18, 1961.

[32] Edgar J. Kelly. "Method for Improving Flavor Constituents." Pat. 3,223,533. Assignee: Libby, McNeill & Libby. United States Patent. Dec. 14, 1965.

[33] Edgar J. Kelly. "Method of Improving Flavor Constituents." Pat. 3,223,534. Assignee: Libby, McNeill & Libby. United States Patent. Dec. 14, 1965.

[34] R. W. Wolford. *Preliminary Studies of Volatile Flavor Components in Citrus Juices Using Gas Chromatography*. Citrus Station Mimeo Report 60-1. Lake Alfred, FL: Florida Citrus Commission and Florida Citrus Experiment Station, Sept. 16, 1959. URL: `https://ufdc.ufl.edu/UF00072390/00001?search=wolford` (visited on 07/23/2024).

[35] Food & Drug Administration. *Orange Juice and Orange Juice Products: Definitions and Standards of Identity*. 1961.

[36] Alissa Anne Hamilton. "Fabricated Fresh: What Industry and the FDA Failed to Tell You About Processed Orange Juice." Doctoral Thesis. Yale University, May 2006.

[37] "Libby Research Develops New Juice Concentrate." In: *Port Huron Times Herald* (Oct. 16, 1962), p. 24.

[38] Andy Fillmore. "Longtime Ocalan 'Key in Moving the Industry Forward.'" In: *Ocala Starr Banner* (Aug. 25, 2016). URL: https://www.ocala.com/story/news/local/2016/08/25/citrus-industry-pioneer-dies-in-ocala/25583041007/ (visited on 04/04/2022).

[39] James B. Redd. "The Volatile Flavors of Orange Juice." In: ASME 1988 Citrus Engineering Conference. Lakeland, FL: American Society of Mechanical Engineers Digital Collection, Mar. 24, 1988, pp. 79–93.

[40] Donald Hendrix. *E-mail to Robert Kryger*. Jan. 19, 2022.

[41] Ellis M. Byer and Alfred A. Lang. "Production of Flavor-Enhanced Citrus Concentrates." Pat. 3,118,776. United States Patent. Jan. 21, 1964.

[42] Ellis Milton Byer and Alfred Allen Lang. "Process of Fortifying and Stabilizing a Citrus Fruit Juice." Pat. 3,117,877. Assignee: General Foods Corporation. United States Patent. Jan. 14, 1964.

[43] "Minute Maid Dedicates Plymouth Research Lab." In: *Citrus Industry* (May 1953).

[44] Jewell Allen Brent. "Orange Concentrate and Method of Making." Pat. 3,140,187. Assignee: The Coca-Cola Company. United States Patent. July 7, 1964.

[45] Jewell Allen Brent, Clarence W. Du Bois, and Carl F. Huffman. "Essence Recovery." Pat. 3,248,233A. Assignee: The Coca Cola Company. United States Patent. Apr. 26, 1966.

[46] James B. Redd. *Memoranda of James Redd to A. E. Staley Manufacturing Company Personnel on the Topic of the FDOC Patents on Essence Recovery and Use*. Unpublished. 1974.

[47] "Title 26 Part 198 - Volatile Fruit-Flavor Concentrates." In: *Federal Register* Volume 14 (Issue 186 Sept. 27, 1949), pp. 5869–5879.

REFERENCES

[48] "Notice of Proposals to Establish Definitions and Standards of Identity for Certain Types of Orange Juice." In: *Federal Register* Volume 21 (Issue 216 Nov. 6, 1956), p. 8511.

[49] "Notice of Proposals to Establish Definitions and Standards of Identity for Canned Orange Juice; Industrial Orange Juice; Orange Juice for Processing; Concentrated Orange Juice; and Sweetened Concentrated Orange Juice." In: *Federal Register* Volume 22 (Issue 107 June 4, 1957), pp. 3893–3894.

[50] "Orange Juice and Orange Juice Products; Definitions and Standards of Identity." In: *Federal Register* Volume 25 (Issue 41 Mar. 1, 1960), pp. 1770–1772.

[51] "Notice of Hearing Re Establishment of Definitions and Standards of Identity for Orange Juice and Orange Juice Products." In: *Federal Register* Volume 25 (Issue 234 Dec. 6, 1960), pp. 12372–12374.

[52] "Orange Juice and Orange Juice Products; Definitions and Standards of Identity; Findings of Fact and Final Order." In: *Federal Register* Volume 28 (Issue 199 Oct. 11, 1963), pp. 10897–10937.

[53] "Title 26 Part 198 - Production of Volatile Fruit-Flavor Concentrates." In: *Federal Register* Volume 28 (Issue 6 Jan. 9, 1963), pp. 219–225.

[54] Internal Revenue Service. *IRS Revenue Ruling 65-253*. 1965.

[55] "Title 26 Part 198 - Production of Volatile Fruit-Flavor Concentrates." In: *Federal Register* Volume 32 (Issue 126 June 30, 1967), p. 9314.

[56] R. K. Eskew et al. "Concentrates, Strips Flavor in 1 Pass Without Vacuum." In: *Food Engineering* Vol. 31 (Jan. 1959), pp. 70–72.

[57] Joseph B. Claffey, Roderick K. Eskew, and Nelson H. Eisenhardt. *An Improved Experimental Unit for Recovery of Volatile Flavors*. Agricultural Research Service Report 73-19. Philadelphia, PA: Eastern Regional Research Laboratory, Feb. 1958.

[58] Stanford Brett Welch. "The T.A.S.T.E. Evaporator, Continuing Progress in Evaporator Technology." In: ASME 1989 Citrus Engineering Conference. Lakeland, FL: American Society of Mechanical Engineers Digital Collection, Mar. 30, 1989, pp. 79–92.

[59] Ralph W. Cook. "Vacuum Evaporator." Pat. 3,141,807. United States Patent. July 21, 1964.

[60] David Walker. *Interview by Robert Kryger.* By Phone. Apr. 6, 2022.

[61] Brett Welch. *Interview by Robert Kryger.* By Phone. Sept. 16, 2021.

[62] C. S. Chen. "Citrus Evaporator Technology." In: *Transactions of the ASAE* Vol. 25 (Issue 5 1982), pp. 1457–1463.

[63] Ralph W. Cook. "Apparatus for Recovering Essence-Bearing Vapors." Pat. 3,293,150. United States Patent. Dec. 20, 1966.

[64] James B. Redd. *Memorandum to H.J. Barnett Concerning Essence History in Florida.* Unpublished. Jan. 3, 1975.

[65] Ellis M. Byer and Alfred A. Lang. "Recovering Aromatics from Coffee Extract." Pat. 3,244,530. Assignee: General Foods Corporation. United States Patent. Apr. 5, 1966.

[66] Ellis M. Byer and Alfred A. Lang. "Production of Flavor-Enhanced Apple and Prune Concentrates." Pat. 3,310,409. Assignee: General Foods Corporation. United States Patent. Mar. 21, 1967.

[67] Alfred A. Lang and Ellis M. Byer. "Process for Fortifying Fruit Juice." Pat. 3,310,410. Assignee: General Foods Corporation. United States Patent. Mar. 21, 1967.

[68] R. W. Wolford et al. *Analysis of Some Recovered Natural Flavor Enhancement Materials.* Citrus Station Mimeo Report 65-8. Lake Alfred, FL: Florida Citrus Commission and Florida Citrus Experiment Station, Oct. 6, 1964. URL: https://ufdc.ufl.edu/UF00072429/00001?search=wolford (visited on 07/23/2024).

[69] F. W. Wenzel et al. *Questions for Consideration in the Use of Natural Flavor-Enhancement Materials in Frozen Concentrated Orange Juice.* Citrus Station Mimeo Report 65-9. Lake Alfred, FL: Citrus Station, Oct. 6, 1964. URL: https://ufdc.ufl.edu/UF00072430/00001/citation (visited on 02/02/2022).

[70] R. W. Wolford et al. *Current Status of Recovery, Characteristics, and Use of Orange Essence.* Citrus Station Mimeo Report 68-8D. Lake Alfred, FL: Florida Citrus Commission and Florida Citrus Experiment Station, Oct. 12, 1967. URL: https://ufdc.ufl.edu/UF00072452/00001/images (visited on 07/23/2024).

[71] R. W. Wolford et al. "Recovered Volatiles From Citrus Juices." In: ASME 1968 Citrus Engineering Conference. Lakeland, FL: American Society of Mechanical Engineers Digital Collection, Mar. 27, 1968, pp. 64–81.

[72] R. W. Wolford et al. *Chemical Characteristic and Use of Orange Essences*. Citrus Station Mimeo Report 69-6A. Lake Alfred, FL: Florida Citrus Commission and Florida Citrus Experiment Station, Oct. 10, 1968.

[73] Matthew K. Veldhuis et al. "Studies on Recovery of Water Soluble Essences and Distilled Oil from Orange Peel." In: USDA Citrus Processing Conference. Winter Haven, FL: US Department of Agriculture, Sept. 26, 1968.

[74] Cedric D. Atkins and John A. Attaway. "Method of Producing Enhanced Citrus Juice Essence." Pat. 3,787,593. United States Patent. Jan. 22, 1974.

[75] Cederic [sic] D. Atkins and John A. Attaway. "Essence for Enhancing the Flavor of Citrus Juices." Pat. 3,782,972. Assignee: Florida Department of Citrus. United States Patent. Jan. 1, 1974.

[76] Cederic [sic] D. Atkins and John A. Attaway. "Distillation Apparatus for Recovering Citrus Essence." Pat. 3,862,014. Assignee: Florida Department of Citrus. United States Patent. Jan. 21, 1975.

[77] James B. Redd. "Processing - Processed O.J., Definition of Quality, Purity and the Effects of Processing on These Characteristics - Part I." In: *Citrus Industry* (Sept. 1983), pp. 8–10.

[78] Tom Millsaps. "Citrus Notes." In: *The Tampa Tribune* (Jan. 7, 1968), p. D10.

6

Birth of the Citrus Flavor Industry 1960–1982

"This was not the only time I had been wrong!"

—James Redd on declining an early purchase of Minute Maid stock, 1988[1].

The commercial need to improve orange juice flavor was well-established, and the necessary raw materials were becoming available through essence collection. However, it remained an open question as to where the expertise would be developed and how it would be commercialized. Most juice companies, while quite knowledgeable about the practical aspects of their products, generally lacked expertise in flavor science. Even the most scientifically advanced companies, like Minute Maid and Libby's, who recognized the potential, faced many competing concerns. For flavor companies outside Florida, who best understood flavor chemistry, citrus juices were very complex, and they had limited experience with 100% juice products. Furthermore, these companies were not very familiar with the new citrus essences, and From-the-Named-Fruit (FTNF) flavors did not align well with their expertise in combining artificial and natural ingredients. One unique Floridian, James Redd, would combine his experience in the citrus industry with scientific insight into flavors and entrepreneurial zeal to create a new flavor industry in Florida.

Who was James B. Redd?

James Beverly[1] Redd was born on December 21, 1918 in Perry, FL[3], located in rural north Florida, east of Tallahassee. His parents, Allen Toy Redd, a railroad employee, and Ella Pitts Redd, raised him as one of four children. James was an extremely bright child who loved science and reading, despite an early eye injury that left him with limited vision. In later life, he rarely spoke about his childhood, but conveyed a sense of having been well-provided for. In the mid-1930s, the Redd family relocated to Weirsdale, FL, northeast of Orlando, after his father took a job with the Atlantic Coast Line Railroad. James began his higher education at University of Florida (UF) in 1936, graduating with a BS degree in 1940. At UF, he joined the Sigma Phi Epsilon social fraternity. One of his fraternity brothers, Charles Brokaw, would later have a long career at Minute Maid, eventually becoming Chief of Quality Control[1]. Brokaw would become just one of Redd's eventual collection of important contacts in the Florida citrus industry.

Following graduation, Redd continued graduate studies in chemistry at UF, and completed his Ph.D. in August, 1943, after only three years. His thesis research was on the oxidation of β-pinene, a terpene found predominantly in turpentine[3]. His thesis advisor was J. E. Hawkins. Although this work was not directly related to citrus, the knowledge he developed in terpene chemistry would be useful later. Redd's thesis was notably concise, reflecting a direct writing style, and he devoted minimal effort to justifying the purpose of his research. The thesis included a short biography and acknowledgement section, but no dedication, and no mention is made of his family.

Redd married Eleanor Marian Roser in June, 1943[4]. Their engagement had been formally announced in the Tampa Bay Times in December, 1942[5]. Eleanor came from a prominent family in St. Petersburg, FL. Redd and Roser probably met at UF. Eleanor's father, Charles, had co-invented the *Fig Newton* snack in Ohio[6] and later became a property developer in Florida. Although Charles had died in 1937, the family remained affluent, owning extensive properties in St. Petersburg and Anna Maria Island, FL.

Shortly after the wedding and graduation, Redd accepted a research

---

[1] Redd rarely used his full middle name professionally. A very close friend of Redd suggested the spelling should be Beverley, but this spelling was not used on his death certificate[2].

position at UF's Citrus Experiment Station (CES) in Lake Alfred, FL. The station's research primarily focused on citrus propagation and cultivation. The facility employed about a dozen scientists. Redd later reflected on how much he learned during this period about the importance of cultivation practices on fruit quality and yield[1]. After a year or two, Redd left the CES and joined the Wm. P. McDonald Corporation in Auburndale, FL. William McDonald, a developer who moved to Florida around 1930, had purchased citrus groves and established a fresh fruit packing house. By the early 1940s, McDonald was producing canned single-strength orange juice primarily for the US Army[7, 1]. At McDonald's, Redd worked on several projects including the installation of new Rotary Juice Presses, a new plate-pasteurizer, and the development of a freeze-dried orange juice product[2]. This position was Redd's second opportunity to work with orange juice. He had previously worked under Dr. Arthur Stahl at UF studying freeze concentration of orange juice as an undergraduate[8, 9]. Redd's early career exposed him to the important impact of juice processing methods on flavor.

In the fall of 1947, at the age of 29, Redd became the inaugural director of the new Citrus School at Florida Southern College (FSC) in Lakeland, FL. FSC's President, Ludd Spivey, seeing an opportunity to educate students for the rapidly growing citrus industry, had recently launched the new program. In addition to Redd, FSC hired other faculty including Dr. Boris Sokoloff, a physician and medical researcher, to begin the program. The FSC Citrus School remains in operation today, known for having produced many citrus industry leaders. Yet, Redd only stayed there four years, resigning in 1951. During his tenure, he collaborated closely with Sokoloff on several research projects, including patenting a process to remove bitter flavor from citrus molasses[10], and researching the isolation and health benefits of a citrus flavonoid extract known as Vitamin P[11]. The flavonoid research led to a patent [12] and a commercialization deal with Vitamerican Oil Corporation of Paterson, NJ[13]. According to a history of the Citrus School compiled in 1993, FSC earned modest patent royalties from this research for several years after Redd's departure[14]. While at FSC, Redd also arranged tours of various citrus facilities for his students and was known for inviting industry representatives to speak at the school. Redd's aca-

---

[2]In 1949, McDonald sold his operation to Clinton Industries, the owner of the popular *Snow Crop* brand of orange juice. Clinton sold Snow Crop to Minute Maid in 1954.

demic position allowed him to engage with the industry without being seen as a competitor.

Several of Redd's colleagues from his later business career described him as a scientist or engineer at heart, not a man who enjoyed routine business activities. He maintained a lifelong interest in the scientific literature and relished solving challenging technical problems, sometimes becoming so absorbed in a new challenge that he neglected his other tasks. He was obviously very intelligent, authoring various research articles and a book in his later years. An academic job might have seemed ideal for him, offering intellectual freedom and security. So why did he resign from the FSC position so quickly? In a 2021 search, the archivist at FSC found no documentation regarding Redd's resignation[15]. However, in a 1984 letter to the then-director of the Citrus School, Dr. Rubert W. Prevatt, Redd stated that he left to commercialize a citrus flavonoid product with a local processing company[16]. Within eight years of finishing graduate school, Redd had held three jobs: two in academic settings and one in industry. Perhaps with age and opportunity, his entrepreneurial spirit was awakening. Maybe the small college atmosphere didn't suit him, or perhaps he was seeking greater economic opportunities, especially given his growing family; by 1949, he and Eleanor had two daughters. His next steps underscored his independence and self-confidence.

At age 32, Redd began a decade of work as an independent consultant for the citrus industry. One early client was Pasco Packing Company in Dade City, FL, the company Redd referred to in his letter to Prevatt. The success of the flavonoid product is unclear, but Redd reported it continued to be manufactured for the US Vitamin Corporation until at least 1958[1]. Between 1952 and 1953, he worked for Dr. George Sperti on an orange juice freeze-concentration process for the Hi-Ester Corporation (see pg. 95). From 1953 to 1958, he also worked with Charlie Hendrix at the Winter Garden Citrus Cooperative on various projects, including a pilot-scale freeze-concentration plant and essence collection from their conventional low-temperature/high-vacuum evaporators (see pg. 125). Redd reported he also experimented with folding peel oils using a continuously-fed, swept-surface evaporator during this period[8].

By the late 1950s, he was regularly collaborating with Charlie Walker's Gulf Machinery Corporation, setting up a small juice concentrate plant in Irapuato, Mexico in 1958, and installing an (unsuccessful) essence unit in Venezuela. He co-developed the new TASTE evaporator concept, helping to install the first unit at Pipkins Dairy in Lakeland, FL in 1960 (see pg. 134). All these projects were recounted by Redd in 1988[1]. According to later colleagues, Redd also consulted for Anthony Rossi, who founded Tropicana[17, 18]. It is likely he was involved in other consulting work. The orange juice concentrate business was growing rapidly and plants were challenged to keep up with the growth.

By the end of the 1950s, Redd had developed extensive experience in many aspects of citrus juice processing including quality testing procedures, processing equipment, and common operational difficulties, including the importance of fruit selection on juice quality. He had also learned about the complex business of selling citrus products, including juice and by-products such as peel waste, citrus molasses, and peel oils. Furthermore, he had established a reputation in the industry and an extensive network of contacts as a result of his work. Known for his friendly demeanor, Redd enjoyed conversation and storytelling, and could communicate well with both management and less-educated plant staff. He particularly valued the insights of day-to-day equipment operators. Despite his academic achievements and the nickname "Doc Redd," his communication style was "down-to-earth," and he felt very comfortable among plant personnel.

Redd Laboratories 1961–1970

Jim Redd's professional relationship with Charlie Walker, owner of Gulf Machinery Corporation, dated back to the mid 1940s during Redd's tenure at Wm. P. McDonald Corp[1]. By 1960, their professional collaboration had evolved into a close friendship. Walker was a mechanically-gifted, but essentially self-trained. He was also a shrewd businessman, with other business interests in addition to Gulf Machinery. Walker's personality was very different from Redd's. He was very competitive, seeing business as a matter of winning or losing, and he never wanted to lose. A very assertive man with a large personality, he could be a demanding boss. An employee once described him as "having ice-water in his veins[19]." But Walker and Redd shared a mutual respect and their personalities complemented each other. Their friendship would be life-long.

The new TASTE evaporator design they jointly developed (see pg.

132) provided both men substantial business opportunities. The demand for these new evaporators obviously benefited Walker's equipment company. But the new evaporator design, incorporating a high-temperature/fast transit time concentration process, produced a different juice concentrate compared to the older, low-temperature evaporators. The product from the TASTE evaporator was essentially sterilized, reducing microbial issues and associated off-flavors, and significantly improving shelf-life. When citrus plants adopted this new type of evaporator, they required extensive training on equipment operation and concentrate handling. While Walker focused on manufacturing equipment, Redd took on the training responsibilities. This arrangement proved fortuitous for Redd, as his increased consulting opportunities came at a time when he needed additional income.

Although Redd had married into a wealthy family in 1943, his marriage unfortunately ended in divorce in the 1950s, leaving him as the single parent of two young daughters and necessitating a financial restart. His consulting work throughout the decade kept him busy but did not provide sufficient economic stability[20]. In August 1961, at Walker's invitation, Redd moved to Clearwater, FL and established a new company called Redd Laboratories Inc. in Largo, FL[3]. Walker supported this new venture as a major shareholder, providing the necessary funds for Redd to make a fresh start[20, 21, 22]. Redd Laboratories became Jim Redd's operational base for the next decade.

Over the next several years, Redd worked to design and install essence units and commission TASTE evaporators across Florida, Puerto Rico, and South America. In 1962, his former colleague from Winter Garden Citrus Cooperative, Charlie Hendrix, joined Redd Laboratories as a consulting chemist. Together, they spent most of 1963 working on setting up the new Suconasa citrus plant in Brazil. This project involved building the entire facility from the ground up, including a new TASTE evaporator and essence unit. By the summer, the plant was operational producing high-Brix orange juice concentrate without cutback juice. In place of cutback juice, Redd's essence and peel oil were added to the concentrate to restore the lost flavor. This innovative product was successfully introduced into the Canadian market by the company Sunny Orange (see pg. 136). Back in Florida, Redd Laboratories also produced beverage bases for Sunny Orange. These beverage

---

[3]The original location was 507 S. Seminole Rd, Largo, FL 33540.

bases, concentrated mixtures of fruit concentrates, sugar, acids, and flavoring ingredients, were designed to be efficiently shipped to beverage facilities where they could be diluted and bottled for local distribution. Throughout the 1960s, Redd Laboratories continued to manufacture these beverage bases for various customers[4].

In 1964, Redd reached an agreement with the M&O citrus plant in Wauchula, FL to build and install an essence unit. This initiative aimed to reduce waste emissions of citrus oils into the Peace River, which were killing fish. In exchange for his expertise and operation of the essence unit, Redd received the collected essence at no cost. Leveraging his experience from Suconasa and this new source of essence, Redd Laboratories began selling essence products, the first company to trade in citrus essence independently of manufacturing orange juice concentrate. While these essences were primarily used in orange juice concentrate, Redd also knew these same ingredients could be used in beverage bases and in other flavoring applications. As Redd gained experience in essence unit operation and the use of peel oils and essence in place of cutback juice, his organization quickly developed unique expertise. The company also needed more space. Consequently, the company relocated to a new site in Safety Harbor, FL, next door to Walker's Gulf Machinery facility. Charles Walker owned this new property and the buildings, which Redd Laboratories leased[20].

Redd and Walker also explored opportunities beyond citrus. Around 1965 or 1966, they collaborated with local businessmen to plan a pineapple processing facility in Honduras[24]. The initial investor group included Frances Marsh, a prominent Clearwater resident and former spouse of the Clearwater Sun newspaper owner[25]. Marsh's CPA and business advisor, Rex Harper, attended investor meetings in both the US and Tegucigalpa. Although the facility was never completed due to financing issues, the venture led to Jim Redd gaining a new business advisor and lifelong friend, Rex Harper. Marsh was impressed enough by Redd and Walker to invest in some of Redd's future business activities.

In 1966, Redd Laboratories published the first edition of a manual for citrus processors entitled "Quality Control Manual for Citrus Pro-

---

[4]Another early employee of Redd's was Jon Jefferson, who was very experienced in base formulation and would later leave Redd to start a separate beverage base business[23]

cessing Plants[5][27]." Charlie Hendrix and Jon Jefferson were credited as the authors, with no mention of Redd himself, although he apparently contributed to later expanded editions which list him as a co-author. This 180-page paperback served as a handy reference featuring juice test methods, charts, and conversion tables. The corporate tagline for Redd Laboratories, displayed on the inside cover, was "Consulting, Analytical and Manufacturing Chemist Serving the Food Industry." Interestingly, the manual made no mention of essence use, perhaps because it was too new.

Later in the same year, Redd hired Howard Trumm from Libby, McNeil & Libby as Executive Vice President[28], apparently aiming to expand the company's activities. Despite Trumm's experience in both citrus and pineapple essence, his stay at Redd Laboratories was short. Trumm departed for a new position within a year[29].

During this period, Redd developed a washed pulp cell product used to enhance the mouthfeel of juice and juice-like beverages. Redd leased space from a citrus plant to manufacture the product, using excess pulp obtained during orange juice extraction. This product was added to the inventory of citrus oils, essences and beverage bases that Redd Laboratories was already selling. Meanwhile, he continued to expand his consulting clientele, both domestically and internationally, with notable clients including Eckes in Germany, one of Europe's largest juice companies, and Del Monte in the UK. Redd also developed a relationship with INA Trading in Japan and began marketing citrus products there using the *REDD* brand[17, 24]. An avid traveler, Redd relished the opportunity to visit plants, meet customers, offer his advice, and tackle new technical challenges on the go.

By 1967, Redd had installed a number of essence units globally and had devised a sustainable business strategy around essence. Large processors, like Minute Maid or General Foods, had developed their own essence units and preferred to manage essence collection and usage internally. Meanwhile, smaller processors, recognizing the cost-savings and other benefits of TASTE evaporators, were less certain about the value of essence units. Redd's approach was to offer to install a Redd-designed essence unit at the processor's facility at his own expense. His team would oversee the unit's installation, operation and essence col-

---

[5]The first edition was self-published and does not show a publication date. According to a later edition, it was released in 1966[26].

lection, with the plant providing an operator to monitor the equipment and utilities. Redd Laboratories would also manage the BATF registration and associated regulatory paperwork. In exchange, Redd would receive a predetermined fraction of the collected essence, typically 40–50%. This arrangement was formalized in an "essence contract" lasting three to five years, with options for renewal or a buyout. The contracts stipulated that Redd would advise on the use of essence in the plant's products and manage the sale of any plant-owned essence, if not used internally, under terms comparable to other essence Redd Laboratories sold.

Redd had established at least five essence contracts by 1970[6]. The benefits for the plants were clear: minimal capital investment, limited operational demands, and the the potential for profit by using or selling their share of the essence. Since essence was a byproduct of operating evaporators, the main challenge was to capture it without disrupting concentrate production. Redd's essence units were designed for ease of operation and had minimal impact on the concentrate process. His engineers managed the units by means of site visits and communication with on-site operators. The goal was to address any problems proactively, ensuring smooth plant operations. For Redd, these arrangements not only provided new sources of essence raw materials, but also positioned him to produce and obtain the highest quality essence from his pool of suppliers. His regular access to these plants also allowed him the opportunity to purchase other byproducts, including premium peel oils. By this time, Redd was also purchasing essence from overseas, including from Brazilian and Mexican plants where he had established relationships[31].

Historically, the citrus industry had learned to add peel oil to orange juice concentrate to mimic the natural oil content in hand-squeezed juice. Later, the idea of restoring other lost volatiles, the water-phase and oil-phase essence, motivated essence recovery for citrus. But in practice, the variability in the sensory impact (both positive and negative) of essence and peel oil to juice hinted at a fundamental truth. Peel oils and essence lots varied significantly from one another, and they influenced the flavor of juice differently. Since these flavor ingredients were complex mixtures, some components had a positive impact on the juice

---

[6]Alcoma, Bordo Citrus, Myakka Processors, Treesweet Products and Sunny Orange/Redd Orange Concentrates Inc.[30].

flavor, while others proved detrimental. By the late 1960s, advances in flavor analysis, particularly through gas chromatography, allowed for the identification of many specific chemicals in citrus oils and essences that were important for juice flavor. This led to a shift in thinking about citrus essences, away from simply restoring lost flavor, and towards the idea of improving juice flavor by careful selection of essences and optimized use rates. Not far behind was the concept of creating a specialized flavoring mixture, produced by combining various oils and essences, that could be added to juice concentrate to improve the flavor. This flavoring mixture, eventually known as a flavor-package or add-back flavor, was designed in a process similar to that of traditional flavor houses, where aroma chemicals and other flavoring ingredients are blended to produce a target flavor profile for a product. For juice, regulatory constraints limited the flavoring ingredients to only peel oil and essence, but batch selection, mixing ratios, and usage rates could be finely tuned. In practice, flavoring orange juice concentrate presented a complex challenge. Concentrates varied widely in their inherent qualities such as sweetness, acidity, and bitterness. Consequently, the impact of a specific essence on one type of juice concentrate did not necessarily replicate on another. Additionally, consumer preferences for juice flavor were not uniform, varying significantly in terms of desired sweetness, acidity, and oil content. For the citrus industry, this transition in thinking about juice flavor occurred slowly, but Jim Redd was at the forefront of the new thinking. Concurrently, Redd Laboratories was transitioning from a consulting and training company into a specialized flavor company.

In 1968, Redd ventured into a new business, incorporating Sunny Orange Concentrates Inc. with Frances Marsh serving as corporate secretary[32]. In collaboration with Charlie Walker, another shareholder, they acquired a small citrus concentrate facility in Lakeland, FL from Universal Food Products. The facility had been owned by J. Stanley Sargeant and his co-investors, but they ran into financial difficulties and owed money to Walker[18]. The new business was kept legally separate from Redd Laboratories, but the organizations worked very closely together, particularly on the production of citrus pulp and beverage bases. Within a few years, the processing business was renamed Redd Orange Concentrates Inc.

By 1970, the Florida orange juice industry was embracing the use of essence products and moving away from cutback juice. New TASTE evaporators and essence units were proliferating, and the global citrus industry was expanding. Florida had become the undisputed hub of the industry, which now stretched from producers in the US, Brazil, and elsewhere in Central and South America to markets across North America, Europe, and Japan. Redd Laboratories was flourishing, employing approximately 8 people[31, 17], and offering consulting services, installing essence units, and supplying citrus essences and oils, beverage bases and pulp cells. Jim Redd had a global network of customers, a strong reputation, and his *REDD* brand of citrus products. However, some segments of the Florida citrus industry viewed Redd with suspicion. Florida citrus growers and processors were concerned about the competitive threat of Brazil's juice industry, and some disliked Redd's involvement with Brazilian processors. Some also feared that the citrus beverage bases that Redd manufactured would compete in the consumer marketplace against 100% juice. Additionally, there was apprehension that the use of citrus essences could reduce the demand for top-quality oranges or facilitate juice adulteration, disadvantaging the Florida citrus growers.

In his personal life, Redd was much happier now. He had remarried in 1964 to Lillian Michaels, a widow with four children. The couple formed a blended family of 6 children, with Redd legally adopting Lillian's two younger children. Redd's business success had greatly improved his finances. In 1967, he and Lillian purchased a beautiful waterfront home on Clearwater Beach. By age 50, Redd had achieved personal and professional success.

Redd Laboratories Sells

An important client for Redd Laboratories was Wagner Fruit Juice Industries based in Chicago, Illinois. This company, which produced 100% fruit juices, fruit-flavored drinks, and fruit syrups, distributed its products throughout the Midwest. The family company had gone public in 1967 under the leadership of its majority shareholder, Frank Wagner. The following year, A. E. Staley Manufacturing Company, a firm headquartered in Decatur, IL that specialized in chemical byproducts from corn and grain processing like starches and sweeteners, acquired Wagner's business. As part of this acquisition, Wagner was appointed as an executive and board member. By 1969, Staley's was looking to further diversify its business portfolio, and Wagner, having developed a friendly relationship with Jim Redd through their business dealings, recommended that Staley's acquire Redd Laboratories[31].

Redd delegated the negotiations to his business advisor, Rex Harper. During the course of 1970, the parties agreed that Staley's would acquire not only Redd Laboratories but the juice concentrate plant, along with the rights to the REDD brand name. However, Staley's was not interested in building essence units or installing them. In response, Redd established a new company in July 1970, Intercit, to house his collaborative projects with Gulf Machinery and related consulting activities. In November 1970, Staley's publicly announced the acquisition of Redd Laboratories and Redd's juice processing company, the newly renamed Redd Orange Concentrates Inc., and the transaction concluded soon after. Terms of the private sale were not disclosed[7]. As part of the sale, Redd signed a non-compete agreement and agreed to work for Staley's for several years.

So why did Redd sell? None of Redd's later business colleagues who were interviewed recalled him specifically addressing this question. At just over 50 years old, Redd was not seeking a sale nor was he ready to retire. Nevertheless, Staley's offer was likely financially attractive and promised fresh investment capital, allowing Redd to continue his technical work with greater support. Charlie Walker, Redd's partner and shareholder, also recognized potential opportunities collaborating with Staley's, given its larger market in the grain business compared to citrus[20]. Redd and Walker likely discussed the advantages and disadvantages of a sale at length. Interestingly, around the same time, Walker was also entertaining the sale of Gulf Machinery[20]. Rumors from at least two sources suggested that Redd might have faced financial difficulties in his concentrate business that instigated the sale of his business. Manufacturing juice concentrate in Florida could be capital intensive, as the fruit had to be purchased in advance, but the concentrate might be held for some time before sale. Unexpected price swings in the concentrate market due to weather or other factors could be large and rapid, leading to large gains or losses. While it is unknown how profitable the juice concentrate business was for Redd, there is no evidence he needed to sell his company.

---

[7]In a 2021 interview, Rex Harper could not recall the sales price.

The Transition Years 1971–1974

After the sale, a number of changes happened quickly at Redd Laboratories. James Redd assumed the role of Director of Research & Development, while E. B. Freyfogle, a Staley's employee, was appointed President of both Redd Laboratories and Redd Orange Concentrates Inc. Charlie Hendrix, who had worked closely with Redd for the past eight years, left to join Citrus Central. For the newly acquired Redd Laboratories, the essence contract business remained important and considerable efforts were directed towards developing a product line of citrus flavor ingredients for both juices and broader food and beverage uses. Memos exchanged with Staley's staff in Decatur suggest that Redd maintained close contact with top management and received substantial corporate support.

One new area of emphasis was using the distillation process to concentrate citrus oils. The process of distilling citrus peel oils for both concentration and increased beverage solubility had been used by the flavor industry for many years. Orange oil, consisting of more than 90% d-limonene, a water-insoluble hydrocarbon with a faintly citrus-like aroma, was a prime candidate. By distilling orange oil under vacuum, a portion of the limonene could be removed, concentrating the oil by a factor from two to ten. The concentrated oil retained most of the original orange flavor and, with reduced limonene, was more soluble in beverages. Historically, the process was known as "folding" and the concentrated oils as "folded oils."

Using folded peel oil had distinct advantages for restoring flavor volatiles to orange juice concentrate compared to single-fold peel oil. Folded oil allowed formulators to adjust the level of limonene independently from other flavor volatiles. However, citrus concentrate producers traditionally used single-fold oil for several reasons. First, the juice concentration process stripped out limonene along with other volatiles, making single-fold oil a straightforward solution. Second, single-fold oil was readily available at every processing plant, while folded oil required specialized equipment and expertise that was not otherwise needed. Finally, in either case, peel oil was only a partial solution of the flavoring problem; water-phase and oil-phase essence or cutback juice were still needed.

Redd was familiar with distillation and had folded orange oil as early as 1953[8]. Although Redd Laboratories had a small stainless steel still before the 1970 acquisition, its use was not an important part of the business activities[17, 31]. However, following the acquisition, commercial distillation equipment was installed and the regular production of folding citrus oils began. By 1974, Redd Laboratories' product list included folded orange, grapefruit, and tangerine oils along with "standardized" water-phase aroma, oil-phase aroma and peel oils from various citrus fruits. They also concentrated oil-phase essence using the same distillation process, with the product list showing folded orange and lemon essence oils.

Flavor packages were also developed, combining folded cold-pressed oil with single-fold or folded essence oils into a concentrated mixture. One example was *REDD Special Orange Oil Concentrate*, which combined seven-fold orange peel oil with three-fold orange essence oil. The 1974 product description read "to secure a uniform flavor level and a bouquet of freshly extracted orange juice," and recommended use in juice and both non-carbonated and carbonated orange-flavored drinks[33]. Additionally, Redd Laboratories began marketing terpenes, a byproduct of the oil folding process, joining Florida Chemical Company.

Redd Laboratories also applied their new distillation technology to water-phase essence. James Redd developed a concentrated water-phase aroma containing about 75% ethanol, achieved by removing much of the water through distillation. He referred to this product initially as "anhydrous aroma" and later as "aroma concentrate." He believed this product was more stable at room temperature compared to regular aroma, and would reduce shipping costs due to its decreased volume[34, 35, 36]. Additionally, the high flavor concentration and water-solubility made it suitable for a wide range of beverages, unlike citrus oils that were difficult to solubilize. The potential market was much larger than just orange juice. However, the high alcohol content presented a challenge as the product no longer met the federal requirements to avoid the excise tax on alcohol, which was levied on any product that the federal government considered potable. Water-phase aroma with alcohol content at or below 15% had received a special exemption in the 1960s (see pg. 131). The excise tax was substantially increased the cost of the new aroma concentrate. In July 1972, Redd Laboratories petitioned the IRS for an exclusion. Jim Redd, working with Staley's Director of Government Relations, visited Washington, DC in February 1973, and returned expecting the petition to be approved within several months. In the summer of 1973, the company prepared product samples and presented them widely to potential customers[35]. There was considerable interest, but the IRS was slow to act. By January 1974, the petition still had not been approved. A December 1973 memo from E. Freyfogle, President of Redd Laboratories, to the Staley lobbyist revealed that the company had invested $200,000 in R&D costs on this product over the past two years, against total company sales of $300,000 for the fiscal year ending September 30, 1973[36][8]. This expenditure evidently included the distillation equipment. A follow up memo in January 1974 showed the product had been rebranded as *Natural Orange Flavor*, with an annual sales forecast of nearly 12,000 pounds[37].

The ultimate resolution to this excise tax issue is unknown, but Freyfogle was willing to launch the product in January 1975, even if it meant absorbing the excise tax costs[34]. This decision was motivated by the interest shown by a diverse group of companies, including juice and beverage producers, dairies, and flavor houses from the US, Canada, England, Japan, and South America, which highlighted Redd Laboratories' client base. Nevertheless, significant changes were looming for both Jim Redd and Staley's in the next two years that would shift their priorities.

Jim Redd managed another major research project at this time, applying liquid chromatography to capture important flavor compounds which remained in the citrus oil distillates. The strength or quality of citrus oils had traditionally been measured by the total aldehyde content, a measurement made using a laboratory titration method. Higher total aldehyde content was associated with better flavor. Redd Laboratories used this analytical method to characterize the strength of their folded oils and flavor packages. Redd noticed that the distillate terpenes removed when citrus oils were folded retained some citrus flavor character, and showed a non-zero aldehyde measurement.

Considering that aldehydes are polar molecules and d-limonene is rather non-polar, he developed a chromatographic separation method using silica gel with mobile-phase solvents including hexane and ethyl acetate. While the process of liquid chromatography was well-known, and some flavor companies had developed their own proprietary applications of the technology to citrus oils, Redd considered his approach novel and the process was certainly new in Florida. Collaborating with a Redd Laboratories' chemist named David Mitchell, he prepared a patent

---

[8]The sales figure excludes internal sales to Staley's entities.

application titled "Recovery of Citrus Flavors and Essences from Citrus Process d-Limonene Byproducts." The patent was prepared with Staley's support and submitted to the patent office sometime before 1974[38, 39, 40, 41, 42, 43]. However, the patent office found the application lacking citing prior art, and despite an appeal, the patent was never granted. Despite the setback, Redd Laboratories successfully utilized the chromatographic process to isolate aldehyde-rich fractions, primarily containing octanal, from their distilled terpenes. They ran the process on a large 8 ft long, 2 ft diameter packed column, and incorporated these new fractions into their compounded flavor products by late 1974.

Around the same time, Redd also filed a patent on an improved apparatus for vacuum drying juice concentrates like orange juice, which was granted and assigned to Staley's[44]. This process aimed to produce very low-moisture orange juice flakes, not unlike the powdered OJ that Vacuum Foods (precursor to Minute Maid) tried to commercialize in the early 1940s (see pg. 63). Redd's patent sought to improve the basic process and product. There is no evidence this product was commercialized by Redd Laboratories.

In 1974, the FDOC patents on essence recovery and use were issued[45, 46, 47] (see pg. 139). Concerns arose at Staley's about potential restrictions on Redd Laboratories' essence-related commercial activities, while Jim Redd was annoyed, perceiving the patents as encroachments on his earlier ideas. Discussions ensued between Redd, Staley's management, and a patent attorney regarding the history of essence collection and the commercial implications of the patents[48, 49]. However, the FDOC never attempted to restrict any commercial activities, and the issue was dropped by Staley's.

In the few short years following the Staley's acquisition, Redd Laboratories had made rapid advancements in utilizing natural citrus flavoring ingredients. Beyond offering essences and oils as flavoring ingredients, they were deconstructing these ingredients and reconstructing new flavoring mixtures, with an aim to reach beyond citrus juice applications. Ingredient selection, distillation and chromatography were all employed to create flavoring fractions, which could then be combined to create specialized flavoring products. The specialized know-how that Jim Redd and his colleagues developed in the character and use of these citrus fractions is more difficult to document. Nevertheless, they were learning how these fractions performed in various juice and beverage applications, and that experience would guide their product development and marketing efforts.

Despite the succeses, Jim Redd grew increasingly unhappy working under Staley's corporate structure, and it seems the discontent might have been mutual. Having been his own boss for the past two decades, and an expert in a field he was deeply passionate about, Redd was accustomed to making quick decisions. Furthermore, he thrived on addressing new challenges, often becoming bored with routine or slow-moving projects. Staley's more methodical style and slower decision making probably chafed against Redd's sense of efficiency and opportunity. Additionally, following an acquisition, the corporate vision of the new owners seldom matches that of the previous one. While no records of any disagreements remain, by 1974 it was evident that Redd was unhappy and would soon leave[31, 24]. In response, Staley's identified a successor, Allen Kryger, a young Ph.D. organic chemist from Decatur, IL. Kryger relocated to Florida in April 1974, and within a year, Jim Redd had left the company. He transitioned full-time to his other business venture, Intercit Inc., which was situated on a parcel of land owned by Charlie Walker, right next door to Redd Laboratories.

Florida Chemical Co. and the Terpene Market

Bert Schulz's early efforts to commercialize the citrus limonene had started slowly (see pg. 99). However, by the early 1960s, his business saw substantial growth after discovering a new market for limonene: adhesive resin manufacturers. These manufacturers traditionally used pine oil fractions, but found that citrus limonene offered manufacturing advantages. In 1961, Bert sold a remarkable 3 million pounds of limonene to these customers, significantly boosting his small business[50]. Subsequently, this resin market became a major, ongoing customer for this Florida citrus byproduct. Around the same time, he secured a contract with a major US industrial chemical manufacturer[9] that required consistent, year-round supply of particularly pure limonene, delivered monthly. By 1963, Bert had renamed his company Florida Chemical Company and constructed a new manufacturing facility in Lake Alfred, where he installed a distillation column to produce the high-quality limonene. He found that directly distilling orange

---

[9]This manufacturer remains a proprietary secret of Florida Chemical Company.

peel oil, rather than re-distilling limonene, yielded a consistently better high-purity product with improved odor. Schulz was also selling small quantities of raw citrus peel oils to flavor and fragrance brokers in the northeast.

By 1972, as Redd Laboratories was expanding under Staley's ownership, Florida Chemical Company had firmly established a market for the industrial use of citrus d-limonene and the chemically similar peel oil distillate, now referred to as citrus terpenes to distinguish it from limonene or stripper oil. The primary industrial applications included chemical processing into adhesive resins and l-carvone, a flavor chemical with a "minty" aroma used in imitation spearmint, and solvent applications such as paints and cleaners. During a 1972 citrus industry conference, Bert estimated industry production of limonene for the 1970-71 season at 10 million pounds, with an additional 1 million pounds of terpenes produced by distilling cold-pressed oil[51]. While Schulz faced little competition in the early 1960s, the market had matured, with some resin producers beginning to purchase limonene directly from citrus plants, and at least one other terpene broker emerging in Florida[52, 53, 54, 55][10].

The limonene market proved very important for Redd Laboratories in the 1970s. As they installed commercial-scale distillation units and began folding citrus oils, their primary interest was in the flavor use of the folded oils, not in the terpene distillates. However, these terpenes comprised a large volume of the original raw material, 80% in the case of five-fold peel oil or 90% for ten-fold oil. By selling these terpenes to Florida Chemical, Redd Laboratories significantly reduced their inventory volume and, more importantly, recovered a substantial portion of their raw material investment. The price differential between the cost of peel oil and the sales price of terpenes was typically small, allowing the company to quickly recoup nearly 80% of each dollar invested in peel oils, once the product was folded to five-fold and the terpenes sold. Much of Redd Laboratories' peel oil inventory was stored after folding, rather than as a single-fold, and blended into finished products as needed. The symbiotic relationship between Redd Laboratories and Florida Chemical benefited both companies, enabling Redd Laboratories to handle larger quantities of peel oil, as well as reduce the cost basis for their flavors, while supplying Florida Chemical with high-

---

[10]That company was called PDM or Pine Derivatives Marketing.

quality terpenes without the complication of in-house distillation. The result was that Florida Chemical became one of Redd Laboratories' largest customers in terms of volume and revenue.

Florida Chemical also purchased distilled terpenes from Coca-Cola Special Products, which was folding peel oils like Redd Laboratories. With two suppliers, Schulz soon found it inefficient to continue operating his own distillation column. By the mid 1970s, he negotiated an agreement with Redd Laboratories to ship distilled terpenes directly to some of his highest-volume customers, and he shut down his distillation equipment in Lake Alfred. The terpene products he purchased met the high purity standards required by his most-demanding customers.

Coca-Cola and Special Products

As one of Florida's original FCOJ producers, Minute Maid was deeply interested in orange juice flavor, and had active research programs in the collection and use of citrus oils and essences. However, the acquisition of Minute Maid by Coca-Cola in 1960, significantly bolstered the organization's dominance in the use of citrus flavoring materials. In addition to juice, Coca-Cola's carbonated beverages were flavored with citrus oils, including oils from lemon, lime, grapefruit and orange. Coca-Cola maintained a global network of suppliers for these oils, and relied on US flavor houses for the processing capacity and expertise necessary to produce the distilled and extracted fractions utilized in their products. Due to the long-standing problem of adulteration in the essential oil industry, Coca-Cola had developed in-house expertise in citrus oil production methods, chemical composition, and analysis techniques to ensure they received authentic, high-quality essential oils which were crucial for maintaining their brands. They cultivated long-term, trusted relationships with their citrus oil suppliers and the flavor houses that processed their oils, using these relationships to stay informed about the latest growing and processing practices.

Coca-Cola cultivated another core expertise: guarding corporate secrets. Protecting the secret formula for Coca-Cola served both as a marketing signature and a corporate mission. The company formulated all their beverages internally, relying on expert R&D and product development teams. Strategic sourcing of flavoring ingredients ensured that no single supplier knew the complete recipe of any beverage. Citrus fractions and oils, for example, were purchased from various suppliers and blended with other flavoring ingredients in Coca-Cola's own limited-access facilities. These "secret" mixtures could then be shipped to bottling facilities to produce their beverage products, effectively protecting their proprietary formulae from suppliers, the public, and nearly all employees. Maintaining this level of secrecy and compartmentalization required considerable effort and expense, but it was integral to Coca-Cola's organization and deeply embedded in the company's culture.

The acquisition of Minute Maid marked Coca-Cola's first foray outside of the soft-drink industry, introducing opportunities for both organizations. The Florida juice industry had already revolutionized the global supply of citrus oils, which were once so costly to manually express, but were now expressed automatically by juicing machines. However, Coca-Cola had not traditionally used Florida citrus oils, and in fact, predominantly used lemon and lime oils which were not produced in large quantities in Florida. By acquiring Minute Maid, Coca-Cola not only entered a burgeoning new beverage market but also gained direct control over a new supply of citrus byproducts. For Minute Maid, the acquisition provided access to Coca-Cola's expertise in citrus essential oils, a large internal customer for their byproducts, and all of the other tools and resources that Coca-Cola could provide.

Integrating these internal citrus byproducts within the newly combined organization was an on-going effort. Coca-Cola's soft-drink business and Minute Maid's juice business had distinct needs and processes. One early decision was to maintain separate research and product development teams for the soft-drink business (in Atlanta) and the juice business (in Plymouth, FL). Florida citrus oils, including the lemon and lime oils that were grown in state, differed in flavor character from oils Coca-Cola purchased elsewhere due to processing methods, cultivar mix, and growing conditions. Additionally, the new essences from Minute Maid's proprietary essence units were novel flavor ingredients for both Coca-Cola and Minute Maid. In response, research teams in both Atlanta and Plymouth explored applications of these ingredients across both carbonated soft-drink and juice products.

Around 1974, Coca-Cola established a specialized division in Plymouth known as "Special Products," adjacent to the existing R&D facility[56, 57, 58, 59, 60]. This division evolved into a manufacturing hub for citrus flavoring ingredients, a center of expertise on essence quality and usage, and a developer of new flavoring ingredients. Starting with equipment inherited from Minute Maid R&D, and utilizing oils and essences from Minute Maid processing plants, Special Products (SP) worked to standardize these ingredients, and to concentrate or fractionate them, for use internally at Minute Maid. Over time, SP expanded it role, manufacturing citrus flavoring products for other Coca-Cola products. Structured to maintain Coca-Cola's strategy of of compartmentalization and secrecy, SP was created within the Minute Maid organization, but reported directly to Coca-Cola's headquarters in Atlanta. Access to the facility was restricted, even to other Minute Maid R&D employees[61, 62]. The new organization was required to operate at a profit, purchasing raw materials from Minute Maid and external suppliers, while selling its finished products internally, to either Coca-Cola or Minute Maid. Carl Huffman, one of Minute Maid's citrus essence technology inventors, served as the first general manager. SP would remain Huffman's responsibility until he retired in the early 1990s. Two key early employees, Wesley Bucek, who had worked at Minute Maid since 1960, and Albert Kruger, sequentially served as general managers following Huffman's retirement.

Operating in parallel to Redd Laboratories, Coca-Cola's Special Products developed a similar expertise in FTNF citrus flavoring ingredients, but under very different conditions. SP had only one large customer, the Coca-Cola organization, and it benefited from Coca-Cola's vast scale and expertise. SP usually became a major global producer for its products, due to Coca Cola's dominant market size. This larger operating scale, compared to Redd Laboratories', more easily justified capital investments for specialized processing equipment or technology. Additionally, SP collaborations with product developers in both softdrinks and juice, allowed SP staff to accumulate highly-specialized applications know-how in FTNF citrus flavors similar to that of Redd Laboratories' staff.

Special Products activities were highly proprietary, but some of their activities during the 1970s can be discerned indirectly. They were folding citrus oils, particularly orange peel oil, for use in Minute Maid OJ concentrate. A Minute Maid employee recalled adding "five fold CPO" to their concentrate under Coca-Cola specifications in the mid 1970s[63]. It is unclear whether this was simply a simple folded cold-pressed oil, or a more complex mixture of folded oils and other ingredients, similar to the add-back flavors being produced at Redd Laboratories at the time. SP certainly had the expertise and capability to produce complex add-back flavors, and it would have been convenient to leave Minute Maid production employees unaware of Coca Cola's flavoring secrets. SP was also responsible for Minute Maid's proprietary aroma, receiving all the aroma produced at the Minute Maid processing plants. As Jim Redd observed in his operations, Minute Maid's essence was subject to a similar variability due to fruit maturity, varietal mix, and other factors throughout the processing season. SP standardized all the Minute Maid essence, by analyzing each lot and blending lots to meet their target specifications, prior to distributing it for use in Minute Maid's OJ concentrate. A university researcher who collaborated with SP personnel during this period also noted that they were processing lemon oils[64].

By the late 1970s, SP had developed an interest in valencene, a trace chemical naturally found in orange essence oil. Valencene has a small flavor impact in orange juice, but could be chemically modified into an important flavor chemical used in grapefruit flavors. The evidence for this interest comes from a USDA researcher who acknowledged receiving a sample of highly-concentrated valencene from Wes Bucek in 1978[65]. While it is possible Special Products received the sample from one of Coca-Cola's flavor suppliers, they likely were isolating it themselves from their supply of orange essence oil, as Redd Laboratories would begin doing in the early 1980s. Around the same time, Coca-Cola supported the master's degree research of Albert Kruger at UCF, who studied the application of production-scale liquid chromatography to citrus oil fractionation[66]. This technology, although it was more complex and costly than distillation or alcohol extraction, provided additional fractionation capabilities for citrus oils. It had found some niche applications in the flavor industry, including the one Jim Redd explored earlier at Redd Laboratories. In 1982, SP moved into a new facility in Plymouth, increasing its manufacturing space and acquiring additional chemical processing equipment. At the time of the move, SP had approximately a dozen employees[59].

Although Special Products operated in secret, they played a crucial role in the development of the specialized citrus flavor industry in Florida, interacting with both the broader citrus industry and the flavor industry in important ways. Initially relying on their internal oils and essences, by virtue of Coca Cola's size, SP soon began to purchase raw materials from other fruit processors, and secondary sources such as Redd Laboratories and its future competitors. In time, SP purchased specialized processed citrus flavoring ingredients from these companies, such as folded and terpeneless oils, and other specialized fractions. Driven by internal capacity issues, limited availability of raw materials, or favorable pricing, SP became a very important customer of processed citrus flavoring fractions in Florida. And Coca-Cola's exacting standards drove suppliers like Redd Laboratories to continually innovate their processes and quality control procedures. SP also produced citrus terpenes from their distillation operations. These terpenes had limited use to Coca-Cola, and SP was selling them to Florida Chemical Company by the mid 1970s[55]. As SP operations grew in size, they became a major supplier of terpenes to the Florida market.

Lastly, SP actively maintained collaborative relationships with university and USDA scientists across Florida and beyond, who specialized in research on citrus oils and flavors. Coca-Cola conducted their own internal research, some of which they published, and sponsored outside researchers with funds and specialized equipment. Given Coca-Cola's extensive worldwide network and SP's operational scale, they possessed key industry insights and had access to specialized materials, such as the previously mentioned valencene, that were difficult for academic researchers to obtain. SP strategically utilized these partnerships to initiate and advance research that, while beneficial to the company, was optimally conducted by independent researchers, possibly due to efficiency or regulatory considerations. Over time, this published research benefited the entire Florida industry.

Redd Laboratories, PFW and Hercules

Following Dr. Redd's departure from Redd Laboratories, the company continued its technical and product development under the leadership of two new employees who had relocated from Staley's headquarters in Decatur, IL: Mike Taylor, a food technologist, and Allen Kryger, a Ph.D. chemist[67, 56, 68]. Both arrived within a year before Redd left, and learned as much about the business from him as they could. With Redd gone, a significant challenge for Redd Laboratories was transitioning to a new sales strategy, one that did not rely on Redd's extensive industry connections[69].

Laboratory notebooks from 1974 through 1976 reveal interesting insights into the company's activities[70, 71, 72]. Projects were documented for about 30 potential customers, 90% of which were beverage companies. Those projects primarily focused on presenting flavor recommendations based on Redd Laboratories' product line. Kryger and Taylor were also trying to formulate cloud and flavor emulsions for use in beverages with their citrus ingredients. Most of the beverage projects during this period were for less than 100% juice products. Several companies had multiple active projects, with the largest number of projects documented for the King Juice Company and Wagner Fruit Juice Industries. The remaining 10% of potential customers were flavor & fragrance companies, including Manheimer, International Flavors and Fragrance (IFF), and Firmenich. Kryger and Taylor collaborated but concentrated on different areas. Taylor's projects mostly involved flavor evaluations and emulsion and beverage formulations. In contrast, Kryger's projects were geared towards chemical separations, utilizing techniques such as distillation, extraction, and chromatography, to create new fractions for particular customer projects. For instance, one of Kryger's projects was an effort to match Firmenich's popular *Orange Tetrarome* product, a concentrated orange oil fraction produced by counter-current extraction. Kryger also pursued new R&D efforts, including isolating natural pigments from citrus oils, and pesticide removal. For both Kryger and Taylor, most work focused on orange, but they also developed some lemon, lime and grapefruit products. It is noteworthy that some process and distillation equipment was located in Lakeland, FL, at the Redd Orange Concentrates plant, instead of Safety Harbor. Both companies had been acquired by Staley's and were operating in collaboration.

Since Staley's acquisition, distillation technology had become a focal point for Redd Laboratories, but the company also invested in developing alcohol extracts of citrus oils and distillates. This involved using ethanol, which they obtained from water-phase aroma by distillation. When ethanol was mixed with a citrus oil, and diluted with water to a specific concentration, the alcohol-water formed an immiscible layer that extracted valuable polar flavor components from the citrus oil, leaving less soluble terpenes and other hydrocarbons behind. The decanted alcohol layer possessed a strong citrus flavor character, and was more miscible in water-based beverages than the original oil. The basic process was widely-known and had been used for decades[73, pg. 246-257]. At Redd Laboratories, the goal was not to produce the alcohol layer but, additionally, to remove the alcohol and water from the extract by distillation, resulting in a very concentrated flavor fraction, with the alcohol being collected and reused. This process was known internally as the LEX process[74], likely short for "Limonene Extraction." One of the earliest uses for the process was extracting distilled terpenes produced when folding oils, which yielded a citrus oil fraction rich in the naturally-occuring aldehyde octanal. Redd Laboratories added this LEX ingredient to some folded oils and flavor packages, often using the terminology "enriched" in the product name. The process was applied to both orange and grapefruit terpenes, and later directly to peel and essence oils[75].

Behind the scenes, Staley's was re-evaluating their interest in the citrus flavor industry, resulting in the sale of Redd Laboratories to Hercules Inc. in June 1976[76]. Hercules, a large and diversified US chemical company, had previously acquired PFW, a well-established US flavor and fragrance company, in October 1973[77, 78]. Following the PFW acquisition, Hercules formed a food and fragrance department, integrating PFW and Hercules' other bulk food ingredients[79]. Redd Laboratories was incorporated into this new department. Staley's sold the Redd Orange Concentrates company to Sunstar Foods Inc., a Minneapolis-based company specializing in non-citrus food products[80]. Following Redd Laboratories' sale, Allen Kryger was appointed General Manager, while Ed Freyfogle, who had been President of both Redd Laboratories and Redd Orange Concentrates business, departed.

PFW, originally known as Polak's Frutal Works, was a family-owned essential oil company started in the Netherlands in 1914. The company established a US-based subsidiary in New York in 1921. At the start of the Second World War, the Polak family relocated to the US, making the US-based operation their headquarters. By 1973, when PFW was acquired by Hercules, it had grown into an international flavor and fragrance company with operations in the US, Canada, England, Holland, Germany, and Australia[81]. Following Redd Laboratories' acquisition by Hercules in 1976, it was slowly integrated with PFW. The merger brought several benefits to Redd, including a new internal customer for its citrus oils, which PFW required for their flavor and fragrance formulations. Moreover, PFW's internal citrus oil processing operations, all located in New York, were evaluated for relocation to Florida, providing new synergies. For example, when producing a citrus oil alcohol extract for PFW in Florida, the waste oil that PFW would normally discard could be used by Redd Laboratories to recover terpenes and other flavor isolates. More significantly, the exchange of know-how between the staff of Redd Laboratories, who were experts in the narrow field of 100% natural citrus essences and fractions, and PFW's employees, knowledgeable in the broader global flavor and fragrance industry, jump-started the future development of the Florida-based citrus flavor industry. Working together, they were able to incorporate Redd Laboratories' products more efficiently into global flavor markets. It would take time, but the size of these markets would support substantial investments in Florida to capitalize on these opportunities.

Coincidentally, around the time of Redd Laboratories' sale in June 1976, Allen Kryger documented an investigation in his logbook to isolate ethyl butyrate (EB) by fractionating orange essence oil[71, pg. 115]. EB's role in enhancing fresh orange and other fruit flavors was well-known in the flavor industry, and being an inexpensive aroma chemical produced synthetically, it was commonly used in fruit flavor applications. However, the importance of ethyl butyrate in orange juice was not yet fully appreciated, and juice regulations prevented any use of synthetic EB in 100% juice. Kryger and his colleagues recognized that natural EB, present in orange essence oil, would have a very different legal standing compared to synthetic EB and could be used both in orange juice and in other products that use only natural flavors. The technical challenge was that EB was present at extremely low levels in oranges. However, EB was already concentrated to 1000 ppm in the essence collection process that produced orange essence oil, and Redd Laboratories was handling increasingly large quantities of this oil, making the isolation of EB potentially feasible.

Kryger's earliest work was in the laboratory. By distillation, he generated flavor fractions rich in EB and other important flavoring aldehydes that were used at Redd Laboratories internally for new product development. Unfortunately, the documentation on how these processes were optimized and scaled to production has been lost. However, by the early 1980s, Redd Laboratories had standardized the production of two distinct fractions from the distillation of orange essence oil – one called "a-phase," which was high in ethanol and water-soluble, and the other called "o-phase," which contained terpenes and concentrated EB – and these fractions were in routine production[82, 56, 74]. This innovative process, and the EB it produced, would play a critical role for the Florida citrus industry over the next two decades.

On a summer evening in 1977, Thursday, July 14th, an unexpected disaster struck[83, 84]. Bystanders reported seeing dense black smoke rising from one of Redd Laboratories' building. Firefighters quickly determined that at least one drum of citrus oil had caught fire. Over the next two hours, additional drums caught fire, with some exploding due to the heat. The fire was contained by 10 pm, but eleven firefighters were injured and a building was extensively damaged[84]. Despite the damage, only a small portion of the company's citrus oil inventory caught fire, and the rest of the facility sustained only minor damage. Business operations were able to resume shortly afterwards. The fire unexpectedly proved to be a windfall for the author, a young science enthusiast, whose father brought home smoke-damaged yet still usable laboratory glassware and equipment salvaged from the blaze. The fire was thought to have been caused by a welding spark that ignited a rag, which smoldered until it triggered the main blaze after everyone had gone home. The incident underscored the fire danger associated with storing and processing citrus oils, which were flammable hydrocarbons. In addition to the obvious fire risk, limonene was known to auto-ignite under certain conditions due to the heat of oxidation, especially on cotton rags used to wipe up spilled oils. Other volatile solvents used in plant operations, such as ethanol or ethyl acetate, further contributed to the fire risk.

In the year after the fire, once operations were fully restored, efforts to integrate Redd Laboratories and PFW resumed. Dennis Kujawski, a young PFW flavorist, was appointed as the flavor liaison to Redd Laboratories. During regular visits to Florida, Kujawski was introduced to all of Redd's products by Kryger and Taylor, and he brought back samples to New York to share with his PFW colleagues. The personal collaboration, rather than simply sending samples by mail, was found to be much more effective for integrating Redd Laboratories' products into new PFW formulations. In 1979, Kryger was promoted to Director of Natural Products for PFW, relocating to Middletown, NY[85], while Taylor assumed the role of General Manager in Florida. Joe Johnson, a chemist with experience at Coca-Cola R&D and Citrus Central Cooperative, was recruited by Taylor to take over Kryger's technical responsibilities[56, 68]. Additionally, Hadi Lashkajani, a young chemical engineer, was hired to manage plant operations. Both Johnson and Lashkajani would become influential figures in the industry. Kryger, on the other hand, would be laid off by PFW during the 1981 economic recession.

Joe Johnson, born and raised in Alabama, brought his background as a trained chemist, with experience in the pharmaceutical industry, to his work at Coca-Cola and the Citrus Central Cooperative, where he developed expertise in orange juice and beverage flavors. Possessing the quiet manners of a genteel Southerner, he arrived to Redd Laboratories where the most advanced flavor packages for orange juice had evolved to include combinations of folded peel and essence oils, fortified with topnotes including EB. The term topnotes described the most volatile natural flavor chemicals in orange juice, including EB, trans-2-hexenal (T2), and acetaldehyde. The oil-soluble flavor packages were purchased by FCOJ producers and added to their concentrate, along with water-phase aroma, to restore and enrich the flavor. FCOJ manufacturers, who were now using orange juice concentrate which was often processed separately and stored frozen in tanks, had to take care to avoid an over-concentration of limonene in their products because the stored concentrate was already typically fortified with peel oil to minimize "cardboard" off-flavor (see pg. 90). Excess limonene negatively affected the flavor and reduced shelf-life. Water-phase aroma, on the other hand, contained essentially no limonene. Once at Redd Laboratories, Johnson used the concentrated EB fractions developed from Kryger's earlier work to formulate a new product he named *Aroma Plus*. *Aroma Plus* was made by using a large tank of standardized water-phase aroma to extract EB and other topnotes from concentrated, oil-soluble EB fractions. This innovative, water-soluble ingredient could be easily added to orange juice to enhance the flavor without altering the oil content, and it quickly became a very popular product. Johnson recalls choosing the name *Aroma Plus* himself, being influenced by a popular General Foods beverage called *Orange Plus*[86]. Yet, the the name had been used internally at Redd Laboratories since at least 1974, when it was used to describe an extraction of essence oil by concentrated aroma in one of Kryger's notebooks[71, pg. 17]. Whatever the source of the name, the newly formulated *Aroma Plus* sold very well, and it became a standard product used by the global orange juice industry.

The success of *Aroma Plus* brought to light a significant challenge for Redd Laboratories in the early 1980s that illustrates a recurring problem in the industry. The demand for EB and other topnotes was growing, but the only source was orange essence oil. However, once these topnotes were removed from the essence oil, there was little use for the remaining essence oil. Redd Laboratories folded the essence oil, to recover and sell as much of the constituent terpenes as practical, but by 1982 they had built up a large inventory of approximately 25-fold orange essence oil with little value. Material imbalances of this type would be a challenge to all market participants. Redd Laboratories produced all of its products using only three raw materials: water-phase aroma, essence oil and cold-pressed oil. Out of these raw materials, a number of intermediate fractions were produced, together with process byproducts, which were either immediately blended into finished products, stored in inventory, or discarded. The apparent profitability of a particular finished product depended on the allocation of costs throughout the complex production process. Careful management of raw material costs, cost allocation, and inventory accumulation was critical for ongoing success. Without meticulous attention, this process could generate apparent profits, leaving behind an over-valued inventory of byproducts. Even with careful attention, there would often be a build-up of certain unused fractions, stored at a low value in inventory, but held for possible future use either because disposal was costly or there was hope of future value.

In 1982, Johnson hired J. D. Vora, a recent master's graduate with a food science degree from UF, for an R&D position[87, 74, 88, 68]. Vora, whose master's research focused on citrus oils and flavors, was tasked with finding value in the large inventory of 25-fold essence oil. He leveraged a new processing tool that Redd Laboratories had recently acquired, a $\sim$ 100 gallon high-vacuum still with 25–30 theoretical plates of fractionating capacity. This still incorporated a specialized, high-vacuum column packing called *Mellapak* from Sulzer Corporation, and was certainly one of the most advanced in Florida at the time. Johnson and Vora developed two new products using the surplus essence oil. The first was a highly-concentrated fraction called *Orange Juice Carbonyls*, produced by removing almost all the remaining terpenes from 25-fold essence oil, and then further distilling the fraction away from the non-volatile polymerized limonene and other waxy compounds found in folded essence oils. This carbonyls fraction was chemically similar to terpeneless orange oil, which was a traditional flavor-industry product produced by a similar process from folded orange peel oil, but it possessed a very different, more "juicy" orange character compared to terpeneless orange oil. The product was initially marketed toward the flavor industry as a new orange flavoring ingredient.

Their second product was an 80% pure fraction of valencene, a rare sesquiterpene found at low concentrations in a few essential oils. Orange essence oil contained about 1% valencene, and the folding process that produced 25-fold essence oil concentrated it to about 15% purity. By applying additional slow, high-vacuum distillations, Johnson and Vora achieved 80% purity. Though sesquiterpenes were not usually recognized for their potent flavor impact, this concentrated valencene fraction imparted a notable juicy/fruity note to orange beverages. Much later, these properties were traced to valencene's own flavor impact, as well as that of other very powerful trace chemicals, like β-demascenone, that are naturally present in the fraction. An even more important factor in the success of this valencene product was that valencene could be chemically converted into nootkatone, a powerful aroma chemical which was very important in grapefruit flavors. Valencene and nootkatone were similar on a molecular level, and organic chemists had developed conversion methods starting in the 1960s[89], but the scarcity of valencene made sourcing the raw valencene difficult. However, an Israeli company Frutarom had successfully commercialized the valencene-to-nootkatone conversion process, and valencene isolated from orange essence oil soon became the dominant raw material. Subsequently, Redd Laboratories' surplus folded essence oil became a new revenue source for the company.

Johnson and Vora also collaborated on one other important effort, the 1983 publication of a scientific paper in the Institute of Food Technologists' journal "Food Technology," which detailed the chemical and flavor properties of commercially produced citrus essences and their fractions[90]. This publication introduced these specialized flavoring ingredients to a broader audience and served as a future reference for both users and regulators. This article was probably the first industry-originated publication on these specialized citrus products.

At this time, Hercules' Florida operation was branded "Redd Citrus Specialties, a part of the PFW Division of Hercules Incorporated." The REDD name, which had been sold by Jim Redd to A. E. Staley Company, was now owned by Hercules and utilized for both the commercial entity and in various product names. Mike Taylor, who had assumed the role of general manager just a few years prior, would go on to lead Redd Citrus Specialties for nearly two decades, overseeing the transformation from a small, "seat-of-the-pants" organization to a more structured corporate entity. Managing the external demands from PFW and Hercules, along with maintaining business growth, presented ongoing challenges for Taylor. Just one example was the extensive effort invested in a new product code system, based upon computerized recipes, that Hercules required in the early 1980s[75, 87]. Before this, the inventory system and blending recipes were manually managed with paper files.

The continuing growth of the Florida citrus industry provided ample sourcing of raw material, and juice markets for the sale of Redd Laboratories' flavoring products. Furthermore, PFW had facilitated Redd Citrus' entrée into larger flavor & fragrance markets, while both Hercules and PFW contributed new expertise in chemical processing and product applications. Meanwhile, aside from Jim Redd's Intercit company (discussed below), Redd Laboratories' competition was very limited because few citrus plants in Florida were chemically-processing their citrus byproducts. One that did was Citrus Central, a cooperative organization the provided centralized services, including R&D, for a group of independent fruit processing plants. Citrus Central began producing a five-fold cold-pressed oil using a *LUWA* falling-film evaporator in the 1970s, some of which was sold to national flavor companies like Firmenich[56, 88, 17]. However, most citrus plants lacked the focus and expertise to compete effectively in these specialized products. Apart from PFW, and Coca-Cola's internal flavor efforts, all other national flavor & fragrance companies in the US operated outside of Florida, procuring raw citrus oils for processing out-of-state, or buying processed ingredients from other manufacturers, including Redd Citrus Specialties.

Intercit 1975–1982

Just before Staley's acquisition of Redd Laboratories, James Redd had established Intercit Inc. to handle his consulting activities, primarily in collaboration with Gulf Machinery for the installation of new processing equipment. Intercit was located next door on Charlie Walker's property, and had one employee, Carlos Odio, a young Costa Rican engineer whom Redd and Walker met in 1966, and hired for Redd Laboratories in 1968[31]. However, following Redd's departure from Redd Laboratories, partly due to frustrations with Staley's conservative approach to business, he began to expand Intercit's operations into citrus essence. Despite being bound by a non-compete agreement after the sale of Redd Laboratories, the specifics of which are unknown, Redd was apparently free of major restrictions on his buisiness activities soon after he left[31, 24].

One of Redd's early moves at Intercit was to hire Johnny Lillard, a skilled operations manager from Redd Laboratories, who had worked for Redd for years, and previously at Citrus Central Cooperative handling citrus oils and other byproducts[17]. Intercit then installed two small distillation units built by Gulf Machinery, marking the beginning of Lillard's long tenure distilling citrus products for Intercit. Redd also worked to establish new essence contracts with Florida citrus processors, now directly competing with his old company. Leveraging his industry reputation and essence expertise, as well as his friendship with Charlie Walker, whose Gulf Machinery was the major builder of evaporators and essence units, Redd soon negotiated a number of new essence contracts. These contracts were very similar to ones Redd negotiated earlier in his career, with Intercit managing the essence unit operations at the plants, conducting regular inspections, and providing advice on essence use in exchange for a portion of the essence. Soon after, Intercit started manufacturing add-back flavors for orange juice[11]. However, unlike Hercules' Redd Laboratories staff, Redd also engaged in consulting work for citrus plants, providing him regular access to the plants, their personnel, and management. His interests extended beyond just essence collection. In 1976, he presented a paper titled "Distillation Systems in the Citrus Industry" at a UF conference. The paper discussed various practical engineering aspects of distillation, including those used in essence units, juice de-oilers, and limonene recovery systems[8].

In the late 70s, Intercit developed an important customer relationship with Firmenich, an international flavor and fragrance company based in Geneva, Switzerland, known for its scientific excellence and expertise in citrus products. Firmenich began buying five-fold coldpressed oil, and over time became one of Intercit's largest customers. In the process, Jim Redd developed important relationships with several key Firmenich employees. Notably, Firmenich also purchased a five-fold orange peel oil from Citrus Central Cooperative, produced on a *LUWA* evaporator[88][12]. The two folded oils, although similarly named, differed significantly due to their distinct distillation processes. Intercit's

---

[11]Golden Gem was reported to be an early customer of these flavors in 1976 or 1977[17].

[12]After the Citrus Central Cooperative dissolved in the early 1980s, the *LUWA* evaporator was operated by Golden Gem Citrus Processors for a time[91].

folded peel oils, similar to Redd Citrus' product, was produced by batch fractional distillation equipment under vacuum, while the continuous wiped-film *LUWA* evaporator lacked a fractionating column. By chemical analysis, the products appeared similar, but their flavor properties were quite different. The situation illustrated how very different products could be developed under similar names. Even when using identical process equipment, a manufacturer had to carefully manage their raw oils and essences to produce a standardized product year after year. The natural lot-to-lot and season-to-season variations in raw materials were a constant challenge, but through close contact with suppliers and process know-how, companies like Intercit and Redd Laboratories learned to keep their finished product variation to a practical minimum. For their customers, the naming ambiguities and product variations reinforced loyalty, as the easiest way to to minimize variability was to purchase the same flavoring materials from the same Florida supplier year after year.

By 1982, Intercit had grown to about 16 employees and mirrored many of Redd Laboratories' business activities, including the essence contracts, production techniques, and product offerings. However, Intercit also leased processing space at various citrus plants to manufacture pulp products, and produced beverage bases, neither of which Redd Laboratories had continued producing. Jim Redd continued to handle much of the R&D and applications work himself, often formulating new flavor blends for specific customers. Redd was both the business owner and the technical expert, although he employed an engineer to help manage the essence units and a chemist for quality-control testing. Intercit was doing reasonably well financially, and Redd enjoyed his work. He especially liked working next door to his friend Charlie Walker, and they often met to discuss citrus industry gossip as well as current engineering or plant problems. Redd also enjoyed traveling extensively on business, visiting plants around Florida and internationally. Meanwhile three related problems were festering at Intercit. First, Redd found business administration responsibilities unpleasant, including human resource issues, customer management, and general record-keeping, but Intercit lacked anyone else to handle these tasks. Second, Redd could become quite enthusiastic about a new technical project, but he often lost interest over time, without necessarily bringing a project to completion. Finally, beyond incremental growth, Redd's plans for Intercit's future were unclear.

The Professional Researchers

Publicly funded research has long been instrumental in supporting the Florida citrus industry, funded through both state and national programs. The USDA was researching citrus horticulture in Florida in the 1800s, and in 1932 created the Winter Haven Citrus Products Laboratory for non-fresh fruit utilization research[92, 93]. The University of Florida's Citrus Experiment Station (CES) in Lake Alfred, FL was established in 1919[94], and various faculty at UF, particularly from the food and agricultural sciences departments, have engaged in research and extension activities supporting the citrus industry ever since. Additionally, the FCC/FDOC continued funding their research programs after the successful introduction of FCOJ in the 1940s.

Early on, much of this research centered on cultivation aspects, including breeding, horticulture practices, pest control and harvesting. However, as the FCOJ industry gained economic significance, research increasingly addressed the citrus processing, juice production and use, and byproduct utilization. Although the topic of citrus flavor was of interest to the entire industry, and aspects of flavor improvement were incorporated into many research efforts, the use of citrus oils and essences for flavoring applications was incorporated into the broad category of citrus processing and byproducts research. J. W. Kesterson's study on Florida citrus oils dating back to the late 1940s was an early example (see pg. 101).

By the early 1950s, several annual meetings were held in Florida to highlight current research on processed citrus and related topics, bringing together academic researchers and industry participants. UF hosted a meeting at the CES, jointly sponsored by the FCC, that was initially called the "Citrus Processors Meeting," while the USDA's Winter Haven group sponsored the "Conference on Citrus Processing." In the 1960s, the USDA added the "Citrus Chemistry and Utilization Conference," while UF introduced the "Short Course for the Food Industry," co-sponsored by the Department of Food Science and the Institute of Food Technologists(IFT)/Florida Section. These meetings served as a platform for researchers to showcase their work and sustain industry support for their research. They also facilitated swift communication of research activities and results to the industry, bypassing the slower peer-reviewed publication process, and provided a valuable forum for informal interactions between scientists and industry representatives.

It was not uncommon for commercial groups to have access to specialized equipment and samples, or insights, that could aid the researchers. From published attendee lists[13], it is evident that Redd Laboratories staff participated in these industry meetings starting in the early 1960s, and Minute Maid personnel who would later establish Special Products were also in attendance by the late 1960s.

Some of the publicly-funded research in byproducts and flavor had already had a critical impact on the nascent citrus flavor industry, such as the work of R. W. Wolford and other scientists, sponsored by the FCC, to chemically characterize the new essence products (see pg. 138). These efforts not only facilitated regulatory approval for add-back flavors to orange juice, but also helped gain broader approval for essence use as a food flavoring ingredient. As the use of Florida's citrus flavoring products expanded, publicly available information on the processing techniques, constituents, byproducts and potential contaminants of citrus flavoring products became increasingly important. Additionally, the scientific understanding of citrus flavor chemistry was still quite limited. New advancements in flavor analysis technology, particularly with the advent of more accessible and sensitive gas chromatography and mass spectrometry instruments, opened new avenues for scientific discovery. Florida researchers were often at the forefront of these investigations, but many other researchers also contributed. Over time, these research efforts grew in importance to Florida's emerging flavor industry, as did the mutual support between the industry and researchers.

From this era, two young scientists began their careers in Florida, destined to have lasting impacts on the local flavor industry. Philip Shaw started working at the USDA Winter Haven facility in 1965 when he was 31. Born in St. Petersburg, FL, and a 4th generation Floridian, Shaw completed his BS at Duke University and his Ph.D. in organic chemistry at Rice University. With a keen interest in citrus flavor chemistry, Shaw utilized gas chromatography and mass spectrometry to conduct detailed studies on the constituents of various citrus essences, and he investigated the odor thresholds of flavor active compounds in citrus, among other aspects of flavor chemistry in citrus juices and beverages. Shaw, known for his methodical demeanor and slow, deliberate speech, collaborated with Manual Mashonas, a wiry, energetic lab technician known for his fast talking. Their lab was a cramped mess, with

---

[13] Not all of these meetings included a list of attendees.

old and new equipment scattered about, but together, the two were very prolific researchers. Furthermore, they welcomed industry visitors and were always willing to share their results and expertise. Over his 35-year career at the USDA, Shaw published more than 150 publications, including several book chapters. Notably, he also co-authored the 1996 edition of the "Quality Control Manual for Citrus Processing Plants" (Volume 3) with Jim Redd[95](see pg. 159).

In 1970, Robert Braddock joined UF's Department of Food Science and the Citrus Experiment Station at the age of 30, following completion of his BS and MS degrees at UF, and his Ph.D. in food chemistry at Michigan State University. He became part of the processed citrus research group working with James Kesterson (see pg. 101). A fifth-generation Floridian, Braddock was tall, thin, and lanky, with reddish hair and complexion, and he was particularly comfortable in agricultural settings, easily communicating with growers, processors, and other non-academics. Despite his "good ol' boy" demeanor, Braddock was well-versed in science and math and known for his willingness to express vocal, contrarian views on technical issues. Unlike Philip Shaw, who worked at the USDA, Braddock worked at a university where he directly trained students throughout his career. His students were highly sought after by the industry, reflecting the practical nature of his research, and his expertise in both teaching and research. Over his 36-year career, Braddock published over 100 research papers and a book, contributing extensively to the analysis of citrus oils and contaminants, examining the effects of horticultural and processing practices on oil yields, and developing various new methods to concentrate citrus oils and essences. Braddock was also very friendly and generous in sharing his expertise with industry personnel, and he was particularly welcoming to young professionals in the industry.

References

[1] James B. Redd. "The Volatile Flavors of Orange Juice." In: ASME 1988 Citrus Engineering Conference. Lakeland, FL: American Society of Mechanical Engineers Digital Collection, Mar. 24, 1988, pp. 79–93.

[2] Beverly Bateman. *E-mail to Robert Kryger*. Aug. 4, 2024.

[3] James B. Redd. "The Oxidation of Certain Cyclic Compounds." Doctoral Thesis. Gainesville, FL: University of Florida, Aug. 1943.

[4] "Redd-Roser Nuptials Solemnized." In: *Tampa Bay Times* (June 7, 1943), p. 7.

[5] "Miss Eleanor Marian Roser to Wed James Beverly Redd." In: *Tampa Bay Times* (Dec. 20, 1942), p. 21.

[6] Dick Bothwell. "Roser Park: Building On Dreams and Fig Newtons." In: *Tampa Bay Times* (Dec. 4, 1976), p. B1–B2.

[7] "Two Big Florida Citrus Deals Made." In: *The Tampa Tribune* (July 26, 1949), pp. 1–2.

[8] James B. Redd. "Heat Transfer in Food Processing - Its Effects on Quality, Economics, Sanitation & Safety." In: *Food Industry Short Course Proceedings*. Food Industry Short Course. Ed. by R. F. Matthews. Gainesville, FL: University of Florida Department of Food Science, 1976, pp. 24–42.

[9] James B. Redd. "Processing - Processed O.J., Definition of Quality, Purity and the Effects of Processing on These Characteristics - Part II." In: *Citrus Industry* (Oct. 1983), pp. 15–18.

[10] Boris T. Sokoloff and James B. Redd. "Method of Treating Citrus Fruit Pulp Liquor." Pat. 2,559,685. United States Patent. July 10, 1951.

[11] Boris Sokoloff and James B. Redd. "The Health Angle in the Consumption of Canned Orange Juice." In: *The Citrus Industry* Vol. 30 (Issue 5 May 1949), p. 8.

[12] Boris T. Sokoloff. "Method of Extracting Vitamin P from Citrus Molasses." Pat. 2,734,896. United States Patent. Feb. 14, 1956.

[13] "Dr. Boris Sokoloff Has 12th Book Published." In: *The Southern* (Sept. 30, 1949), pp. 1–2. URL: https://archives.flsouthern.edu/digital/collection/Southern/id/1516/rec/352 (visited on 01/19/2021).

[14] Thomas B. Mack. *Documented History of the Citrus Institute*. Unpublished. Copy in McKay Archives, Florida Southern College, Lakeland, FL. 1993.

[15] Gerianne Schaad. *E-mail to Robert Kryger*. Oct. 19, 2021.

[16] James B. Redd. *Memorandum to Dr. Rubert W. Prevatt*. Unpublished. Copy in McKay Archives, Florida Southern College, Lakeland, FL. Oct. 11, 1984.

[17] Donald Hendrix. *Interview by Robert Kryger*. Winter Haven, FL. Oct. 12, 2021.

[18] David Walker. *Interview by Robert Kryger*. By Phone. Apr. 14, 2022.

[19] David Walker. *Interview by Robert Kryger*. By Phone. May 12, 2022.

[20] David Walker. *Interview by Robert Kryger*. By Phone. Apr. 6, 2022.

[21] Rex Harper. *E-mail to Robert Kryger*. Sept. 17, 2021.

[22] Brett Welch. *Interview by Robert Kryger*. By Phone. Sept. 16, 2021.

[23] M. J. Potter. "Nerve, Know-How and Taste." In: *The Orlando Sentinel* (Oct. 14, 1969), p. 35.

[24] Beverly Bateman and Rex Harper. *Interview by Robert Kryger*. Lakeland, FL. Feb. 11, 2021.

[25] "John Marsh, 53, Florida Newsman." In: *St. Petersburg Times* (Nov. 19, 1992), p. 15. URL: https://www.tampabay.com/archive/1992/11/19/john-marsh-53-florida-newsman/ (visited on 01/05/2023).

[26] V. C. Praschan. *Quality Control Manual for Citrus Processing Plants*. Intercit Inc., 1981.

[27] Charles M. Hendrix Jr. and Jon E. Jefferson. *Quality Control Manual for Citrus Processing Plants*. Redd Laboratories, Inc., 1966.

REFERENCES

[28] "Howard Trumm to Assume Post." In: *The Orlando Sentinel* (Nov. 20, 1966), p. 1.

[29] "Trumm Heads Research with Golden Gem." In: *Ocala Starr Banner* (Oct. 4, 1967), p. 19.

[30] E. B. Freyfogle. *Letters of Renewal of Essence Contracts between Redd Laboratories and Sunny Orange Concentrates, Alcoma, Myakka Processors, Treesweet Processors, Bordo, Florida Home Juice and Peace River Processors.* Unpublished. June 1976.

[31] Carlos Odio. *Interview by Robert Kryger.* By Zoom. Oct. 4, 2022.

[32] Sunny Orange Concentrates Inc. *Corporate Filing on Name Change with Polk County FL.* June 15, 1970. URL: `https://www.polkcountyclerk.net/187/Public-Records-Searches` (visited on 01/06/2023).

[33] *1974 List of Redd Laboratories Inc. Technical Data Sheets.* Unpublished. Apr. 29, 1974.

[34] E. B. Freyfogle. *Memorandum to Wm. Allen.* Unpublished. Dec. 6, 1973.

[35] James B. Redd. *Memorandum to Wm. F. Allen.* Unpublished. Dec. 26, 1973.

[36] E. B. Freyfogle. *Memorandum to Wm. Allen.* Unpublished. Dec. 27, 1973.

[37] E. B. Freyfogle. *Memorandum to Wm. Allen.* Unpublished. Jan. 18, 1974.

[38] H. J. Barnett. *Memorandum to D.T. Mitchell.* Unpublished. Jan. 9, 1974.

[39] H. J. Barnett. *Memorandum to E. Landon Hope, J.B. Redd, and D.T. Mitchell on Patent Examiner Evaluation.* Unpublished. Oct. 11, 1974.

[40] James B. Redd. *Memorandum to H.J. Barnett on Patent Examiner Comments.* Unpublished. Dec. 17, 1974.

[41] Allen Kryger. *Memorandum to E. B. Freyfogle.* Unpublished. Dec. 26, 1974.

[42] D. T. Mitchell. *Notes on Invention.* Unpublished. Jan. 2, 1974.

[43] D. T. Mitchell. *Memorandum to E. B. Freyfogle, A. Kryger, J. Redd and L. Hope on Chromatographic Extraction.* Unpublished. Written in 1974 or 1975.

[44] James B. Redd. "Vacuum Dehydration of Heat Sensitive Materials." Pat. 3,969,183A. Assignee: Tate and Lyle Ingredients Americas LLC. United States Patent. July 13, 1976.

[45] Cederic [sic] D. Atkins and John A. Attaway. "Essence for Enhancing the Flavor of Citrus Juices." Pat. 3,782,972. Assignee: Florida Department of Citrus. United States Patent. Jan. 1, 1974.

[46] Cedric D. Atkins and John A. Attaway. "Method of Producing Enhanced Citrus Juice Essence." Pat. 3,787,593. United States Patent. Jan. 22, 1974.

[47] Cederic [sic] D. Atkins and John A. Attaway. "Distillation Apparatus for Recovering Citrus Essence." Pat. 3,862,014. Assignee: Florida Department of Citrus. United States Patent. Jan. 21, 1975.

[48] James B. Redd. *Memorandum to C. J. Meyerson on US Patent 3,782.972.* Unpublished. Feb. 6, 1974.

[49] James B. Redd. *Memorandum to H.J. Barnett Concerning Essence History in Florida.* Unpublished. Jan. 3, 1975.

[50] Henry Elbert Schulz. *Bert's Story - The Life & Heritage of Henry Elbert Schulz.* Lakeland, FL: Genie Publishing, 2000. ISBN: 1-889137-13-8.

[51] H. E. Schulz. "d-Limonene Recovery in the Florida Citrus Industry." In: ASME 1972 Citrus Engineering Conference. Lakeland, FL: American Society of Mechanical Engineers Digital Collection, Mar. 29, 1972, pp. 1–6.

[52] Paul Schulz. *Interview by Robert Kryger.* By Phone. Mar. 10, 2021.

[53] Paul Schulz. *Interview by Robert Kryger.* Winter Haven, FL. Mar. 24, 2021.

[54] Paul Schulz. *Interview by Robert Kryger.* Winter Haven, FL. June 24, 2021.

REFERENCES

[55] Paul Schulz. *Interview by Robert Kryger.* By Phone. May 11, 2022.

[56] Joe Johnson. *Interview by Robert Kryger.* By Phone. Sept. 24, 2020.

[57] Joe Johnson. *E-mail to Robert Kryger.* May 11, 2022.

[58] Eric Bennett. *Interview by Robert Kryger.* By Phone. June 27, 2022.

[59] Susan Martin. *Interview by Robert Kryger.* By Phone. Aug. 18, 2022.

[60] Tim Anglea. *Interview by Robert Kryger.* By Phone. Mar. 15, 2021.

[61] Jerry Sachs. *Interview by Robert Kryger.* By Phone. Nov. 19, 2020.

[62] Susan Martin. *E-mail to Robert Kryger.* Aug. 27, 2022.

[63] Dan Mouton. *Interview by Robert Kryger.* Lakeland, FL. Oct. 6, 2020.

[64] R. J. Braddock. *Interview by Robert Kryger.* Auburndale, FL. Sept. 28, 2020.

[65] Charles W. Wilson III and Philip E. Shaw. "Synthesis of Nootkatone From Valencene." In: *Journal of Agricultural and Food Chemistry* Vol. 26 (Issue 6 Nov. 1, 1978), pp. 1430–1432.

[66] Albert Joseph Kruger. "A Study on the Concentration of Citrus Essential Oils by Adsorption." Masters Thesis. Orlando, FL: University of Central Florida, 1980. URL: `https://stars.library.ucf.edu/rtd/495`.

[67] Chris Li. *Interview by Robert Kryger.* By Phone. Aug. 9, 2022.

[68] Joe Johnson. *Interview by Robert Kryger.* By Phone. June 23, 2022.

[69] Unknown. *Redd Laboratory Memorandum on Sales Strategy.* Unpublished. Written ca. 1973.

[70] Mike Taylor. *Redd Laboratory Notebook 22W for Mike Taylor 1974–1976.* Unpublished. Original at Givaudan's Facility in Lakeland, FL.

[71] Allen Kryger. *Redd Laboratory Notebook 23W for Allen Kryger 1974–1976*. Unpublished. Original at Givaudan's Facility in Lakeland, FL.

[72] Allen Kryger. *Redd Laboratory Notebook 44B for Allen Kryger 1976–1979*. Unpublished. Original at Givaudan's Facility in Lakeland, FL.

[73] Giovanni Fenaroli. *Fenaroli's Handbook of Flavor Ingredients*. Trans. by Thomas E. Furia and Nicolo Bellanca. 2nd ed. Vol. 1. Cleveland, OH: CRC Press, 1975.

[74] J. D. Vora. *Interview by Robert Kryger*. By Phone. Apr. 6, 2021.

[75] *Hercules Redd Laboratory Formula and Specification Notebook ca. 1990*. Unpublished. Copy located at Givaudan's facility in Lakeland, FL.

[76] E. B. Freyfogle. *Letter from E. B. Freyfogle to Max J. Hanke Concerning Sale of Redd Laboratories*. Unpublished. June 1, 1976.

[77] "Hercules Buys Flavor Maker." In: *The Philadelphia Inquirer* (Oct. 6, 1973), p. 16.

[78] "Hercules Inc. Acquires Polak's Frutal Works." In: *Food Technology* (December 1973 Dec. 1, 1973), p. 85.

[79] "Product-Group Shifts, Management Changes Slated by Hercules." In: *The Morning News* (Jan. 16, 1975). Wilmington, DE, p. 26.

[80] "Sunstar Foods Buys Citrus-Concentrate Firms From A. E. Staley." In: *The Star Tribune* (Apr. 15, 1976). Minneapolis, MN, p. A15.

[81] *Polak's Frutal Works, Inc. v. United States of America*. Legal Decision. Case: 281 F. 2d 261 (2d Cir. 1960). US Court of Appeals, 2nd Circuit, July 21, 1960. URL: https://law.justia.com/cases/federal/appellate-courts/F2/281/261/60504/ (visited on 03/16/2024).

[82] Joe Johnson. *Redd Laboratory Notebook 43BB for Joe Johnson 1979–1983*. Unpublished. Original at Givaudan's Facility in Lakeland, FL.

[83] "Citrus Food-Testing Lab Gutted by Fire." In: *The Tampa Tribune* (July 15, 1977), p. B3.

REFERENCES

[84] Steve Hasel. "11 Firefighters Overcome in Laboratory Blaze." In: *The Tampa Tribune* (July 15, 1977), p. 3.

[85] Dennis Kujawski. *Interview by Robert Kryger*. By Phone. Nov. 11, 2022.

[86] Joe Johnson. *E-mail to Robert Kryger*. Sept. 26, 2020.

[87] J. D. Vora. *PFW Redd Laboratory Notebook 369 for JD Vora*. Unpublished. Original at Givaudan's Facility in Lakeland, FL. 1982.

[88] J. D. Vora. *Interview by Robert Kryger*. By Phone. Sept. 15, 2021.

[89] G. L. K. Hunter and W. B. Brogden. "Conversion of Valencene to Nootkatone." In: *Journal of Food Science* Vol. 30 (1965), pp. 876–878.

[90] J. D. Johnson and J. D. Vora. "Natural Citrus Essences." In: *Food Technology* (Dec. 1983), pp. 92–97.

[91] Donald Hendrix. *E-mail to Robert Kryger*. Jan. 19, 2022.

[92] Harry W. von Loesecke. "Four Years of Citrus Products Research in Florida." In: *Proceedings of the Florida State Horticultural Society* Vol. 49 (1936), pp. 64–68.

[93] Harry W. von Loesecke. "The Chemist Looks at the Citrus Products Industry in Florida." In: *Proceedings of the Florida State Horticultural Society* Vol. 51 (1938), pp. 105–108.

[94] Tom Nordlie et al. *The 100-Year Journey of the UF/IFAS Citrus Research and Education Center*. UF/IFAS Communication Department, 2017.

[95] James B. Redd et al. *Quality Control Manual for Citrus Processing Plants*. Vol. 3. Agscience, 1996.

7
The 1980s — The Flavor Industry Grows

"[The Freezes of the 1980's] rank collectively as the greatest agricultural disaster in the history of Florida."

—John Attaway, *A History of Florida Citrus Freezes*, 1997[1].

The OJ Wars

The decade of the 1980s brought important changes to the US consumer orange juice (OJ) market, predominantly supplied by Florida's oranges. Up to this time, the main consumer product was frozen concentrated orange juice (FCOJ), which consumers had to thaw and blend, and the market was very fragmented. There were a few national food company brands, including Minute Maid (MM), General Foods, and Kraft, additional brands associated with Florida grower cooperatives or individual citrus processors, and a host of regional and private label brands. In 1981, Minute Maid had the largest market share but this amounted to only about 20% of the market[2]. Tropicana, originally a local Florida company that had been purchased by Beatrice Foods in 1978[3], was a much smaller regional brand that specialized in a niche not-from-concentrate (NFC) product. This NFC product was ready-to-drink, requiring no consumer thawing or mixing. It was more expensive to ship and store, but Tropicana had invested in a special distribution system using custom train cars to ship refrigerated juice each week to the northeast US markets from Florida. The selling point of NFC, justifying the higher production costs, was that it was fresher and better tasting. Also competing against both FCOJ and NFC was chilled-OJ, reconstituted from concentrate by the manufacturer before packaging and sold ready-to-drink. For example, Minute Maid had successfully introduced a nationally-branded reconstituted product in 1973[4]. However, in total, the entire reconstituted OJ and NFC market was still small compared to FCOJ in 1980.

By the late 1970s, Procter & Gamble (P&G) had identified OJ as a fragmented market that they could potentially dominate. P&G's corporate strategy across many different consumer products was to combine technical superiority in design, and a keen analysis of what consumers "really wanted," with their national marketing prowess. They identified superior and consistent OJ flavor as a very important attribute and began an extensive research effort into OJ processing and flavor. Jim Redd recalled a visit to P&G's research facility in Cincinnati around this time, where he walked past an open door and saw pilot-scale freeze-concentration equipment for OJ. Redd commented to his hosts that it was a great process, but far too expensive to commercialize[5]. This research was indicative of the breadth of P&G's research investment in OJ. In 1981, P&G purchased a large citrus processing plant in Frostproof, FL. The following year, they test-marketed a new OJ product in Indiana and Iowa[6]. In 1983, P&G launched the *Citrus Hill* OJ brand nationally, including both FCOJ and reconstituted products, with an extensive marketing budget. In fact, the marketing budget was rumored to be the largest ever for a single-item packaged good and more than five times that of Minute Maid's or Tropicana's advertising spending[7]. The primary marketing tagline was "a whole year of sunshine in every sip," with a clear focus on flavor. By 1984, P&G had achieved a 7% market share in all OJ categories and 9% in chilled ready-to-drink juice (NFC and reconstituted together). Minute Maid remained the leader with 21% and 16%, respectively, while Tropicana held 13% of the total OJ market and 25% of chilled juice[8]. P&G's market entry forced all participants to respond, with superior flavor and consistency becoming key attributes. Tropicana's VP of Marketing, Tom Thompson, remarked in 1984 about the net positive effect on consumers: "*Citrus Hill* has created a lot of interest in the orange juice business[9]."

Following the launch, P&G continued an intensive research effort in both Frostproof and Cincinnati to improve both processing methods and flavor for OJ. The flavor lost via the juice concentration process was of high concern. At one point, almost overnight, a large, covered vertical silo was erected at the P&G processing plant in Frostproof. Located in a small, rural town, it was highly visible and was colloquially referred to as the "missile-silo." This "silo" included custom essence capture equipment that P&G had designed and enclosed to keep as secret as possible[10]. P&G was deeply interested in the flavor profile of fresh OJ, particularly which natural aroma chemicals contributed the best flavor and how processing affected these aroma constituents. Collecting and restoring the "best" flavor back to their juice was a major focus. P&G soon became a major customer of both Hercules Redd Citrus and Florex Flavors (discussed below), both to supplement their internal add-back flavors and to monitor external flavor innovations. In 1987, P&G filed a patent that outlined the importance of ethyl butyrate (EB) to the flavor of OJ, especially the ratio of EB to certain other flavor components[11]. A close reading of the patent reveals the detailed research P&G was undertaking at the time. The patent filing created quite a stir, not so much for the information it contained – much of which was already known to experts in the flavor industry – but because of the public nature of a patent filing. The Florida citrus flavor industry had traditionally protected their flavor know-how as trade secrets. Since US law did not require any disclosure of the presence or chemical makeup of from-the-named fruit (FTNF) add-back flavors in juice, flavor suppliers and almost all juice producers preferred to protect their know-how by secrecy. However, unlike patents, trade secrets impose no right to restrict their use by competitors. Initially, there was considerable concern about how a flavor patent like this might be used by P&G, for example, to challenge competitor products. The patent was not issued until 1990; soon after, it became irrelevant to P&G (see below). Nevertheless, the importance of EB and its ratio to other important aroma chemicals in OJ was now widely publicized within the OJ industry.

As P&G entered the market, Minute Maid strove to maintain its market-leading position. In 1983, Minute Maid operated three citrus processing plants in Florida (located in Altamonte Springs[1], Leesburg,

---

[1]This plant was closed in 1986[12].

and Auburndale) and partnered with others in Florida, as well as maintaining a relationship with the Cutrale family in Brazil. This processing base gave Minute Maid an extensive supply of juice and add-back flavor components to formulate their products, along with a network of locations to test new processing techniques. By mid-1984, they had their traditional FCOJ product on the market, along with a reconstituted ready-to-drink OJ, a reduced-acid orange juice, orange juice with extra pulp, and other citrus-based products like *Five-Alive*. In 1986, they introduced a calcium-fortified OJ[13], and in 1988, a not-from-concentrate OJ[14] to compete directly with Tropicana's product. All these products required managing a complex variety of different juices and concentrates throughout the year. Furthermore, each product utilized a customized add-back flavor that was sometimes modified during the processing-year to compensate for changes in the juice flavor profile[15]. The add-back flavors were formulated by the Special Products group, which used as raw materials their own peel oils and proprietary "HVE essence" collected on their secret essence recovery equipment[16]. MM was as knowledgeable as P&G about the important flavor role of EB, and this aroma chemical was an important part of their add-back flavors. Apparently MM's demand for oils and essences exceeded their internal production because by 1986, they were a significant customer of these products from Florex Flavors[17]. By the late 1980s, they were also purchasing large quantities of EB-containing orange fractions from Florex Flavors[18], as well as Redd Citrus[19].

Tropicana's response to P&G was to emphasize the flavor superiority of their flagship NFC product[9]. Unlike concentrated OJ, their product was bulky to store and ship. To produce a consistent product year-round, Tropicana developed a method to freeze and store industrial-sized blocks of OJ at their Bradenton, FL processing plant. This process was more expensive than producing FCOJ, making their product pricier for consumers. However, with the backing of Beatrice Foods, Tropicana had access to a significant marketing budget, which they used to highlight the purported flavor superiority of NFC OJ. As the freezes hit Florida in 1980s (discussed below), Tropicana had a particularly difficult time managing the fruit disruption. Unlike FCOJ producers, Tropicana could not rely on imported juice; imported NFC did not yet exist in Florida. Consequently, they were forced to significantly raise their prices. Unexpectedly, they found that consumers were willing to pay more for the convenience of ready-to-drink juice and the perceived higher quality of NFC juice. Despite supply and pricing challenges, Tropicana continued to grow their market share. By 1986, US sales of chilled ready-to-drink juice (all brands, NFC and reconstituted) surpassed sales of FCOJ, and by 1990 Tropicana claimed to have overtaken Minute Maid in total market share for OJ sales (22.3% vs. 22.2%)[20]. Over just a decade, Tropicana had displaced the market leader to become a national brand. However, the NFC portion of the market was still small (only 14.3% of the market in the 1988/89 season[21]), but Tropicana also produced FCOJ at their citrus processing facility and also sold FCOJ juice and reconstituted orange juice. Consequently, they operated their own essence collection equipment and utilized add-back flavors. By the late 1980s, they were also a large customer of add-back flavor fractions including EB from Florex Flavors, similar to Minute Maid[18].

The result of all this competitive activity was a bifurcation of the OJ market into premium products and lower-priced brands. Prior to 1980, generic brand-independent advertising for OJ, managed by the Florida Department of Citrus for the benefit of the entire Florida OJ category, was roughly on-par with brand-based advertising. However, in this decade, OJ advertising increased almost threefold, with the three national brands – Minute Maid, P&G, and Tropicana – dominating the spending oriented towards their specific brands[3]. Their premium products had superior flavor and were produced to be as consistent as possible year-round, even though the fruit variety mix changed constantly throughout the processing season. For consumers willing to pay, they could enjoy products more akin to home-made, fresh-squeezed juice from optimally-ripe fruit. They also enjoyed the convenience of the ready-to-drink products without the hassle of reconstituting FCOJ themselves. A taste test published in The Orlando Sentinel in 1988 evaluated national and regional OJ brands, illustrating the rising consumer expectations[22]. The article highlighted the different flavor profiles, as well as other attributes like color and pulp consistency, across different OJ brands. Producing these products required careful attention to fruit supply, processing conditions, and the incorporation of sophisticated add-back flavors. During this time, new technology was developed allowing for bulk aseptic storage of NFC juice for extended periods, significantly reducing the cost of producing consistent NFC products year-round. This set the stage for further NFC product growth in the subsequent decade. However, the less-than-premium juice market suffered from an excess of producers relative to available fruit due to the freezes, and a less-profitable revenue stream as the highest-paying consumers opted for premium products. Competition was fierce and costs were rising faster than sales prices. Some prominent OJ processors exited the market, including Kraft Foods which sold its citrus operations in 1988[23]. Even P&G decided to pull out of the OJ market completely in 1992, after more than a decade of effort, having peaked in market share in 1989[20] and concluded they could not achieve their corporate goal of being either the first or second top brand.

For the Florida-based citrus flavor industry, the so-called "Orange Juice Wars" were very good for business. FCOJ products, which were stored frozen until the consumer reconstituted them, and ready-to-drink juices shipped refrigerated to consumers experienced significantly different changes in flavor during their shelf-lives. Consequently, they required distinctly different add-back flavors to optimize product flavor. Even NFC orange juice lost important flavor components during the deaeration and pasteurization processes, as well as upon refrigerated storage. The different production methods used for NFC juices meant that the add-back flavors needed for these products differed from those used in other juices. For a juice company collecting their own peel oil, water-phase aroma and essence oil, simply adding these back to their product could never produce the flavor quality the market now demanded for premium products. Instead, very specific fractions had to be isolated from the raw essences to produce flavors suited to particular classes of finished products. The citrus processing plants and the juice packaging companies lacked this expertise, as did the national flavor companies, which had no specific expertise in orange juice. Instead, the Florida-based citrus flavor companies were best positioned to produce these products. They had access to the raw materials, the necessary fractionating equipment and know-how, and they were very experienced with the orange juice product. As consumer demand for better tasting juices grew, so did sales of their add-back flavoring products.

The 1980s Freezes

The productivity of Florida citrus growers depends on the weather. The state usually provides an excellent subtropical climate for the cultivation of citrus, with ample rainfall and enough cool winter nights that enhance the sugar/acid balance in the fruit. However, citrus is susceptible to damage if temperatures drop below freezing for a sufficient duration, an event that occasionally happens in Florida. Growers have learned to contend with the occasional freeze, but the unusual weather during the 1980s was devastating, leading to long-term changes for the entire citrus industry.

Cool winter nights are beneficial for growing citrus, but if the ambient temperature drops below approximately 28°F, the interior of the fruit will start to freeze. If frozen fruit is harvested soon after a freeze, it remains edible but will become soft and "mushy" as it thaws. If left unpicked, this fruit usually falls from the tree. When temperatures drop below 28°F for more than four hours, damage to the tree begins to occur. The initial damage includes partial or total leaf loss and the death of the small branches. For prolonged freezes, major limbs are killed or even the entire tree down to the roots. It typically takes several weeks after a freeze to fully assess the tree damage. Thus, a minor freeze might lead to some fruit loss without major long-term consequences, while a major freeze can lead to reduced fruit yields for several years, or in the worst cases, the death of entire groves.

Just before the start of the 20th century, a series of three severe freezes in the 1890s nearly wiped out commercial citrus growing in Florida. Due to prolonged multi-day sub-freezing temperatures across the state, most citrus trees were killed[1, pg. 37]. The industry only restarted after new trees were planted. However, that was unusual; the normal pattern was for moderate freezes to occur a couple of times a decade. Since the 1940s, Florida growers had developed several techniques to mitigate the effects of freezes as weather forecasting improved and they received some advance notice of impending cold weather. Techniques included lighting fires and smudge-pots inside groves to warm the trees, using large fans to displace cold air with warmer air[2], or spraying the trees with water[3]. Prior to 1980, the last severe freeze occurred in 1962, just after Jim Redd started his company, Redd Laboratories. That freeze killed quite a few citrus trees in Florida and raised

---

[2]The ambient air 10–200 ft above a grove can sometimes be warmer than the air right at the surface. Just a few degrees of temperature difference can have a large effect.

[3]Surprisingly, freezing water on the surface of fruit and trees releases some heat and can protect them from colder temperatures for a time.

concerns among the national OJ brands about their product supply dependency on one geographic location. Following that freeze, investment in Brazilian citrus operations substantially increased, much to the disappointment of Florida growers. On the other hand, this investment in Brazil proved quite beneficial for Jim Redd as he developed his essence units and essence use technology, providing new processing facilities for his new equipment.

Following the 1962 freeze, the weather in Florida largely returned to normal, with only occasional moderate freezes. For example, prior to 1980, the most significant recent freeze occurred in January 1977, when approximately 12% of the orange crop was lost[1, pg. 146-148]. A freeze of this magnitude did not severely affect the operations of the Florida citrus industry. Freezes typically occurred in December or January, when the first half of the orange crop, the early-maturing varieties, was either already harvested or nearly ready for harvesting. Following a freeze, growers would rush to pick any suitable damaged fruit as quickly as possible and have it processed for juice, also recovering the peel oil and essence by-products during processing. The latest maturing fruit, the Valencia oranges which yielded the highest quality essence, could also suffer damage and some portion of those by-products might be lost along with the fruit. For the citrus flavor industry, as long as the availability of good essence exceeded the demand, which had been the case in the early years of the industry, the overall effect on their industry was minimal.

Unfortunately, the 1980s proved to be an exceptional decade in the worst possible way for freezes. Over eight years, there were seven major freezes, including three very severe ones in December 1983, January 1985, and December 1989. The aggregate effect on the citrus industry was stunning. However, it is important to remember that industry participants viewed each freeze as a singular "once-in-a-decade-or-two" event, and they expected the weather to return its average behavior. Viewed in retrospect, it is much easier for us to understand the overall effect than it was for those who experienced it as it unfolded to comprehend what was happening.

At the start of the decade, Florida was producing its largest crop ever. The 1979/80 citrus season yielded 206 million boxes[4] of oranges[24]. Orange juice continued to sell well with growing consumer

---

[4] A standard box of oranges contained 90 pounds of fresh fruit

demand, but the greatest concern for Florida growers was that the fruit supply was growing much faster than demand. A classic oversupply problem was developing, which had the potential to substantially drive down fruit prices. That concern, however, soon became moot.

In January of 1981 and 1982, Florida experienced two major freezes, at least by recent historical standards. In the first, approximately 15% of the orange crop was lost and approximately 22% the following year. However, it was the unexpectedly severe freeze in December 1983 freeze that surprised everyone. In many ways comparable to the 1962 freeze[1, pg. 175], it caught the weather forecasters by surprise, giving growers little notice and almost no opportunity to prepare their groves. The result was an approximate 31% loss of the orange crop and many dead citrus trees, especially in the northern citrus growing counties in Florida. Overall, 13.6% of the citrus acreage in Florida was lost in this freeze. The combined impact of the three freezes in 1981, 1982 and 1983 resembled the "triple blast" in the 1890s that had previously destroyed Florida's citrus industry[1, pg. 192]. As a result of these freezes, Brazilian orange production surpassed that of Florida for the first time. While Brazil had produced 85 million boxes of oranges in the 1975/76 season, by the 1981/82 season, Brazilian output had risen to more than 180 million boxes, surpassing Florida's reduced production. Brazil's dominance in orange production became a permanent reality, and US OJ producers began importing increasing amounts of Brazilian concentrate to meet demand, much to the continuing dismay of Florida growers.

Growers who lost trees had to decide whether to replant. Newly planted, juvenile trees would be particularly susceptible to cold for several years until they reached maturity. Many growers chose not to replant in northern Florida, and new groves were preferentially established in southern parts of the state, where the likelihood of another freeze was smaller. The selection of fruit variety was a critical decision when replanting or creating new groves, with growers carefully weighing the advantages and disadvantages of various options. Ultimately, these decisions were driven by the demand for fresh fruit and juice, with fresh-fruit sales generally resulting in the highest economic return to the grower. However, the essence byproducts were only collected from the fruit which was processed for juice. As fruit cultivars and availability shifted, flavor companies had to adapt to the changing availability of raw materials.

Unfortunately, another severe, tree-killing freeze occurred in January 1985. The crop loss was smaller this time, only about 13% of the orange crop, primarily because more citrus trees were now located in South Florida. However, many juvenile trees in North Florida, replanted after the 1983 freeze, were killed. A similar amount of citrus acreage to the 1983 freeze was lost again[1, pg. 205]. For North Florida growers, the decision regarding replanting became clear: it was too risky to grow citrus there. The surviving growers regrouped and focused on groves located in the southern half of the Florida peninsula. The final severe freeze in December 1989 reinforced this trend. After this freeze, most groves north of mid-state were gone. This last freeze also decimated the commercial supply of seedy grapefruit trees, destroying over 50% of the remaining trees. Since seedy grapefruit had fallen out of favor with consumers, there was little incentive for growers to replant these trees. If they replanted at all, they chose other citrus varieties. The loss of certain citrus varieties was keenly felt by some fruit connoisseurs and occasionally had a significant impact on the flavor industry. In total, the seven freezes of the 1980s devastated Florida citrus production. During the 1984/85 season, production fell to 104 million boxes, half the amount from five years earlier[1, pg. 204]. By the 1990/91 season, even with replanting and recovery time, production had only reached 152 million boxes[1, pg. 151].

For the citrus flavor companies in Florida, this sequence of freezes brought significant challenges. Both their suppliers (the processors) and their customers (the juice companies) were under repeated stress. As consumer demand for juice continued to grow, demand for FTNF juice flavors also increased despite the lower availability of high-quality essences from Florida. In fact, juice quality itself declined due to the effects of the freezes, increasing the importance of FTNF flavors for overall product quality. Juice companies responded to the limited fruit supply by importing Brazilian FCOJ. Hercules Redd Citrus and Intercit also increased their purchases of Brazilian peel oil and essence byproducts. Compared to the best Florida essences (particularly those recovered from Valencia oranges), the Brazilian products were less flavorful, but they were very consistent and readily available. By the end of the 1980s, Brazil had become a regular supplier of these products to the Florida market, on par with local supply from Florida citrus processing plants. The citrus flavor industry became reliant on this supply. The loss of certain citrus varieties, such as the seedy grapefruit discussed above, was also felt. The peel oils from mature, seedy grapefruit had exceptional grapefruit flavor, while those from the newer, seedless varieties were less flavorful. For the citrus flavor companies, this meant dealing with the limited availability of a desirable ingredient, including by reformulating existing products and limiting the use of this ingredient in new formulations. Another example was Dancy tangerine oil, obtained from a seedy tangerine variety primarily grown in Florida. Many of these trees were killed during the 1980s, and as this seedy tangerine was less desired by the fresh-fruit consumer than newer seedless varieties, few Dancy trees were replanted. But the peel oil from the Dancy tangerine was nearly unique in its attractive sensory properties. Unfortunately, the flavor industry found this raw material increasingly difficult to source after the 1980s[25].

Finally, the freezes caused supply and price volatility in the terpenes and essence markets, on which the flavor industry relied. Market disruptions could create short-term winners and losers and each participant needed to learn how to manage their risk effectively. For instance, Paul Schulz from Florida Chemical Company recalled an incident where a citrus flavor company had agreed to supply a large quantity of terpenes at the market price just before a freeze. Florida Chemical had already committed to supplying these terpenes to their customers based on this agreement. However, when the freeze hit and terpene prices more than doubled, their terpene supplier found an excuse to back out of the deal and sold the product elsewhere at the higher post-freeze price[26], leaving Schulz scrambling to economically source his raw material. Another example occurred just after the 1985 freeze, when Mike Taylor from Redd Citrus offered to buy a large lot of grapefruit essence oil from Jim Redd at Intercit. Somehow, Taylor managed to secure pre-freeze pricing on the product despite the fact that the market price soon more than doubled. This transaction reportedly left Redd feeling exploited, while Taylor's company profited handsomely when this product was resold[27]. Given the small and tight-knit nature of the Florida citrus flavor industry, the ill-feelings from these exchanges could influence commercial relationships for years to come.

Florex Flavors

In the summer of 1984, a new competitor named Florex Flavors entered the Florida citrus flavor market, based in Lakeland, FL. Florex was a partnership between Allen Kryger, formerly of Redd Laboratories and PFW, and Hadi Lashkajani, who had managed operations at Redd Citrus until 1983. The third partner in the venture was the Todd family, owners of the Michigan-based flavor company AM Todd. Established in 1869, AM Todd initially specialized in mint products before expanding into a broader range of flavoring products[28]. In this partnership, Kryger and Lashkajani contributed their Florida citrus experience, while the Todd family provided financial backing, business acumen, and a network of contacts in the flavor industry. For Kryger and Lashkajani, Florex represented their first entrepreneurial endeavor, whereas the Todd family brought significant experience in launching new business ventures.

The genesis of Florex is somewhat unclear. Kryger and Lashkajani, having previously worked together at Redd Laboratories, reportedly held considerable mutual respect for each other[29]. After Kryger left PFW in 1981, he attempted to start a citrus byproducts company in Brazil with a former PFW colleague, but the project never materialized. Instead, Kryger joined a soft-drink company in Michigan in 1982, where he made connections with the AM Todd Company[30]. One industry story suggests that Lashkajani conceived the idea for Florex while pursuing an MBA, subsequently recruiting Kryger, who then involved the Todd family[29]. Regardless of its origins, Lashkajani departed Redd Citrus in 1983, and Kryger left his position in Michigan in June, 1984. Florex Flavors was officially incorporated in March, 1984.

By the fall citrus season in 1984, Florex Flavors was operating out of a small, rented warehouse in Lakeland. The company's business model closely mirrored those of Intercit and Redd Citrus. Florex purchased citrus peel oils, essence oils and water-phase aroma as raw materials and produced standardized essences, folded oils and a selection of more sophisticated natural citrus flavors and fractions. In addition to blending and storage equipment, Florex had custom distillation equipment built very quickly after opening. Drawing on their familiarity with the Redd Citrus stills, Kryger and Lashkajani designed similar equipment.

As a newcomer, Florex faced significant challenges. Their relationships with Florida citrus fruit processors were not as established as those of Redd Citrus or Intercit, making the acquisition of raw materials more difficult. Consequently, they relied heavily on Brazilian suppliers for most of their raw materials. Additionally, lacking the established sales reputation that their competitors enjoyed, Florex found it challenging to compete, especially with the largest customers. Nevertheless, Florex responded in some innovative ways.

Recognizing that their byproduct terpenes could be highly profitable, they adopted a strategic approach to managing this resource. Unlike Intercit or Redd Citrus, who sought to sell-off terpenes as quickly as possible[31], Florex stored terpenes and tried to capitalize on the seasonal fluctuations in limonene production at the citrus plants. They also engaged with a diverse customer base, including Florida Chemical Company, resin-manufacturers like Arizona Chemical, and other end-users, in an attempt to profitably sell their terpenes year-round. Under the direction of Hadi Lashkajani, who was responsible for the terpene strategy and sales, Florex developed a very profitable terpene business[32].

Florex Flavors also diversified beyond the traditional citrus flavor products in search of profitable products. Under Kryger's direction, they established a successful line of standardized apple aromas for addition to apple juice, utilizing apple essence sourced globally from apple processors, similar to the way orange essence was used for orange juice. Although no apples were grown in Florida, the same distillation equipment, flavor analysis techniques, product formulation, and sales strategies used for citrus could be applied to apples. Florex also ventured into raspberry, pineapple, strawberry, cherry, and passionfruit essences, though with lesser success. Kryger commercialized a number of natural, but not FTNF, flavors by fortifying FTNF fruit aromas such as apple, orange, and raspberry essence with key flavor chemicals obtained from other (typically non-fruit based) natural sources. These WONF flavors (made with other natural flavors) mimicked the fruit's natural flavor but could be made less expensively than a product derived entirely from the fruit's own essence. While 100% juice products required FTNF flavors, WONF flavors were cost-effective for use in less-than-100% juice beverages when natural flavors were desired. Advances in flavor analysis technology, especially gas-chromatography, facilitated the identification of key chemical constituents in natural aromas, aiding the creation of WONF flavors. Florex also created citrus oils with WONF enhancements, including lemon oils with enriched citral. Natural lemon oils with high citral content had long been preferred due to their strong flavor character, but the supply was limited and these oils expensive. Florex utilized an inexpensive natural citral isolated from lemongrass to fortify less-expensive lemon oils, resulting in a WONF product suitable for certain applications. Florex also expanded into mint oil distillation, capitalizing on their vacuum distillation technology and the Todd family's expertise in sourcing mint products.

By head count, Florex was a small operation, similar in scale to Intercit or Redd Citrus. But as the newest competitor in the marketplace, they were forced to hire and train mostly new staff, although some industry veterans joined the team including Paul Jones, a former operational specialist from Redd Citrus, and Phil Capasso, a former PFW salesman. Joe Johnson also joined in 1985, shortly after his stint at Intercit. Among the new hires, Gil Escobar, a recent food science/MBA graduate from Wisconsin, was brought on for a sales role in 1986, and Tim Anglea, a fresh Ph.D. graduate in natural products chemistry from Clemson University, was hired in 1987. Both would go on to have long careers in the industry.

Despite the disruptions caused by the severe freezes, Florex Flavors quickly achieved remarkable success. By their second year, annual sales exceeded $5 million and doubled by their fourth year. Coca-Cola (Special Products) and Tropicana were soon among their largest customers, facilitated perhaps by AM Todd's established relationship with Coca-Cola[19], and by Joe Johnson, who was well-known to Florida clients. Additionally, Florex secured a Japanese agent through AM Todd's relationships in Japan, capitalizing on a citrus flavor market that had grown substantially since it was initially developed by James Redd in the late 1960s. By 1988, Florex's combined business in Japan ranked as their fourth largest customer. The company had quickly outgrown initial rented warehouse, moving into a custom-built leased facility before finally constructing a larger, state-of-the-art facility they owned on the western outskirts of Lakeland[5].

The rapid success of Florex Flavors did not go unnoticed in the US flavor industry, which was keenly aware of Hercules' activities with PFW and Redd Laboratories, alongside the burgeoning demand for citrus-flavored beverages and juices in the US. Several flavor companies visited Florex to propose joint ventures or an acquisition. For Kryger and Lashkajani, the interest was welcome and the prospect of significant financial return from their risky venture was enticing. In 1988, they evaluated several purchase offers, eventually agreeing to sell to Hercules

---

[5]This facility was located at 4705 US Highway 92 E. in Lakeland and is still utilized by Givaudan today.

(discussed further below). The transaction concluded on April 3, 1989, for a purchase price of $13.2 million (net of debt)[33] plus the acquisition of their brand-new facility in Lakeland. Established just five years prior, Florex Flavors had proven to be a remarkably successful financial investment, drawing attention to the business potential within the niche industry. Florex also provided a valuable training ground for future industry leaders including Kryger, Lashkajani, Escobar, and Anglea.

Hercules Redd Citrus

With Florex's entry into the market in 1984, Hercules Redd Citrus faced two direct competitors. However, Redd Citrus had several competitive advantages. First, as a 20-year-old company, it was the largest and most established of the flavor companies in Florida, positioning it well to compete for raw materials from the fruit processors. Second, it had profitably managed the material balance between purchasing raw materials and selling all of the byproducts. Additionally, Redd Citrus' institutional experience in add-back flavors placed it at the forefront of this market just as the OJ wars were driving demand for better-tasting juices. Finally, the influence of its large parent company, Hercules, encouraged processes and procedures that enhanced manufacturing reliability and bolstered its reputation as a supplier, especially with major customers like P&G and Minute Maid/Coca-Cola.

On the other hand, Redd Citrus also faced challenges. Hercules was a vast industrial conglomerate with many diverse business interests. In 1984, Hercules reorganized its food ingredient assets, including Redd Citrus and PFW, along with its gums and pectin businesses, into the Food and Flavor Ingredients Group (FFIG). Hercules hoped that a "one-stop shop" approach to supplying food ingredients would prove successful[34, pg. 422][35]. However, Redd Citrus' products were highly specialized. For example, their add-back flavors sold to juice companies didn't synergize well with Hercules' other products that were not used in juices. Additionally, their flavor fractions and isolates required further processing into complex compounded flavors before they could be marketed to beverage or other food companies. The sales staff at PFW likewise found the FFIG consolidation difficult, with vary different sales cultures present among the flavor and gums/pectin customers[35].

Ideally, close collaboration between PFW in New York and Redd

Citrus in Florida could have been mutually beneficial, but this was challenging due to their geographic separation and Hercules' management structure. The two organizations reported within Hercules through separate management lines, subordinating longer-term collaborations to more immediate concerns for both organizations. Redd Citrus and PFW had relied on separate sales staff, until Hercules consolidated all sales staff within the FFIG, but the integration was complex, time-consuming and led to dissatisfaction among the sales people[19, 35]. The main connection between Redd Citrus and PFW remained Dennis Kujawski, the liaison established in the late 1970s. He and the Redd technical staff communicated weekly by phone, and Kujawski made several brief visits to Florida. However, "success" for Redd Citrus in this arrangement was slow to materialize. Redd's products had to be incorporated in the PFW ingredient library and used to formulate new flavors, and then these new flavors had to be successfully sold to external companies before Redd Citrus could see significant benefits.

Employee turnover posed yet another challenge for Redd Citrus. Experienced employees were prime targets for recruitment, both by the in-state competitors as well as out-of-state flavor companies. One key employee, Hadi Lashkajani, had even departed to establish the competitor company, Florex Flavors. Two more examples included Joe Johnson, who joined Intercit in 1984, and J. D. Vora, who moved to the international flavor & fragrance company Firmenich in 1986. Each departure strained the company's operations, as there was no readily available pool of trained workers for these specialized roles. New hires required extensive training to reach the proficiency of their predecessors, though they could bring new expertise or industry contacts. Typically, recruits came from the broader citrus industry, but this sometimes necessitated careful consideration to avoid conflicts of interest with suppliers or customers. One example was Chris Li, who joined Redd Citrus in 1987 for a technical role after Vora and Johnson left. Li had previously worked for P&G on OJ research, but moved to Pepsi in 1985. Hired by Redd Citrus from Pepsi, he brought valuable customer insights into P&G's operations without the complications that might have arisen from directly poaching a P&G employee.

At the start of the 1980s, Redd Citrus' operations were highly seasonal, with Florida citrus plants operating for only 9 months each year. Consequently, the company's operations largely mirrored this schedule, typically running a single, extended shift for distillation five days a week during the citrus season[36]. However, production planning had to ensure product availability year-round. With the many freezes in the 1980s and the accompanying disruptions in the supply of oils and essences from the Florida processors, Redd Citrus began purchasing more raw materials from Brazilian citrus processors. These South American byproducts were produced on a different seasonal schedule from Florida's byproducts. This broader supply of byproducts, combined with the company's organic growth, necessitated a shift in production scheduling. By 1987, operations had expanded to run 24 hours a day, five days a week throughout the year[36].

Mike Taylor was tasked with managing these challenges as Hercules' site manager for Redd Citrus. Despite various hardships, the company significantly benefited from the organic growth of the OJ market and the intense competition among major players like P&G, Minute Maid, and Tropicana to deliver better-tasting juice. A common Redd Citrus sales demonstration at the time involved purchasing a potential customer's retail juice, and then presenting that customer their raw juice with samples that had added Redd Citrus FTNF flavors. The enhancement in flavor was usually unmistakable, and even more so when a customer voluntarily provided their unflavored juice in advance. This allowed a Redd Citrus application specialist to add different add-back flavors and mimic the pasteurization and packaging of the juice, demonstrating the different flavor profiles that could be offered for their finished product[35]. Taylor adeptly managed the raw material supply, operational issues and sales strategy to expand the business throughout the 1980s, achieving notably high profit margins. These margins were exceptional within Hercules, earning Taylor significant goodwill from senior management[35, 10]. However, most of the business growth was driven by add-back flavors, rather than through collaborations with PFW or Hercules' other operations. By the late 1980s, approximately 70–80% of Redd's sales stemmed from these FTNF juice flavors[31], which were marketed not only in the US but also in Japan, Europe and Australia[35]. Another significant revenue stream was the sale of grapefruit oils to Japanese flavor companies, who highly valued this citrus oil for creating beverages. Although grapefruit production in Florida was ten times smaller than orange production, Florida was the largest global source of grapefruit. Consequently, Florida freezes significantly impacted pricing for these oils and essences, often resulting in profitable opportunities for Redd Citrus due to their ability to purchase and store grapefruit oils efficiently. The third tier of Redd Citrus' business involved selling oils and citrus fractions within the US, to PFW and other flavor or consumer-product companies, or distributing these products through PFW's Netherlands site for the EU market[19].

In comparison to local competitors, Redd Citrus was performing well. Intercit, although well-established, lagged behind in size and technical sophistication. Jim Redd's focus on consulting and pulp products at Intercit diluted his attention to flavors, and his role as the sole technical expert on staff limited innovation. The newest competitor, Florex, still a young company, faced disadvantages in reputation with the largest customers. Despite Taylor being aware that Florex Flavors was breaking new ground with terpenes, apple aroma and WONF flavors[10], Redd Citrus' successful growth and profitability provided little incentive for him to implement major changes.

Around 1987, Mike Taylor was promoted within Hercules and relocated to headquarters in Wilmington, DE. One colleague said he had grown bored in Florida and aspired for something new[10]. However, he was quickly unhappy in the new role and missed his previous position in Florida. Possibly as a means to return, Taylor advocated from Wilmington for Hercules to acquire Florex Flavors. By then, Florex was five years old and the Florex owners had made known their potential interest in selling the company. Hercules had a long history of strategic acquisitions, so Taylor was able to tap their corporate expertise through Jim Rapp, a Hercules acquisition specialist who had previously worked with Taylor on an unsuccessful bid to acquire Intercit. During 1988, Taylor and Rapp negotiated with the Florex owners, who were also entertaining other offers, and ultimately Hercules presented the best offer. The purchase transaction for Florex Flavors was completed in April 1989.

Mike Taylor returned to Florida to manage the integration of the combined business, evidently relieved to be back. There was much to be done. Redd Citrus operated out of their older facility in Safety Harbor, FL, while Florex's newer facility was located 50 miles away in Lakeland, FL. Additionally, given the common business activities, there were staff redundancies across many positions. As often happens with acquisitions, the Florex employees were particularly anxious about their job security.

Shortly after the acquisition, key staff from Lakeland were summoned to Safety Harbor. Two Florex employees, Escobar and Anglea, recall receiving little advance notice to prepare a formal presentation for management the following week, each suspecting their jobs might be at stake. Escobar was tasked with reporting on Florex's sales accomplishments and future sales pipeline, while Anglea was to report on product development activities. The following week, the meetings were held with Mike Taylor and his management team, and included similar activity reports from Redd Citrus personnel. After these high-stress meetings, the critical personnel decisions were swiftly made. Anglea was appointed Technical Manager for Redd Citrus, leading the integration of Florex's products, including FTNF apple flavors, mint fractions, and other WONF fruit flavors, into Redd's product portfolio. Escobar was incorporated into the sales organization, soon taking primary responsibility for terpene byproducts. His position became particularly challenging when Redd Citrus lost one of Florex's largest customers, the terpene purchaser Arizona Chemical, soon after the acquisition. The terpene market was already in flux due to crop freezes and competition from non-citrus terpenes, so while the loss wasn't directly Escobar's fault, the timing raised suspicions. Rumors soon circulated that the Florex owners had known this Arizona business was temporary[37, 32].

The Florex acquisition also brought Joe Johnson back to Redd Citrus, highlighting the fluid nature of employment in this industry. Johnson had left Redd Citrus in 1984, worked for Intercit and then Florex Flavors, and found himself back at Redd involuntarily through the acquisition. Johnson's experience underscored the importance of maintaining professional relationships with past, and potentially future, employers in the small, close-knit flavor community.

Ultimately, the merger resulted in few job losses, although some roles and responsibilities shifted, and several long-time Redd Citrus employees opted for retirement[27]. Hercules decided to continue operating both the Safety Harbor and Lakeland manufacturing sites. Although few citrus groves were still left in Pinellas County by this time, most Redd Citrus staff were opposed to moving inland closer to the citrus-growing regions in Florida. Everyone was relieved by the decision to keep both facilities operating. However, this decision would prove to be temporary.

Following the acquisition, there was a renewed effort to integrate PFW and Redd Citrus more closely. In 1990, a PFW flavorist from the UK, Colin Scott, was transferred to Florida for a one-year assignment[38]. Certified flavor chemists, like Scott, are highly-paid specialists who have completed an extensive apprenticeship under a senior flavorist[6]. In the US, these specialists were geographically concentrated in the NY/NJ area and a few other cities, where their special credentials were recognized and many employers were located, making it challenging to persuade them to relocate. Scott, along with Dennis Kujawski, was part of an internal PFW "Task Team" created to share citrus information, and he had visited Redd Citrus several times before. In agreeing to the temporary assignment, Scott planned to set up a flavor compounding laboratory in Lakeland. However, by the time he arrived five months later, Mike Taylor had decided against Scott formulating any non-FTNF citrus products in Florida. Taylor was motivated in part by the desire to segregate FTNF and non-FTNF flavor production, to avoid suspicion among his important juice customers that their flavors were not 100% FTNF[7]. Pivoting from his initial plans, Scott focused on creating new FTNF flavors for use in juices, which was Redd Citrus' primary business, and improving Redd's citrus flavor fractions for non-juice applications, which was the larger market served by PFW. Scott also trained the Florida technical and sales staff on sensory tools and flavor applications. His flavorist expertise brought a new creative approach to product development at Redd Citrus, and this time is recalled by several of Scott's colleagues as particularly productive for the business[32, 39]. However, the process was not without challenges as disagreements about expertise occasionally arose between Scott, an outsider, and the local in-house experts who were much more familiar with the citrus juice market.[32].

As the 1980s came to a close, Redd Citrus was bustling with activity. Following the acquisition of Florex, they solidified their position as the largest producer of FTNF citrus flavoring ingredients, supplying all of the OJ industry leaders including Minute Maid, Tropicana and P&G. While laboring intensely to integrate the Florex business, they diligently worked to expand the combined operations to justify the acquisition costs. However, at the corporate level, Hercules still felt that the combined flavor business of PFW and Redd Citrus was not

---

[6]The apprentice-based training program requires the flavorist to master the odor, flavor, and use of over 2,000 flavoring ingredients approved for foods. Successful flavorists combine both technical and creative aptitude and excellent olfactory ability.

[7]It was well known that natural, non-citrus flavor chemicals could be used to manufacture flavors more cheaply than FTNF citrus ingredients. These products were considered adulterated if labeled as FTNF flavors from citrus. Nevertheless, there was a strong economic motivation for this type of cheating.

yet operating optimally. Furthermore, Hercules had publicly expressed interest in further acquisitions to enhance its food business[34, pg. 426]. Dramatic changes were on the horizon in just a few short years.

Intercit and the Firmenich Acquisition

At Intercit as the 1980s unfolded, Jim Redd's interests continued to drive the business activities. In addition to producing oils, aromas and add-back flavors, Intercit continued manufacturing specialized pulp products and Redd served as a consultant to citrus processing plants. Intercit's products were sold both in the US and internationally, notably in Japan, which Redd visited annually. Redd also engaged in at least two other business ventures during this time. In one venture, he collaborated with his old friend Frank Wagner, who had been instrumental in Staley's acquisition of Redd Laboratories in 1970. Together, they formed Wagner Excello, a company focused on manufacturing mixed drink blenders in the Chicago area. Wagner, whose family had been in the beverage business, provided the marketing expertise, while Intercit was responsible for manufacturing the beverage bases and sourcing some of the ingredients. Their products included a piña colada mix utilizing coconut concentrate from a Dominican Republic processing plant where Redd had consulted. Unfortunately, Wagner died unexpectedly in 1985, after a tumultuous year marked by an investment scandal and heart disease[40, 41], leaving Redd in charge of a venture far from his core interests and home. He soon sold what remained of the business[42, 43].

Redd also collaborated with Haitian businessman Harold Bussenius to establish a lime processing facility near Port-au-Prince, Haiti[42, 43]. Haiti had a long history of lime cultivation, but political instability and poverty had hindered industry development. This venture aimed to produce lime juice and concentrate, pectin from lime peels, and distilled lime oil. Redd provided his expertise in citrus processing and was particularly interested in the lime oils, while Bussenius, a lime grower, managed operations amidst the challenging local conditions. A fruit processing facility was constructed, along with specialized equipment for distilling lime oil, and the essential oil part of the project was named Reddy Flavors, which Redd co-owned. Through this venture, Intercit was supplied with lime oils.

In 1983, Redd finally addressed the administration issues at Intercit, by hiring Beverly Bateman, a mid-level administrator from Myakka Processors, a citrus plant where Intercit was leasing space for manufacturing pulp products. Bateman, a sixth-generation Floridian from rural Arcadia, FL, was not actively seeking a new position and initially viewed Redd's offer with skepticism. Despite her reservations, Redd's persistance persuaded her, and she eventually accepted a vice-president position at Intercit. However, her job was contingent upon passing a final hurdle – an interview with Charlie Walker, whose opinion Redd greatly valued. Clearing that hurdle, Bateman started in February 1983, and she described the situation she inherited at Intercit as a "mess" which took considerable time to rectify. Redd had allowed many administrative and personnel issues to fester. Within a few years, Bateman became a highly trusted colleague of Redd's and was made a shareholder in Intercit, along with a select group of other key employees[42].

Now well in his 60s and with his day-to-day business concerns effectively managed, Redd began to contemplate the future of Intercit. His children had not been involved in his business endeavors nor expressed any interest in doing so. Redd cared deeply for his employees and was considering some form of business transfer to one or more of them, yet, no one seemed to possess his technical skills or appeared as an obvious successor. Moreover, Redd himself was increasingly engaged in external interests, including spending longer weekends away from the office. Over time, one of Bateman's primary responsibilities became assisting Redd in deciding the future of Intercit, and then preparing the company for this transition.

In 1984, Joe Johnson left Redd Citrus to join Intercit. He brought along his industry experience, and particularly his expertise with the enriched aroma product that had been highly successful at Redd Citrus. However, Johnson's tenure at Intercit lasted less than a year, due to his perception that opportunities might be limited under Redd's uncertain commitment to the company's direction[44]. Subsequently, Johnson moved on to a position with Florex Flavors[45].

Around the same time, Redd and his engineer, Brett Welch, collaborated with Gulf Machinery Corporation to design and build new distillation equipment for Intercit, as they had outgrown their original, decade-old stills. In addition to increasing the distillation capacity, the new stills had enhanced fractionating performance[46].

In 1986, Intercit hired Charlie Hendrix, Redd's longtime colleague from the earliest days of Redd Laboratories, and Charlie's son, Don Hendrix. Charlie was hired in a consulting role, leveraging his extensive contacts at various citrus processing plants to represent Intercit, while Don was hired for a technical and quality control role. Don had been working at Florida citrus plants since 1972 and experienced firsthand the introduction of add-back flavors as routine ingredients in juice. He was well-acquainted with essence collection technology and the challenges associated with using essence and add-back flavors in juice concentrate manufacturing. In his first year at Intercit, Charlie authored a short, self-published paper titled "A History of Juice Enhancement," which is believed to be the first written history of the Florida add-back flavor industry[47]. Much of this information was incorporated in Redd's 1988 presentation given to the Citrus Engineering Conference[48], and was subsequently included in Redd, Hendrix and Hendrix's updated 1992 edition of the "Quality Control Manual For Citrus Processing Plants, volume II[49]."

It is not precisely clear when the final decision was made, but as Jim Redd neared age 70, he decided to sell Intercit. He approached his key employees to gauge their interest in purchasing the business, but without his ongoing involvement in the business, they did not see themselves succeeding. Consequently, it then fell to Bateman and a core group of employees to prepare the business for sale to an external party. Redd engaged in acquisition discussions with several potential buyers, including Hercules, Mallinckrodt (Fries & Fries), and Firmenich. Ultimately, Firmenich made the most attractive offer to Redd, aided by the friendly relationships Redd had with Firmenich, and the internal efforts of a J. D. Vora. Vora, who had worked at Hercules Redd Citrus before joining Firmenich in 1986, was well-acquainted with the niche citrus flavor industry in Florida. Seeing the business potential of combining the natural citrus flavoring ingredients of Intercit with Firmenich's expertise, he championed the acquisition internally[50].

In 1987, as Firmenich's interest intensified, Redd, Bateman, and Redd's business advisor Rex Harper traveled to Firmenich's headquarters in Geneva for a meeting with their Board of Directors. After the meeting, Redd delegated the negotiation responsibilities to Bateman and Harper. Firmenich's point person was Peter van Houten, the North American President. A deal was reached a few months later. Harper later described it as one of the easiest deals he ever negotiated and successfully closed. Harper and van Houten reached a verbal agreement first and only then involved outside legal counsel, with instructions that the attorneys were to conduct all communications through Harper or van Houten[42].

The sale to Firmenich was finalized on November 8, 1988, just shy of Redd's 70th birthday. Redd also exited his other businesses at this time, with Firmenich purchasing the Haitian Reddy Flavors business as well. Almost all Intercit employees remained with Firmenich after the sale, with Bateman and Don Hendrix assuming significant leadership roles. Redd had a three-year consulting agreement and retained an office at the Safety Harbor facility. However, aside from collaborating with Firmenich's technical staff on a handful of projects, his business involvement quickly decreased over time.

Firmenich's acquisition introduced a second major flavor and fragrance company to Florida, joining Hercules' PFW & Redd Citrus. Firmenich had a long history of processing citrus, with a proprietary, continuous citrus oil extraction facility in Geneva and another citrus oil facility in Brazil. However, most of this prior experience focused on peel oils. Intercit allowed Firmenich to expand into juice-derived byproducts, such as essence oil and water-phase aroma, and the FNTF-based juice flavor business that relied on these ingredients. Following the acquisition, Robert Otterbein was appointed site president[51], and a new main office was constructed on the Safety Harbor property. Over time, Firmenich would dedicate considerable resources into the Safety Harbor site, internally known as **FIRHARBOR** and externally marketed as their Citrus Center of Excellence[52]. This site coordinated worldwide citrus purchasing for Firmenich and all citrus ingredient processing, though other manufacturing operations continued in Geneva and Brazil. However, Firmenich soon exited both Intercit's pulp business and the Haitian lime business.

Notably, one of Firmenich's early investments in Safety Harbor was hiring a flavorist. Margrit Messenheimer, a Firmenich flavorist who had retired to Sarasota, FL, agreed to work part-time to aid the integration of Intercit into Firmenich[52, 53]. Her hiring predated Colin Scott's transfer to Redd Citrus in 1990 and may have influenced Hercules' decision to act. Redd Citrus was likely aware that Firmenich had an onsite flavorist in Florida and may have seen it as a competitive threat[53].

Sunpure and Florida Treatt

In 1988, anticipating the sale of Florex Flavors, the owners – Kryger, Lashkajani, and the Todd family – purchased an old citrus processing plant in Avon Park, FL, and established a company called Sunpure Ltd. Refurbishing the facility and installing new processing equipment, they started producing FCOJ. However, their plans for Sunpure also included re-entering the flavor business. Shortly after the sale of Florex, Sunpure installed new distillation equipment and began processing and selling apple aroma products. Hercules had not included apple aroma in their non-compete agreement with the previous owners of Florex; instead, they entered into a supply agreement with Sunpure for this product. Meanwhile, Lashkajani and Kryger faced the challenge of finding and training a new team, having lost nearly all their knowledgeable staff in the sale of Florex. Over the next few years, they maintained a low profile in citrus flavors while adhering to their five-year non-compete agreement and learning the intricacies of citrus fruit processing, a business very different from manufacturing citrus flavors.

In 1989, the English flavor company R. C. Treatt established a subsidiary named Florida Treatt in Haines City, FL. Founded in 1886 by a London essential oil merchant, R. C. Treatt had been involved with lime oils since the 1930s, due to its client relationship with the producer of *Rose's Lime Juice*. Treatt, who primarily sourced its lime oil from West Africa and the West Indies, also developed some lemon oil business. Around 1970, R. C. Treatt began purchasing Brazilian orange peel oil through a relationship with Jean van Iperen, a Dutch broker of citrus juices and other products for the Cutrale family in Brazil. At that time, Brazil had an excess of peel oil, which Treatt acquired on generous payment terms. With a small vacuum still in England, they produced five-fold oil and sold the distilled terpenes into the European solvent market, where terpene prices were higher than in Florida due to limited availability and trade and duty regulations. This arrangement allowed Treatt to produce the five-fold oil at a competitive price for sale in Europe or for internal use. During the 1980s, they also began producing terpeneless orange oil and a decanal fraction, which they were able to sell quite profitably to several US customers. By 1990, they had also started producing a natural sinensal fraction from this orange oil[54, 55].

R. C. Treatt went public on the London exchange in 1989, and around the same time, the CEO Hugo Bovill decided to start Florida Treatt. In addition to his other connections, Bovill was informed about the Florida market through his relationships with van Iperen and Jan Soudijn. Van Iperen was well-acquainted with various citrus processors in Florida and maintained his relationship with the Cutrale family in Brazil. Soudijn, a former sales executive with Tropicana, started the Florida WorldWide Citrus Products Company (FWW) in Bradenton, FL in 1985. FWW handled numerous citrus byproducts, including citrus oils, but did not distill or further process them[56, 57]. Both van Iperen and Soudijn saw a market opportunity for Treatt in Florida and received an ownership percentage in exchange for their efforts in helping establish Florida Treatt[54].

However, Florida Treatt encountered significant challenges from the onset. Although knowledgeable about the technology of citrus peel oil processing, Treatt was far less familiar with essence oil and water-phase aroma. Florida citrus plants often sold their byproducts to Redd Citrus, Intercit, or Florex, expecting them to handle the bulk of the products produced rather than cherry-pick lots. Given that the market demand for peel oil, essence oil, and aroma could fluctuate drastically, the citrus plants, whose primary economic focus was on juice, did not have the space or desire to store these byproducts any longer than necessary. As a result, Florida Treatt had to quickly adapt to handle all these products to compete for raw materials effectively. Moreover, the distillation technology used by Treatt's competitors in Florida differed significantly from Treatt's equipment in England. After installing a Florida-built still, it took some time for them to learn how to use this equipment effectively. Additionally, the terpene market in Florida presented a less favorable cost-structure compared to the European market for their folded peel oil. These factors combined to create a steep learning curve for Florida Treatt. Finally, Bovill acknowledged that Florida Treatt was under-capitalized from the start, as R. C. Treatt did not have an abundance of capital available at that time[54].

Interestingly, Florida Treatt was the first company to enter the Florida citrus flavor industry with technical expertise independent of either Jim Redd or Coca-Cola. Leveraging R. C. Treatt's established flavor expertise in Europe, their early product focus was quite different from many of their Florida competitors. However, it wasn't until later in the 1990s that they established a significant market presence in Florida.

References

[1] John A. Attaway. *A History of Florida Citrus Freezes*. Florida Science Source, 1997. ISBN: 0-944961-03-7.

[2] George Lazarus. "Minute Maid Expands." In: *The Chicago Tribune* (Mar. 11, 1981). Section 4, p. 3.

[3] Robert A. Morris. *The U.S. Orange and Grapefruit Juice Markets: History, Development, Growth, and Change*. EDIS Document FE834. IFAS, University of Florida, Gainesville, FL, June 2010. URL: https://journals.flvc.org/edis/article/download/118658/116582/ (visited on 07/23/2024).

[4] Margaret D. Pacey. "The Business Front: Chilled or Frozen; Orange Juice is Steadily Winning Fresh Adherents." In: *Barron's National Business and Financial Weekly* Vol. 54 (Issue 52 Dec. 30, 1974), p. 11.

[5] Donald Hendrix. *Interview by Robert Kryger*. Winter Haven, FL. Oct. 12, 2021.

[6] Dan Tracy. "Newcomer May Squeeze Juice Giants." In: *The Orlando Sentinel* (Oct. 17, 1982), pp. F1, F10.

[7] Patricia Bellew. "Procter & Gamble Squeezes New Juice Into Staid Industry." In: *Miami Herald* (Dec. 12, 1983). Section: Business, p. 14.

[8] Mary Lou Janson. "Competition Withers the 'Sunshine Tree.'" In: *The Tampa Tribune* (Dec. 23, 1984), p. J4.

[9] Nancy Giges. "Tropicana Puts Ad Squeeze on Foes." In: *Advertising Age* (June 14, 1984), pp. 1, 43.

[10] Chris Li. *Interview by Robert Kryger*. By Phone. Aug. 9, 2022.

[11] Robert L. Swaine Jr. et al. "Commercially Processed Orange Juice Products Having a More Hand-Squeezed Character." Pat. 4,938,985. Assignee: The Procter & Gamble Company. United States Patent. July 3, 1990.

[12] "Citrus Processing Plant Closing Due to Freezes." In: *The South Florida Sun Sentinel* (Feb. 10, 1986), p. A8.

[13] George Lazarus. "Minute Maid Expands Line." In: *Chicago Tribune* (Aug. 21, 1986). Section 3, p. 4.

[14] Kevin Spear. "Minute Maid Squeezing Into Juice Market." In: *The Orlando Sentinel* (June 18, 1988), pp. L3, 10.

[15] Jerry Sachs. *Interview by Robert Kryger*. By Phone. May 17, 2021.

[16] Jerry Sachs. *Interview by Robert Kryger*. By Phone. Nov. 19, 2020.

[17] *1986 Florex Flavors Customer List and Sales Projections.* Unpublished. June 13, 1986.

[18] Allen Kryger. *1988/89 Florex Flavors Customer List and Sales Projections.* Unpublished. 1988.

[19] Peary Marro. *Interview by Robert Kryger*. By Phone. Jan. 16, 2023.

[20] Paul Power Jr. "Tropicana Squeezes Minute Maid." In: *The Tampa Tribune* (May 1, 1991). Section: Business & Finance, pp. 1, 3.

[21] Will Mims, Al Wysocki, and Richard Weldon. *Understanding NFC and RECON Orange Juice Demand.* UF IFAS EDIS Document FE 175. University of Florida IFAS, July 2000. URL: https://ufdcimages.uflib.ufl.edu/IR/00/00/18/92/00001/FE17500.pdf (visited on 09/23/2023).

[22] Charlotte V. Balcomb. "The Taste Test Champ." In: *The Orlando Sentinel* (Sept. 25, 1988). Section: Florida Magazine, p. 10.

[23] Gaynell Terrell. "Erly Buys Kraft Plant in Lakeland." In: *The Tampa Tribune* (Sept. 30, 1988), p. D7.

[24] *USDA NASS Citrus Summary 1999 - 2000.* United States Department of Agriculture, Jan. 22, 2001. URL: https://www.nass.usda.gov/Statistics_by_State/Florida/Publications/Citrus/Citrus_Summary/index.php (visited on 07/01/2023).

[25] Robert Kryger. "Florida Tangerine Peel Oil–The Changing Cultivar Landscape." In: *Perfumer & Flavorist* Vol. 27 (Jan./Feb. 2002).

[26] Paul Schulz. *Interview by Robert Kryger*. By Phone. Feb. 6, 2023.

[27] Jeff Dodson. *Interview by Robert Kryger*. By Zoom. Dec. 1, 2022.

[28] Matt Roush. "Diversification has put Kalamazoo's A.M. Todd Co. In Mint Condition." In: *Kalamazoo Gazette* (June 3, 1990), pp. H1–H2.

REFERENCES

[29] J. D. Vora. *Interview by Robert Kryger.* By Phone. Mar. 2, 2023.

[30] Luis Haro. *Interview by Robert Kryger.* Lakeland, FL. Mar. 22, 2023.

[31] Chris Li. *Interview by Robert Kryger.* By Phone. Sept. 16, 2022.

[32] Gil Escobar and Tim Anglea. *Interview by Robert Kryger.* Clearwater, FL. Sept. 22, 2022.

[33] *Stock Acquisition Agreement by Hercules Incorporated.* Unpublished. Apr. 3, 1989.

[34] Davis Dver and David B. Sicilia. *Labors of a Modern Hercules - Evolution of a Chemical Company.* Boston, MA: Harvard Business School Press, 1990.

[35] David Rosen. *Interview by Robert Kryger.* By Phone. Dec. 13, 2022.

[36] Charles Thomas. *Interview by Robert Kryger.* By Phone. Nov. 21, 2022.

[37] Gil Escobar. *Interview by Robert Kryger.* By Phone. Dec. 7, 2022.

[38] Colin Scott. *Interview by Robert Kryger.* By Phone. Feb. 27, 2023.

[39] Cathy Conway. *Interview by Robert Kryger.* By Phone. Nov. 15, 2022.

[40] "Obituary - Francis H. Wagner." In: *Chicago Tribune* (May 26, 1985). Section 3, p. 7.

[41] Maurice Possley. "How Naive Investors Fall Victim to Greed." In: *Chicago Tribune* (May 12, 1985). Section 7, p. 2.

[42] Beverly Bateman and Rex Harper. *Interview by Robert Kryger.* Lakeland, FL. Feb. 11, 2021.

[43] Beverly Bateman. *E-mail to Robert Kryger.* Mar. 12, 2021.

[44] Joe Johnson. *Interview by Robert Kryger.* By Phone. June 23, 2022.

[45] Joe Johnson. *Interview by Robert Kryger.* By Phone. Sept. 24, 2020.

[46] Brett Welch. *Interview by Robert Kryger.* By Phone. Sept. 16, 2021.

[47] Charles M. Hendrix Jr. *A History of Juice Enhancement*. Unpublished. 1986.

[48] James B. Redd. "The Volatile Flavors of Orange Juice." In: ASME 1988 Citrus Engineering Conference. Lakeland, FL: American Society of Mechanical Engineers Digital Collection, Mar. 24, 1988, pp. 79–93.

[49] James B. Redd, Charles M. Hendrix Jr., and Don L. Hendrix. *Quality Control Manual for Citrus Processing Plants*. Vol. 2. Agscience, 1992.

[50] J. D. Vora. *Interview by Robert Kryger*. By Phone. Apr. 6, 2021.

[51] "Industry News." In: *Perfumer & Flavorist* Vol. 14 (July/Aug. 1989), p. 74.

[52] Beverly Bateman. *E-mail to Robert Kryger*. May 23, 2023.

[53] J. D. Vora. *Interview by Robert Kryger*. By Phone. Apr. 4, 2023.

[54] Hugo Bovill. *Interview by Robert Kryger*. By Zoom. Aug. 4, 2022.

[55] Hugo Bovill. *E-mail to Robert Kryger*. Aug. 15, 2022.

[56] "New Citrus Firm." In: *The Bradenton Herald* (Aug. 13, 1985), p. A7.

[57] James A. Jones Jr. "Florida Worldwide Citrus Brings Fruit Flavors to the World." In: *The Bradenton Herald* (Apr. 3, 2017), p. A8.

8
The 1990s — The Golden Years

"There is never a dull moment in the Florida citrus industry."

—Editorial, *Tampa Morning Tribune*, 1950[1].

The Florida OJ Market

After increasing for decades, growth in the world's largest market for OJ, the US, had slowed considerably by the late 1980s and was essentially flat entering into the 1990s. Meanwhile, the drastic changes in the product category that began in the last decade continued into the 1990s. Consumers increasingly purchased ready-to-drink orange juice, either not-from-concentrate (NFC) or reconstituted frozen concentrated orange juice (FCOJ), while demand for traditional thaw-and-dilute at home frozen concentrate was falling. Manufacturers experimented with new ways for consumers to enjoy juice, moving beyond product requiring continuous refrigeration to options that could be stored at ambient (room) temperature but tasted much better than the old-style canned juice. Packaging options for ready-to-drink juice included traditional gable-top cardboard packaging, as well as glass and plastic bottles, and aseptic "juice-boxes." The different storage temperatures and packaging materials strongly influenced the flavor of OJ under storage, and these products required customized from-the-named fruit (FTNF) flavors for optimum taste. In addition, the market-leading companies continued to produce specialized OJ products, including low and high-pulp juices, low-acid juice, calcium-fortified juices, and low-sugar orange juice. They also introduced blended juices and juice-containing drinks, such as the *Tropicana Twisters*, to expand customer reach. These specialized juices and some of the blended juice products also used FNTF flavors. Within this market environment, two major changes occurred in the early 1990s. First, Minute Maid, one of the oldest and most successful of Florida's OJ companies, lost its market-leading position in OJ to Tropicana. Second, P&G gave up on the OJ market, concluding their product sales would not catch up to Tropicana and Minute Maid. P&G discontinued their Citrus Hill brand in 1992 and sold their citrus processing plant.

Tropicana had a remarkable run during the 1990s. Between the 1988/89 and 1998/99 citrus seasons, NFC production in Florida increased by 295%, while frozen concentrate production decreased by 45%[1], all while total OJ consumption increased only 22% over those 10 years[2]. Good-quality NFC orange juice, more expensive to produce year-round than FCOJ, continued to be favored by a growing number of consumers. As the NFC category leader, Tropicana drove this trend with their well-advertised *Pure Premium* brand and benefited from the increasing demand. They invested heavily in aseptic storage technology for NFC orange juice, moving away from frozen blocks of juice, to more efficiently produce a standardized NFC juice which was available all year long, even outside of the citrus growing season. Using enormous aseptic tanks, holding millions of gallons of juice, they grew their *Pure Premium* product to a national brand. In addition to carefully storing and blending NFC juices to achieve a standardized product, Tropicana also made careful use of add-back FTNF flavors to help achieve this goal. Unlike Minute Maid's Special Products, Tropicana did not have an internal FTNF flavor production department. Instead, they relied on external suppliers within the Florida citrus flavor industry and the flavor expertise of their in-house product specialists, supported by a team of flavorists at their parent company, Seagram Co. Remarkably, by early 2000, Tropicana's *Pure Premium* became the 4th largest grocery brand in the US[3], trailing only behind Coca-Cola Classic, Pepsi Cola, and Campbell's soup. Tropicana even managed to successfully export

---

[1]Comparison made on a single-strength juice basis.

their *Pure Premium* juice to Europe and Japan[4]. In 1998, Seagram sold Tropicana to Pepsi, placing the top two OJ brands into the midst of the ongoing marketing battle between soft-drink giants Coca-Cola and Pepsi Cola[5].

For second-place Minute Maid, the 1990s were more challenging. More invested in the FCOJ process, Coca-Cola emphasized their reconstituted ready-to-drink OJ as a response to consumer demand for convenience rather than NFC. Minute Maid was convinced of their technical ability to make a reconstituted OJ that tasted just as much like fresh juice as Tropicana's product, and to make it at a lower cost than NFC. While they also produced a NFC product, it was not their priority. In 1995, a Coca-Cola Foods VP of Marketing described their NFC product as only a "regional weapon in development of markets where they care[6]." This reference to a "regional" product here was an allusion to Tropicana's particular strength in the Northeast US. Around this time, Minute Maid also changed their OJ package graphics, subordinating the very long-standing "Black Box" containing the Minute Maid name against an orange background, and highlighting green and orange "Grove Colors" more akin to Tropicana's packaging. This change coincided with an FTNF flavor reformulation that increased their use of ethyl butyrate and other essence-oil related fractions in the search for a fresher juice flavor[7, 8]. In 1997, they dropped their NFC product entirely, believing that "a better product can be produced by concentrating juice at its peak of quality and then blending juice from those concentrates to produce the best-tasting juice possible[9]." Given Coca-Cola's world-class expertise in flavor science, their in-house experts in FTNF flavors at Special Products, and long experience in orange processing, there was quite a bit of internal confidence in their ability to succeed. But whether NFC was really a better product or not, consumer sentiment increasingly favored NFC. In 2001, Coca-Cola changed direction again and launched their *Simply Orange* brand of NFC orange juice. Despite all the effort and confidence, Coca-Cola's second-place standing behind Tropicana was firmly confirmed by this time. The future battle for the premium OJ market between Pepsi and Coca-Cola would entirely be over NFC orange juice.

The role of Coca-Cola's Special Products division in these flavor reformulations and new product formulations is a closely guarded secret, but the division remained a significant participant in the Florida citrus flavor market. However, Special Products was undergoing many internal changes. In the late 1980s, Carl Huffman, the original General Manager of Special Products, retired and was replaced by Wes Bucek, a long-time employee. Bucek, in turn, retired around 1996 and was succeeded by another veteran employee, Al Kruger, who retired in 2000[10, 11]. During Kruger's tenure, Special Products purchased significant amounts of specialized fractions containing ethyl butyrate from both Tastemaker/Givuadan (successor owners of Redd Laboratories as discussed below) and Firmenich, as their internal production capability was exceeded[7]. To maintain the secrecy of their FTNF flavors, Kruger would purchase "pieces" of their final flavors from different suppliers and blend them in-house. Special Products also continued to manage the production and use of their proprietary water-phase aroma, obtained from Minute Maid's customized essence units[7] as previously discussed (see pg. 127).

Given the dominance of top OJ brands and the rising NFC market, the citrus processing plants making FCOJ faced increasing economic pressure. Although total juice demand was slowly increasing, most demand shifted towards NFC and branded products, while FCOJ demand declined sharply. Only a few Florida processors sold juice under their own brand; most were producing either bulk FCOJ or packaging for third-party brands, known as "private label" production[12]. Competition in this declining market segment was fierce, and profitability decreased over time. Some processors attempted to establish their own brands. Citrus World, a citrus-grower cooperative dating back to the 1930s, successfully launched the *Florida's Natural* NFC brand in 1987, achieving national distribution in 1995 and becoming the third largest branded OJ[4, 13][2]. However, creating a national brand was challenging. Lykes Pasco, another long-time Florida citrus processor, launched a ready-to-drink OJ under the *Sunkist* brand in 1996, but high advertising and start-up costs led to steep initial financial losses, and Lykes exited the market after a few years[14]. Ultimately, there seemed to be room for only a few national OJ brands, and perhaps Lykes entered too late. The net result was financial pressure on the bulk FCOJ producers, and an industry consolidation. Once, Florida had more than 50 FCOJ processors, but by the early 1990s, only about 25 major plants remained[15]. As the decade progressed, a handful of plants associated with top brands consolidated the bulk of the Florida fruit supply

---

[2]The brand was originally named *Fresh n' Natural* when launched.

and expanded capacity, while the remaining plants competed for the leftovers. Some plants closed, while others merged operations with another facility or owner. By 1999, the Tampa Tribune reported that 22 plants handled 95% of the fruit in Florida, but only 15 of these operated at more than 50% capacity[16]. The Florida processing industry received a shock in 1996 when Minute Maid sold its two remaining Florida processing plants to the Brazilian OJ company Sucocitrico Cutrale Ltda[17]. Minute Maid was one of the oldest juice processors in Florida, dating back all the way to the origin of FCOJ in the 1940s. The Brazilian OJ industry, the world's largest producer since the early 1980s and a major competitor in global OJ markets with Florida, was not viewed kindly by some in the Florida industry. Minute Maid continued in the OJ business with their successful brands, but no longer operated processing plants. Soon after, another major Brazilian OJ processor, Citrosuco, purchased a different Florida processing facility. Despite the consolidation in Florida and these other changes, the total fruit processing capacity in Florida remained larger than ever.

A significant change from the previous decade was the improved growing conditions for citrus in Florida. Following the catastrophic freezes of the 1980s, the winter weather during this decade was milder. It certainly helped that more groves were now located in southern Florida, as few trees in the north were replanted. Between 1990 and 2000, there were only a few nights with dangerously freezing temperatures. Some fruit loss occurred, but the damage to citrus trees was minimal. In fact, the number of bearing commercial orange trees in Florida grew from 40.7 million in the 1990 census to 78.7 million in 2000[18]. As a result, fruit availability increased faster than juice demand, creating an ongoing concern about oversupply. Florida produced its largest orange crop ever in the 1997/98 season, reaching 248 million boxes of fruit. Reinforcing this problem, Brazil's orange crop was also at or near record levels during the same period, growing from 242 million boxes in the 1990/91 season to 355 million boxes in 2000/01[18]. Both growers and fruit processors experienced downward pressure on profitability as OJ prices fell. On the other hand, the lower prices made orange juice more economical for consumers, and as an ingredient in other beverage products. The Florida citrus industry had faced this oversupply issue several times before in its history, so it was not a new problem. Growers could reduce expenses by reducing grove care, and the planting of new or replacement trees could be delayed, while processors could reduce the amount of fruit processed or capital investments while waiting for demand to catch up with supply. The mix of fruit grown in Florida was also changing. Valencia oranges, the most desirable juice orange for its flavor and color, remained popular and commanded a premium price over other juice oranges, while earlier-maturing orange varieties saw less growth. Traditional tangerine varieties, sometimes blended into orange juice at low levels to improve the color, were replaced by easy-to-peel, seedless cultivars, which consumers preferred for fresh fruit. Unfortunately, the peel oils from these new varieties, like Sunburst or Robinson tangerines, were not very flavorful or interesting from a flavor industry perspective.

The situation with grapefruit was more problematic. Growers had been replacing seedy-grapefruit varieties with seedless ones, which were preferred in the fresh fruit market. Additionally, US consumer preferences were shifting toward colored (red or pink) grapefruit over the white-fleshed varieties. Consequently, processors increasingly segregated grapefruit juice and peel oils by color, responding to the growing price differential between colored and white grapefruit products. The market shift contributed to a nearly 40% increase in the number of bearing grapefruit trees from the 1989/90 to the 1999/2000 citrus seasons, with colored grapefruit varieties increasing faster than white[19]. However, grapefruit drinkers tended to be older consumers who enjoyed the perceived health benefits but did not mind the sometimes bitter, astringent character of the juice. With proper care, the juice could be produced with a delightfully sweet flavor, but this older consumer had traditionally been less sensitive to taste than other consumers. Unfortunately, in 1989, medical researchers discovered that certain natural chemicals in grapefruit juice could interfere with the function of a large class of medicines, including cholesterol-lowering drugs, which were increasingly prescribed to older adults. As the "Grapefruit Drug Interaction" became well-known, older adults were sometimes medically advised against consuming grapefruit juice. Just as the grapefruit supply was substantially increasing, total juice demand began to decline. Other effects also likely contributed including the growing availability of competing juice blends. Between the 1989/90 and 1999/2000 citrus seasons, juice demand decreased 13%, a drop of over 40% on a per-capita consumer basis[18]! This led to a significant oversupply of grapefruit, and the economic returns from harvesting and juicing fell below the costs. During the three seasons starting in 1995/96, many grapefruits were left unharvested in the groves[19], and some growers even removed healthy trees, reducing the grapefruit tree count from 14.2M trees in the 1996/97 season to 12.2M trees by 1999/2000.

These trends significantly impacted the citrus flavor industry. Despite the rising orange crop, the availability of essence oil from Florida decreased as more fruit was processed for NFC orange juice, which does not undergo the concentration process that allows for the recovery of water- and oil-phase essence. Consequently, demand for essence oil from Brazil rose. Oil-phase essence was the only source of the valuable flavor topnotes, including ethyl butyrate, which were crucial for the fresh, juicy flavor of premium orange juice. At the same time, growth in premium orange juice sales, including NFC, increased demand for these topnotes. For the flavoring companies, competition over the best raw materials grew, while the consolidation in number of juice processors reduced the number of suppliers. The remaining plants, which controlled larger portions of the essence in Florida, negotiated package deals that bundled essence products together. This forced flavoring companies to accept lower-quality essence lots and products they did not always need, such as d-limonene or water-phase aroma, to secure essence oil. Purchases of essence from Brazil, now the largest FCOJ producer in the world, increased and the flavor companies looked to other citrus growing regions, like Mexico or Costa Rica, for raw materials. Within the tight-knit Florida citrus flavor industry, the adage "You made your money on the purchasing" was commonly acknowledged[3].

In response to growing variety of juice products, the citrus flavor industry increased its investment in applications expertise for the design and use of FTNF flavors. By this time, the basic science of orange juice flavoring was largely resolved, but challenges persisted in selecting fractions to construct FTNF flavors for specific juice applications and in testing and presenting these products to customers. These application specialists were in some ways similar to flavorists, but applied a much more specialized knowledge focused predominantly on juice beverages. There was no official training for these specialists, and candidates typically gained juice expertise working within the Florida juice industry before transitioning to the flavor companies. Firmenich and Hercules Redd Citrus were among the first companies to recognize the impor-

---

[3]I first heard this expressed by Wesley Beck, an owner of Florida Flavors. I am sure there were many variants and the original source is unknown to me.

tance of this role. Firmenich, in particular, after acquiring Intercit, was the first company to invest in specialized applications laboratories equipped to mimic commercial-scale juice pasteurization and packaging[20, 21]. Others in the industry soon followed.

The increased production of NFC juice, which reduced the availability of essence oil, had little impact on the availability of peel oil, as it was still recovered from the processed fruit. With the rising crop sizes in Florida and Brazil, orange peel oil and distilled terpenes from the oil were abundant and reached historically low prices. By the late 1990s, some Brazilian processors even began using d-limonene as boiler fuel. In Florida in 1998, Wesley Beck from Florida Flavors recalls purchasing good-quality Valencia orange oil at prices as low as $0.17 per pound[22], compared to the average historical price of around $1 per pound. This surplus facilitated new product innovations. For example, the low cost of terpenes, combined with their positive perception as a natural, environmentally-friendly solvent compared to petrochemicals, opened new markets in products such as cleaners, degreasers and paint-removers. In the flavor industry, excess peel oil was often folded to sell the terpenes separately, but inventories of folded peel oils exceeded market demand. This surplus let to efforts to isolate various natural aroma chemicals and new fractions from the peel oil for non-FTNF applications. One example was nonanal or C-9 aldehyde, a potent aroma chemical that is rare in nature and present at only about 0.1% in good quality orange peel oil. At this concentration, it took more than 1,000,000# of processed oranges to produce three pounds of pure nonanal. In combination with all the other things that could be isolated from peel oil, it became feasible to try to commercialize these types of products. Florida Flavors and Tastemaker were among the companies that offered nonanal during this period. Additionally, several other peel-oil derived fractions were commercialized across the industry.

While orange oil was in surplus, sourcing for grapefruit and Dancy tangerine oils was more difficult. Few new Dancy trees had been planted following the freezes in the 1980s, replaced instead by new seedless, easy-to-peel varieties, which were not suitable substitutes. Dancy oil became increasingly difficult to purchase. In the case of grapefruit, colored oils became increasingly available compared to white grapefruit oil. However, white oils often contained higher levels of nootkatone, a key indicator of grapefruit oil quality. Additionally, some customers perceived flavor differences between the colors, favoring one over another for specific applications. Over time, white oils became more expensive, a trend reinforced by the higher average nootkatone content and the growing number of colored grapefruit trees. The economic abandonment of grapefruit in the last half of the decade preferentially affected white grapefruit, the least desirable for fresh fruit or for juice. The Florida flavor companies passed these increased raw material costs on to their customers. However, customers could choose to reformulate their products to minimize or avoid using these costly ingredients. If one or more large customers reformulated, demand for a specialized oil could drop sharply, destabilizing the price. Since the flavor industry needed to purchase these products seasonally and maintain sufficient inventory for annual production, a sudden price drop could lead to substantial financial losses due to the inventory held. Moreover, once a customer undertook the difficult process of reformulating a product, they rarely reverted even if prices later moderated.

The World Flavor Market

As the decade of the 1990s began, the flavor industry as a whole was operating quite optimistically. Growth in the 1980s had been very strong, around 8.5% per year, with expectations for continued growth at the 5–6 % per year rate for the next decade[23, 24]. Trade barriers worldwide were falling, and markets in Asia (due to economic growth) and Europe (due to the fall of communism and the rise of the EU[4]) were expected to grow rapidly. The largest flavor and fragrance (F&F) companies were all looking to expand their business by taking advantage of international markets. Several of these large F&F companies were owned by much larger chemical and pharmaceutical companies, which had been acquiring flavor companies since the 1960s. The growth expectations and margins in the F&F business were quite attractive for these owners, and the technology overlapped well with their core businesses. Yet, the flavor industry remained fragmented, with the top 10 flavor companies accounting for only approximately 60% of worldwide flavor sales[23]. As the industry grew worldwide, a number of important trends influenced the industry and consequently the niche citrus flavor

---

[4]East and West Germany united in October, 1990 and the Euro currency came into formal existence on Jan 1, 1999, after a decade of planning.

industry in Florida.

First, the largest flavor use for citrus oils worldwide was for beverage flavors, including carbonated and non-carbonated soft-drinks, juices, and to a lesser degree, alcoholic products[25]. The beverage industry was one of the largest markets for the flavor industry as a whole. Within the beverage category, orange and lemon/lime-flavored beverages were the second largest sellers, behind colas which also utilized citrus oils within their formulations. World demand for these beverages had been growing strongly for some time and was expected to continue growing at 3–5% per year, driving increased demand for citrus oils, fractions, and compounded flavors[25]. Consequently, all major flavor companies wanted to be proficient in citrus flavors.

Second, the formation and acquisition of small flavor companies remained a constant feature of the industry. The barriers to entry into the flavor business were rather low, with moderate equipment costs and technical sophistication, for persons with the right know-how and customer access. While supplier reputation was critically important for food companies purchasing flavors, since these manufacturers risked ruined products and disappointed customers if something went wrong with the flavor, the personal reputations of the owners or key employees of a new flavor company could suffice, especially if the company possessed critical know-how, favorable raw-material access, or other advantages. Consequently, small privately-owned flavor companies with expertise in one area could start and operate, similar to Florex Flavors in 1984, but these organizations would struggle to grow beyond a certain market size associated with their product area of expertise. At the same time, the larger flavor companies faced difficulties with organic growth in new product areas since success and expertise in one area of flavors, say mint products, did not easily transfer to other flavor areas. Instead, they often found it easier to acquire product expertise and existing sales by purchasing successful smaller companies. This dynamic drove a constant stream of small acquisitions by the larger flavor companies. The purchase of Intercit by Firmenich in 1988, or Florex Flavors by Hercules in 1989, were in no way unusual for the flavor industry.

There was also strong consolidation pressure among the largest companies driven by two main forces during this time. First, the largest consumer-products companies, which were the major customers of the flavor companies, were looking for core suppliers who could provide as many of their flavor needs as possible, especially under some sort of volume pricing. Being approved as a core supplier required a certain size and scope that smaller companies found more difficult to achieve. Many of the consumer product companies were also moving to outsource more of their product development steps to the flavor companies, requiring more in-house (and expensive) expertise from the suppliers in areas such as consumer testing, finished-product chemistry, shelf-life evaluation, and regulatory issues. Second, the combination of two large flavor companies always provided a tempting means to acquire both expertise and enhanced profit margins through synergies achieved by combining corporate support operations such as accounting or regulatory support, reducing the total headcount, and still supporting the increased total sales. Hence, of the largest ten flavor companies in 1990, three would be acquired by the other seven by the year 2000. By way of example, PFW, which was owned by Hercules in 1990, would be merged with Fries & Fries in 1992 and the combined company would later be purchased by Givaudan in 1998.

Another important trend was the increased consumer interest in natural, or at the very least, non-artificial flavors. In both the US and European consumer markets, while flavor ingredients did not need to be disclosed, the product ingredient list was required to disclose the type of flavor used. In Europe, three main categories were recognized: artificial flavors, natural flavors, and nature-identical flavors. The latter utilized the same aroma chemicals found in nature, but these chemicals could be sourced from cheaper, non-natural sources. In the US, only two main categories were recognized: natural or artificial flavors[5]. Throughout the 1990s, consumers increasingly associated the term "natural" as a positive descriptor of foods. Consequently, food manufacturers and their flavor suppliers, especially in the US where nature-identical flavors were not an option, were pushed toward natural flavors. This drove demand both for citrus flavors in general, which were relatively easy to manufacture as all-natural given the availability of citrus oils and essences, and for certain citrus fractions which were economical, all-natural sources of particular concentrated flavor chemicals. For example, artificial grapefruit flavors had been made for some time by combining folded grapefruit oils with synthetic nootkatone, a powerful aroma compound with grapefruit character. Producing an all-

---

[5]FTNF flavors, such as were used in orange or apple juice, were considered "juice" and not "flavors" under existing food regulations. To the extent these flavors were used in non-juice products, they were simply natural flavors.

natural grapefruit flavor was more expensive and required the type of nootkatone fraction that the citrus flavor industry in Florida specialized in producing. As consumer product companies reformulated or introduced new products to meet consumer demand for natural flavors, the Florida-based industry saw rising demand for their natural citrus-based products.

Finally, as the largest flavor companies competed for growth throughout this decade, two in particular, Firmenich and Tastemaker, did very well in growing their worldwide business and reputations. Firmenich was introduced earlier in the discussion of the Intercit acquisition. Tastemaker, a new company formed in 1992 and including Hercules' Redd Citrus business, is discussed in more detail below. The success of these two companies was due to many varied factors, but it was a fact that both companies had major citrus-oriented operations located in Florida. Within their marketing strategies, they emphasized their excellence in citrus to their customers. Unlike their competitors who purchased citrus raw materials from Florida and processed them elsewhere, both Firmenich and Tastemaker would highlight their investment in location, facilities, and expertise in the "heart of the citrus industry." Furthermore they marketed that their day-to-day presence in the citrus market allowed them access to the "best" raw materials and the newest and most sophisticated citrus flavoring products. This was a compelling story and certainly didn't hurt their sales efforts. In addition, as Florida was a warm and sunny place, especially in the winter, it was popular to invite key customers for a tour of their facilities and a citrus grove or fruit processing plant. How important this was to their overall success is debatable, but the undisputed result was to drive interest in "citrus centers of excellence" among other large flavor companies. Thus, the other flavor companies would routinely visit Florida looking for opportunities to partner with fruit processing plants for specialized raw materials, or for acquisition opportunities similar to those of Intercit or Florex Flavors, or even to start a new operation. This provided attractive business opportunities for any independent citrus flavor business as they could leverage this interest into product sales and possible partnerships or an acquisition. It also offered interesting employment opportunities for knowledgeable specialists in the Florida industry.

The Florida-based citrus flavor industry was swept along with these major trends affecting the world-wide flavor industry. It was a very favorable environment for growth, but each of the local companies responded in their own particular ways.

Hercules Citrus Specialties and Tastemaker

Following the acquisition of Florex Flavors by Hercules in 1989, the integration of Florex (in Lakeland) and Redd Citrus (in Safety Harbor) proceeded, with both production facilities remaining operational. Mike Taylor managed the two facilities from his Safety Harbor headquarters. During this time, Hercules made a more concerted effort to integrate the Florida citrus operations with the PFW flavor business. Although some long-time employees retired after the acquisition, and a few others were reassigned within Hercules, the combined staff in Florida was still the largest and most experienced among the competitors. The organization was now called Redd Citrus Specialties, and was primed for continued success as its largest customers, the juice and beverage producers, were expanding their sales worldwide.

However, on a broader scale, Hercules' Food and Flavor Ingredients Group was experiencing difficulties. The effort that began in the early 1980s to combine the sales efforts for such a diverse set of products had not been particularly successful for their flavor business. In practice, their customers' purchasing processes for low-cost, bulk food ingredients differed greatly from those for high-priced, low-volume flavor products. Additionally, the skills required of successful salespeople in these different product categories diverged[26]. The anticipated efficiencies of the combination were slow to materialize. In fact, total sales of PFW and Hercules Redd Citrus together between 1990 and 1991 increased by only 1.4%, reaching $96.6 million[27].

In December 1991, Hercules, along with the major pharmaceutical and chemical company Mallinckrodt Specialty Chemical Co., announced the formation of a joint venture to combine both of their flavor-related businesses into a new independent flavor company[28]. Hercules would contribute PFW and Redd Citrus Specialties to the joint venture with total sales of around $100,000,000 per year. Mallinckrodt would contribute Fries & Fries, a Cincinnati-based flavor company with annual sales of around $70,000,000 that Mallinckrodt had acquired in 1970[29]. The joint entity was legally formed in February 1992, named Tastemaker a few months later, and, based upon total sales, was the fifth largest flavor company in the world[30, 31].

For the Florida-based Redd Citrus team, this was a big change. Fortunately, although the Fries & Fries company had its own internal citrus oil processing in Cincinnati, the scale was much smaller than that in Florida. An important focus in Cincinnati was on alcoholic-extractions of citrus oils, a process largely ignored in Florida, which very much complemented the overall citrus portfolio for the combined company. There was very little overlap that might signal consolidation and future job losses. Mike Taylor remained in charge, now with the new title of Vice-President and General Manager of Citrus Specialties[32]. Following the formation of Tastemaker, it was decided that Redd Citrus would consolidate its two facilities into the newer Lakeland site. Redd Citrus had occupied their Safety Harbor facility since the late 1960s when Pinellas County was a major citrus growing region. However, since then, much of the citrus industry on Florida's West Coast had moved elsewhere, and Pinellas County was rapidly urbanizing. For the employees, living near Lakeland, in central Florida, was much less desirable than coastal Pinellas County. As a result, a number of staff resigned, and Firmenich, located right next door in Safety Harbor, was able to hire some very experienced people. Nevertheless, the consolidation into the Lakeland facility was carried out in 1992 and 1993, with distillation stills and other processing and laboratory equipment moved to the Lakeland site. Following the move, the old Safety Harbor site, dating back to Jim Redd's Redd Laboratories, was sold to Firmenich[33].

The Tastemaker joint venture proved quite successful. The new organization was highly focused with experienced flavor industry personnel from both Fries & Fries and PFW in senior management positions. The Fries & Fries sales team was particularly strong in the US, while PFW had a stronger international team. The product portfolios of the two companies also meshed well. Once operational, Tastemaker invested heavily in flavorists for product development and applications specialists who supported sales by demonstrating how their flavors could be incorporated into customers' finished products. Additionally, Tastemaker introduced an important innovation linked to the growth of overnight shipping during this period. Traditionally, flavor samples for customer evaluations were made to order, a process that ensured freshness and minimized waste, but it could take a week or more to make and deliver samples. Tastemaker developed a 24-hour turnaround model for their flavors, utilizing carefully-managed sample stocks and extended-hour sampling lab operations, along with overnight delivery. This innovation was very attractive to customers and pressured all of Tastemaker's competitors to respond similarly.

For Tastemaker's citrus operation in Florida, and all the Florida competitors, the change in sampling expectations was particularly challenging. Traditional compounded flavors made outside of Florida were usually produced with nearly pure flavor compounds that tasted identical lot-to-lot. Even for natural extractions and essential oils, which were chemically complex, the flavor industry was very adept at minimizing flavor variation within its raw materials. However, controlling this variation was more difficult for the Florida industry, which derived all its products from raw oils and essences that could exhibit large natural flavor variations, even when coming from identical fruit varieties. Lot-to-lot flavor variations were common from the beginning of the season to the end, from one processing plant to another, and from the same plant from one season to the next. A further complication was that small differences in the raw materials could be magnified during distillation or extraction processes. Managing this variation was a constant production challenge in Florida. For add-back juice flavors, the acceptable amount of flavor variation was decreasing over time as orange juice manufacturers became more sophisticated in standardizing their product flavors all season long. Additionally, flavor customers outside of the juice industry were already accustomed to smaller lot-to-lot flavor variations. One common way to mitigate this problem had been to generate custom flavor samples from raw materials currently in inventory that could subsequently be held for a specific customer. But this process was difficult to implement with very rapid sample turn-around times, as product samples had to be available before being requested by customers. The challenge of implementing rapid sample turnaround affected all aspects of traditional operations and impacted almost every employee. It was a continual source of internal friction as habits were changed, new processes implemented, and the inevitable mistakes were made.

Within Tastemaker, the Florida citrus operation continued to promote FTNF flavors for juice, but there was a new effort to produce specialized citrus flavor fractions and other fractions, using similar technology, for non-juice applications. Tim Anglea led this activity, developing several citrus isolates such as c9-aldehyde, as well as mint oil isolates (trans-2-hexenal and cis-3-hexenol) and concentrated fractions from apple aroma. A number of these products were commercially successful, sold both as concentrated fractions to external customers (for use in manufacturing their own compounded flavors), and used internally by Tastemaker for their own compounded flavors. Apple aroma, a standardized water-soluble FTNF flavoring material from apple juice, was a particular growth area for the Florida operation. Anglea, who had previously developed similar apple products with Allen Kryger at Florex Flavors, also experimented with pineapple and tomato aromas, but these were not as commercially successful.

Sales of citrus products to Japan continued to expand during the 1990s. Tastemaker had a strong sales presence in Japan, where consumers were particularly receptive to innovative new beverage products, many of which were citrus-flavored. Grapefruit oils remained a product in high demand, and this market was also favorable for the specialized citrus fractions that Tastemaker was now producing. The Japanese were known to pay well for new and innovative flavoring ingredients. Additionally, Tastemaker's growth in other areas of Asia, including China, was strong.

During Tastemaker's first five years in operation, the company emphasized its expertise in citrus flavors. They also made significant investments in the Florida facility and hosted many customers and guests for tours. The site became a popular stopover, especially in winter, combined with activities like golf, fishing, or visits to theme parks.

In 1997, Tastemaker was acquired by the Swiss company Givaudan, another major flavor company, to form the world's first or second largest flavor and fragrance company[34]. As with any acquisition, major changes were expected in the transition. Mike Taylor retired shortly after the sale, and Tim Anglea left for a position at Coca-Cola in 1998. Over the next few years, Givaudan transitioned the Florida site into a manufacturing facility, moving most of the the other activities including R&D, product management, sales coordination, and most purchasing to its US headquarters in Cincinnati, OH.

Firmenich

Firmenich was operating its Florida-based Citrus Center at the old Intercit site in Safety Harbor, adjacent to Hercules's Redd Citrus facility. Given the close physical proximity and overlapping business interests, both parties were generally aware of each other's activities. In the first few years following the acquisition of Intercit, Firmenich invested considerable resources in the operation, upgrading the facilities, investing in state-of-the-art product applications laboratories, and bringing in new staff with worldwide coordination responsibilities. Firmenich worked diligently to integrate the new citrus portfolio into its worldwide flavor and fragrance operations, resulting in a significant increase in both purchasing of raw materials and internal sales from Florida.

In 1991, Firmenich acquired MCP Industrial Foods, a manufacturer of powdered and encapsulated fruit flavors based in Anaheim, CA[35]. Utilizing this technology, Firmenich developed their *Durarome* line of dry, encapsulated flavors. A manufacturing line for mostly citrus-based *Durarome* flavors was installed in Safety Harbor and soon operated 24 hours a day[36]. Firmenich also began citrus oil washing operations in Florida using batch-based alcohol extraction, a traditional process ubiquitous in the flavor industry, but not previously conducted on a large scale by either Intercit or Redd Citrus. Additionally, Firmenich hired Nick Tarquinio as a permanent, Florida-based flavorist to replace the part-time flavorist hired after the acquisition. Tarquinio would remain in Florida for over a decade[37]. Finally, when Tastemaker announced the consolidation of its Safety Harbor site into Lakeland, Firmenich was able to recruit a number of experienced employees from Tastemaker who preferred not to relocate.

In the first five years following the acquisition, Firmenich's Safety Harbor staff increased from about 40 to 60 employees[37]. Sales out of Florida increased about 500% in the same time-span[38]. By the year 2000, Safety Harbor would grow to approximately 120 employees[37]. Like their main competitor, Tastemaker, the primary focus remained on FTNF products, both for juice add-back flavors, and as internal ingredients to support Firmenich products compounded elsewhere. However, there were important points of differentiation from Tastemaker. First, Firmenich maintained a citrus oil processing facility in Brazil. As Brazilian essences and aromas became increasingly important, Firmenich was able to concentrate some of these products in Brazil, shipping the most important flavor volatiles to Florida while managing the bulk byproducts locally. Second, Firmenich was committed to a "full-service" citrus operation in Florida, housing purchasing, flavorists, applications specialists, and sales staff all in one location. In contrast, Tastemaker was less committed to enhanced technical, purchasing and sales roles in Florida. Finally, Firmenich was particularly focused on using its citrus fractions in internally-compounded flavors rather than selling them externally. In contrast, Tastemaker was more open to supplying its citrus fractions to companies that compounded their own flavors. Some of these fractions were quite profitable to sell, especially when manufactured as a byproduct of other internal processes. However, the buyers of these concentrated fractions were generally quite different from the customers for finished flavors, which was Firmenich's preferred market. Interestingly, Firmenich chose not to produce FTNF apple flavors, unlike many of their Florida competitors.

Sunpure

In 1988, just prior to the sale of Florex Flavors to Hercules, the owners Kryger, Lashkajani, and the Todd family formed a new company named Sunpure Ltd. Following the sale of Florex, the principals were bound by a non-compete agreement, and Sunpure's initial activity was to acquire and refurbish an old citrus plant in Avon Park, FL. They also installed a distillation column and soon began processing apple aroma to make standardized FTNF apple flavors, which were not retricted by their non-compete agreement. The early years presented difficulties for Sunpure, as the major December 1989 freeze impacted their first year of fruit processing, and the US entered a recession in 1990 that dampened the outlook for juice sales. By late 1991, they were forecasting annual sales of nearly $32,000,000, mostly from juice sales but nearly 12% resulting from apple flavors[39].

In early 1992, a bitter dispute arose between Lashkajani and Kryger. The initial cause is unknown, but it quickly escalated into an unmanageable situation, leading to very uncomfortable standoffs where employees were forced to choose between conflicting instructions. Unable to resolve their disagreement, they invoked an existing forced buy/sell agreement among the owners, with the Todd stuck in the middle. Over a few months, the details were negotiated, and in the end, Kryger sold his interest in Sunpure, officially exiting the business in September 1992 with a plan to create his own new company.

Sunpure continued operations without Kryger. A number of key employees left over the next six months to join Kryger's new venture, but this gave Lashkajani the opportunity to hire his own hand-picked staff. Anticipating the end of their five year non-compete agreement with Hercules, Sunpure set out to create a flavor division. An experienced professional chemist from the US flavor industry, Jim Mazetis, was hired in June 1993, and Sunpure acquired land in Lakeland, FL in February 1994 to construct a new flavor facility. For Lashkajani, this would be the fourth citrus flavor facility he had built over his time at Florex Flavors and Sunpure. New office buildings and production facilities were completed in 1995, and distillation stills were designed and installed. Sunpure also relocated the Avon Park distillation equipment to their new Lakeland facility.

In 1996, Sunpure completed the construction of a 445,000 ft^3 tank farm at the Lakeland site for the refrigerated storage of citrus oils and terpenes[40]. This tank farm proved important for Sunpure, as Lashkajani recognized that grapefruit and orange terpenes contained trace levels of important and expensive flavor components like nootkatone and valencene, which he could recover and sell by efficiently distilling large quantities of terpenes. The distilled terpenes, which were of excellent quality after distillation, could be sold into the existing market, and the flavor components could be recovered and further purified for sale. Lashkajani also developed the innovative idea of offering "participation" to some of his terpene suppliers, whereby they would receive a cut of the profits generated from Sunpure's storage and handling of their terpenes. In order to improve the processing throughput, Sunpure designed and installed a new still allowing them to process a full tanker of terpenes (80+ drums) in one batch[41]. It was the largest still in the industry at that time.

In 1997, Sunpure bought the Indian River Foods citrus processing plant, giving Sunpure more direct access to grapefruit products[42]. In the year 2000, Sunpure and Cargill created a joint venture to operate their citrus processing facilities in Florida together[43]. FCOJ processing plants in Florida were consolidating under reduced consumer demand, and neither company possessed a national OJ brand like Minute Maid, Tropicana or Florida's Natural. Sunpure was positioning themselves to exit the juice processing business and retain the more profitable citrus flavor business in Lakeland.

Florida Flavors

In the summer of 1992, as Allen Kryger was embroiled in his dispute with Lashkajani, he incorporated a new company called Florida Flavors Inc. Following his departure from Sunpure in September, he set out to establish a new citrus flavor company, leaving the FCOJ business behind. Joining him were his son-in-law Wesley Beck and a small group of former Sunpure employees. Kryger, a chemist, had always been more interested in technical matters than in day-to-day business affairs. At both Florex Flavors and Sunpure, he had relied on Lashkajani to manage those details. Now, he relied on Beck, who had degrees in business and accounting and experience working outside the citrus industry. For Kryger, there were many challenges ahead, but he was financially comfortable and, for the first time in his life, the sole business owner. During his time at Sunpure, he witnessed the substantial capital requirements and risks associated with the orange juice processing industry. He was happier now to focus on the flavor business, working with a team of employees he truly enjoyed.

Kryger purchased a small warehouse and office building in Lakeland as a base of operations for his new company. However, he was still theoretically bound by his April 1989 non-compete agreement with Hercules, which limited his citrus activities for five years. The formation of Tastemaker had complicated the exact status of this agreement, originally signed with Hercules, at least from Kryger's perspective. Initially, this wasn't a problem as the facility needed extensive renovations, and specialized equipment, including tanks, distillation columns, and laboratory equipment, had to be designed and installed.

By 1993, the last year of the Hercules non-compete agreement, the new facility was fully operational and Kryger had begun purchasing and distilling citrus oils and essences. Not giving much thought to the agreement (and never one to fuss over inconvenient details), Kryger began to test the limits of the agreement by selling some citrus products. Additionally, in October 1993, Florida Flavors hired Gil Escobar from Tastemaker, one of Kryger's former employees from Florex Flavors. Kryger had earlier also hired two other former Tastemaker employees for Florida Flavors. Apparently, this was the last straw for Tastemaker's Mike Taylor, Kryger's old colleague from Redd Laboratories. In December 1993, Tastemaker filed a lawsuit against Kryger for breach of the non-compete agreement, seeking an immediate injunction to shut down

Florida Flavors[22]. Kryger responded by hiring Holland & Knight, a major Florida law firm, to contest the suit. Extensive legal maneuvers took place over 1994 and 1995. In the end, a settlement was reached in July 1995, whereby Florida Flavors paid compensation to Tastemaker in exchange for dropping all claims regarding past activities under the now-expired non-compete agreement. The compensation was paid in the form of 23,400 pounds of white grapefruit oil and 7,800 pounds of Dancy tangerine oil[44]. Kryger harbored bitter feeling regarding this lawsuit for some time afterward.

Despite the lawsuit, Florida Flavors managed to grow rapidly during this period in both sales and employees. Kryger's son, this work's author and a Ph.D. physicist, joined the company in a technical role in early 1995. At that time, there were approximately 25 employees. Once free of the legal distraction with Tastemaker, Allen Kryger and his team could fully focus on their business. Unlike Sunpure, where juice concentrate was the largest product, Florida Flavors was in many ways a reincarnation of Florex Flavors, competing mostly in the FTNF flavor business. But unlike Florex, Florida Flavors was competing against two multinational corporations, Firmenich and Tastemaker, as well as Sunpure and Treatt USA.

Lacking the infrastructure of a large flavor company, Florida Flavors had to operate leanly and with a sharp focus. Allen Kryger himself led the technical activities and product development for the company. His right-hand technical man was a bright, intense young Ph.D. chemist named David McKeithan, whom he had first started training a few years earlier at Sunpure. He also had to train his son Robert, the author. Beck and Escobar managed the operations and sales activities for Florida Flavors. Initially, the product mix focused on those products Allen Kryger had produced at Florex or Redd Laboratories, including basic peel oils, FTNF flavors, enriched aromas, terpenes and apple aromas. Later on, Florida Flavors hired some juice applications experts and even a flavorist and developed a number of new and successful citrus flavors. In time, Florida Flavors was supplying both Tropicana and Coca-Cola's Special Products along with other customers. Outside of the US, sales into Japan and Germany were significant. Meanwhile, McKeithan and Robert Kryger developed some new citrus fractions which were commercialized, primarily using the abundance of low-cost orange peel oil available at the time, as well as apple and mint fractions. One notable fraction they developed was orange polymethoxylated flavones

(PMFs), isolated from leftover orange peel oil after most of the primary flavor-active components and all of the terpenes had been removed. The naturally occurring PMF's were of increasing interest during this time for their possible health benefits, and they were also found to possess some secondary mouthfeel character in citrus flavors[45]. Allen Kryger was quite supportive of these types of R&D efforts, and many different projects were explored, but in the end the most profitable business for Florida Flavors remained the EB-containing FTNF flavors.

By 1997, Florida Flavors was operating profitably with just over 50 employees, but future growth opportunities were limited. OJ sales were no longer growing, and FTNF flavor production was in any case limited by the availability of ethyl butyrate and related topnote fractions. Florida Flavors had made some efforts to expand into natural, non-FTNF flavors but with limited success. They didn't possess the infrastructure to develop, manufacture and sell hundreds or thousands of flavors that their multinational competitors had. Meanwhile, Givaudan had just acquired Tastemaker, including its Florida citrus flavor operation, and "citrus expertise in Florida" was a topic of discussion among the top flavor companies. Several of these flavor companies made visits to Florida Flavors expressing interest in partnerships or outright sales. Allen Kryger had experienced this before at Florex Flavors and knew what to expect. However, this time he was the majority owner of his company and felt no particular need to sell. His son and son-in-law, who were now minority shareholders, however, were looking at the industry with a longer time horizon in mind and they were less optimistic about the future. In 1998, tragedy struck when Allen's wife was killed in an automobile accident. Following this accident, the tide slowly turned toward a serious consideration of offering the company for sale. It would take a couple more years, but Florida Flavors was sold in 2001 to the Danish flavor company Danisco, which was trying to build a large flavor company through acquisitions.

Treatt

In the early 1990s, Florida Treatt faced challenges operating in Florida as they were newcomers to the state, a topic discussed in the previous chapter. However, over time, they gained experience with the competitive markets in Florida, and with their new processing equipment.

They also hired some experienced local personnel who brought important know-how and connections. One significant mid-1990s hire was Tom Antonik as General Manager, who had previously worked at both Sunpure and Florida Flavors. Gradually, Treatt began to emphasize their point of differentiation as a supplier of flavoring ingredients to the flavor market, positioning themselves not as competitors but as partners to the major flavor companies.

In the late 1990s, Treatt purchased a Spinning Cone Column concentrator (SCC) and began developing water-soluble citrus essences as well as isolating essences from other food products such as teas, non-citrus fruits and vegetables. The SCC concentrator was capable of processing thick juices and purees, including those from cucumbers or watermelons. This technology, distinct from a TASTE evaporator with a standard essence unit, originated from the Australia wine industry in the late 1980s[46]. Treatt marketed these SCC-derived essences as an additional point of differentiation from other local flavor companies.

Takasago

In 1992, joining two other top-10 flavor companies, Tastemaker and Firmenich, Takasago began a significant relationship in Florida. They started importing grapefruit juices and essences under a multi-season agreement with the Indian River Foods citrus processing plant in Ft. Pierce, Florida[47, pg. 40-53]. The Japanese flavor industry had long been an important consumer of grapefruit products, including oils and essences, from Florida. As the largest Japanese flavor company, Takasago considered Florida grapefruit essential for its home market and aimed to establish a strong relationship with a Florida grapefruit processor. In 1996, Takasago further installed specialized essence recovery equipment at the Indian River plant, including a SCC concentrator, under a supply agreement[48]. The Indian River plant was acquired by Sunpure in 1998, and Takasago continued their supply agreement for grapefruit products with Sunpure.

Local Industry Trends

During this decade several external factors affected all the competitors in the Florida citrus flavor industry. These included important developments in technology, business practices and consumer trends.

One of the most important technological factors was the growing sophistication of chemical analysis capabilities in the industry. Gas chromatographs (GCs) had become routine instruments for analyzing citrus oil fractions. These devices could separate very small quantities of a citrus oil into its chemical constituents, which could then be detected and quantified. The separation process typically took 30 to 60 minutes per sample. In combination with a chemical detector that was sensitive to hydrocarbons, a GC analysis could provide a relatively quick snapshot of most chemical constituents in a citrus oil. Early GC detectors were not very sensitive, but as both separation and detector technology improved, it became feasible to quantify more than 100 individual chemicals in a citrus oil in under 60 minutes. This data complemented the traditional quality parameters for citrus oils, such as the refractive index, density, appearance, total aldehyde content as measured by titration, and a human odor and flavor evaluation. All this data had to be evaluated quickly to make raw material purchase decisions, guide manufacturing processes, or ensure the quality of finished products. One complication was that while the flavor industry had established standard analysis methods for the more traditional tests used for citrus oils, such as the total aldehyde test, there were no standard GC methods at this time. Each company developed its own methods.

Sometimes, certain trace chemicals present at only a few parts-per-million or less in a sample could significantly impact its value. In such cases, quantifying these trace chemicals was crucial, even if routine GC analysis lacked the necessary sensitivity. Examples included trace pesticide or fungicide contaminants in a citrus oil that restricted its use in certain countries, or specific chemicals that could indicate intentional adulteration of a citrus oil sample. In these cases, additional GC measurements with specialized detectors might be required. One increasingly common specialized detector was the mass spectrometer, which when combined with the GC was called the GCMS. During the 1990s, these instruments became increasingly common in Florida. The GCMS not only separated the input sample into its many chemical components, but also broke up the components into hundreds of chemical fragments in a way that allowed more accurate identification, especially the less-intense, trace compounds. However, the consequence of this new sensitivity was the collection of thousands of times more raw data for each sample analyzed. Alongside the use of GC and GCMS machines, high-pressure liquid chromatography (HPLC) was also beginning to be used for the analysis of certain less-volatile citrus oil constituents that were difficult to measure by GC. In each case, these new tools were generating significant quantities of data which were useless without human interpretation.

As companies grew in size and complexity, they were evaluating more and more raw materials for purchase and managing a greater breadth of simultaneous manufacturing processes. The large quantity of samples requiring rapid analysis and the resulting volume of raw data needing quick evaluation and interpretation motivated several changes in laboratory practices. First, there was an increasing need for more highly trained chemists and chemical analysis specialists to staff these laboratories. Traditionally, the citrus flavor analysis methods had been rather simple, and technicians were relatively easy to train. Perhaps the most challenging training involved sensory testing, which required both a specific aptitude and considerable practice. But these newer more sophisticated tools required significant expertise. They also required regular maintenance and calibration, and their results often required individualized interpretation. It became increasingly common for Ph.D. chemists to be hired to oversee and operate these laboratories, and the lab staff, in general, needed more technical training. A related problem was managing the use and storage of all this data. For a prospective orange oil sample being considered for purchase, what analysis data was needed? How much time was available for analysis? What sort of interpretation was required from the lab? What data would the purchasing staff actually need to see? Once purchased, what sort of data needed to be kept as a permanent record? Likewise, as an oil sample passed through the manufacturing process where it might be distilled into many different fractions, each fraction might be separately analyzed, and decisions regarding interpretation and record-keeping needed to be made again. The process flow considerations and record-keeping decisions regarding all of this data were daunting. Fortunately, the cost of computer data storage hardware was decreasing and the power of laboratory data management software systems was increasing. However, no off-the-shelf software existed for this niche industry, nor was there existing software from some outside industry that was easy to adapt. In particular, the software systems used by the wider flavor industry were not well-suited for the Florida flavor industry. While flavor companies typically blended ingredients, the Florida industry focused on separating components. Custom software was always a possibility, but the upfront and long-term costs were always larger than expected and development times long. Each individual company faced compromises on how to integrate purchasing, inventory, and finished product systems with the vast quantity of laboratory data.

Much of the driving motivation behind sample analysis was to identify the best raw materials and guide the production process. However, the additional problem of avoiding adulterated raw materials was also an ongoing concern. The adulteration of citrus oils for economic benefit has a long history. Diluting authentic, expensive citrus oils with carefully selected, less-expensive turpentine oils or petroleum-derived oils, in a manner designed to fool chemical tests for density or refractive index, dates back to the 1800s[49, pg. 29]. Dishonest traders have always existed on the periphery of legitimate commercial trade, attempting to pass adulterated oils off as authentic for financial gain. Of course, buyers used their best wits to avoid adulterated materials. As chemical analysis techniques improved throughout the 20th century, there was a constant struggle between more sophisticated chemical tests, on the one hand, and new, harder-to-detect methods of adulteration, on the other. The citrus flavor industry had to be concerned about suspicious samples. In most cases, adulteration was never proven absolutely but only suspected. Yet, the potential for financial loss was high, as merely the suspicion of offering adulterated products was enough to tarnish the business reputation of a legitimate company with an important customer. GC technology was very useful for screening for some types of adulteration, especially when used by experienced analysts, and this was a routine part of analyzing potential raw materials. It certainly made adulteration more difficult, but sophisticated methods were still possible. One insidious example was adding synthetic EB, or natural EB isolated from non-citrus sources, to orange essence oil which was valuable primarily for the topnotes and EB present, crucial for FTNF juice flavors. Low-quality essence oil could be "improved" by the addition of non-citrus EB, a form of economic adulteration. Adulterating grapefruit oils with non-grapefruit sourced nootkatone or octanal was another difficult-to-detect example, as was diluting pure lemon peel oils with washed lemon oil, left over from water-soluble alcohol extractions of lemon oil. Some very expensive and high-technology tests were developed to "catch" some of these types of problems, including even particle accelerator-based measurements of isotopic ratios of certain atoms making up flavor molecules. This technology, developed originally by nuclear physicists, was far too expensive for routine use. Invariably, the economic temptation to create these products always existed and a certain amount of adulterated material went undiscovered. Fortunately, these types of economic adulteration posed no safety risk to consumers and the citrus flavors companies were highly motivated to identify and avoid these materials.

Distillation technology, so crucial to the citrus flavor industry, also experienced important changes. Unlike the complex, automated, continuous distillation systems used by the petroleum industry, the manual, batch systems used for citrus products were optimized for much smaller product runs and process flexibility. The same still would often be used to manufacture a number of different products. Energy efficiency, in terms of either heating or cooling, was a minor cost of the entire process and generally ignored. Instead of being automated, stills had always been run by skilled operators who learned the processes on the job and could easily adapt processes to changing raw materials. Yet, as the processed quantity of both raw materials and finished products grew during this decade, stills became more specialized by process, with larger batch sizes. The higher capital cost of a larger still was offset by the throughput, as process time largely remained independent of batch size for a properly designed still. Also, stills optimized for high-value isolates like valencene were very different in design from those for folding peel oil. In this decade too, manual pressure and temperature monitoring and controls were replaced, first by simple recording and Proportional-Integral-Derivative (PID) control technology, and eventually by computerized control systems. However, to the author's knowledge, no fully automated production stills were operating in the Florida industry before the year 2000.

Most distillation used during this period was either vacuum or ambient-pressure fractional distillation. In some cases, a still could operate by bypassing the packed column, which sped up the distillation and improved the performance for some specialized applications where speed was more important than fractionating capacity. Another technology gaining ground was molecular or short-path distillation. This relatively expensive distillation process utilized very specialized, high-vacuum equipment, well-suited for for high-boiling citrus fractions like nootkatone. The technology, commercialized in the 1930s for vitamin recovery[50], had been used by the flavor and fragrance industry only sparingly for expensive materials that could justify the cost. Interest was further spurred by a patent published in 1996 by a Cargill researcher, which examined pesticide removal in citrus oils by molecular distillation[51]. Several Florida companies experimented with this technology on a laboratory scale or took advantage of toll-processing arrangements offered by manufacturers. The technology was particularly suitable for recovering important high-boiling/low-volatility natural aroma chemicals such as valenecene, α- and β-sinesal, and nootkatone from residual distillation residues of citrus oils. As citrus raw material prices were generally low and peel oils available in excess, the technology became increasingly commercially viable. Other improvements in the distillation process were constantly being sought after. The Spinning Cone Column process, discussed above, was also introduced into Florida during this period.

Complementing distillation technology, the worldwide flavor industry had long used alcohol extractions of citrus oils to manufacture flavors, but this had never been widely used in Florida. Alcohol extracts for lemon and lime were particularly important for carbonated soft-drinks, and facilities had been developed elsewhere in the US for manufacturing these products long before Dr. Redd started Redd Laboratories. Nevertheless, most citrus flavor companies in Florida performed some specialized batch extractions of citrus oils or fractions using ethanol for small-scale applications. It was relatively easy to use a mixing tank with temperature control for the extractions, and ethanol was generally available as a byproduct from orange water-phase essence. However, it could be time-consuming, especially on larger batch sizes, and occasionally the process suffered a phase-separation failure. In such cases, seemingly occurring at random and inconvenient times, manual intervention was required to get the process back on track. It was a well-known problem in the industry[6]. Given these difficulties and the lack of a competitive advantage compared to older sites already performing these extractions, most Florida companies had not invested much effort in this process. Yet, as multinational flavor companies arrived in Florida, they brought renewed interest in citrus ethanol extractions, either transferring processes they conducted elsewhere to Florida or expanding their company-wide citrus capabilities. In the 1990s, a

---

[6]Allen Kryger had occasionally quipped, "More jobs were lost in the flavor industry to failed extractions than any other reason!"

relatively new continuous counter-current extraction process that replaced batch settling tanks with continuous-flow centrifuges was being touted by the equipment manufacturer Robatel Inc.[7] and others. The equipment had been developed for non-food applications, but Robatel was exploring a number of new uses, including citrus extractions. Tastemaker/Givaudan, in particular, made a significant investment at their Lakeland facility to install such a counter-current extraction system around 1997. The system included dedicated alcohol-recovery stills to recycle their extraction ethanol[52]. Most of the other flavor companies in Florida also studied this new technology.

In addition to the usual distillation and extraction methods, among the technical staff, there was constant interest in new technologies that might yield better flavor fractions. Solid-phase extractions were one area of continuing interest. Extractions using silica gel had been done on a small scale for some time. Other adsorbents, such as teflon[53, 54] or polypropylene, were occasionally investigated. Membrane-based separation methods like pervaporation also generated interest during this decade[55, 56]. However, many of these new techniques were limited by throughput and cost. Although they might yield different fractions, determining whether a new material was "better" was challenging, as any sensory improvement was subjective and, ultimately, success depended upon finding a customer. Unless the result had an obvious benefit, such as improved purity for a known natural aroma chemical, reduction of a detrimental contaminant, or the improvement of a well-known product limitation like lemon-oil stability in acidic beverages, the process of introducing new citrus fractions commercially was time-consuming.

Another important technological factor was the biotechnology revolution. Although not utilized to any great extent for citrus in Florida, biotechnology began to have a growing impact on the flavor industry. There had long been a theoretical interest in genetically-modified (GM) citrus crops, to speed up the painstakingly-slow process of traditional citrus breeding. The USDA had been breeding citrus in Florida for more than a century, but new cultivars could take decades to develop. In theory, genetic modification could expedite crop improvements, such as freeze tolerance, ripening schedules, easy peeling, and enhancing juice color and flavor, changes that would certainly affect the properties of the citrus raw materials used by the flavor industry. However, early

---

[7]The company later became Rousselet Robatel.

successes with crops like soybeans or tomatoes did not easily translate to citrus. The slow growth rate of citrus trees made them difficult to experiment upon with GM techniques, requiring too long for a new tree to bear fruit, thus hindering the efficient cycle of gene modification, evaluation, and re-modification. As consumer fears regarding biotechnology use in food production increased, the fact that all FTNF citrus flavoring products were derived from non-GM citrus trees became increasingly convenient for the flavor industry. Nevertheless, some of the value of citrus oils stemmed from the flavor chemicals that could be isolated from them, such as trans-2-hexenal or nootkatone. These were valuable flavoring ingredients when extracted from any natural source, with citrus oils being the most commercially viable sources. Early in the 1990s, it was recognized that modern biotechnology could be applied to yeasts or other organisms to produce these aroma chemicals as byproducts of modified metabolic pathways[57]. These "fermentation" products, meeting the criteria for natural aroma chemicals, could potentially compete with traditional isolation methods. Extensive research was conducted primarily outside Florida, as the requisite biotechnology expertise differed significantly from the traditional citrus and essential oil knowledge that the Florida industry specialized in. Over time, many key aroma chemicals found in citrus oils began to see alternative production sources, which put downward pressure on prices. For applications in juices and other products requiring 100% FTNF citrus flavors, these biotech-derived ingredients usually could not be used, but the new technology undeniably impacted the broader citrus flavor industry.

The number of flavor-related professionals in Florida had grown considerably, including employees at Coca-Cola/Minute Maid, Firmenich, Givaudan, Treatt, Sunpure, Florida Flavors, and juice experts at various processing companies including Tropicana and Citrus World. The localized nature of the industry fostered interactions between these employees despite the competitive pressures and the flavor industry culture of secrecy. This localization also created opportunities for employees to transfer to different positions around the industry, underscoring the importance of maintaining industry contacts. Nearly everyone had former business colleagues or friends working at competitor companies, fostering a regular exchange of industry news and gossip. Additionally, certain professional meetings served as forums for these types of exchanges. The local Florida section of the Institute of Food Technologists (IFT) was very active, holding monthly meetings where sales and technical staff mingled. Annually, the IFT held a large national meeting, functioning as both a scientific conference and a trade show, attended by all the major flavor companies. Both sales and technical staff from Florida were commonly in attendance. Another important annual event was the University of Florida Citrus Short Course in Clearwater, FL. This three-day-long conference, focused on citrus juices and related beverages, drew a global mix of attendees from fruit processors, beverage companies, flavor companies, and other industry suppliers. UF first held this conference in 1961 in Gainesville, but its increasing popularity necessitated a relocation to Clearwater in 1995[58]. The conference participants included all of the major citrus juice manufacturers, and the nearby location fostered broad participation of technical and sales staff from the local flavor industry, providing an intense period of meetings, dinners, intelligence gathering, gossip and reunions. The extent to which each flavor company encouraged their employees to attend these meetings varied widely, influenced by sales strategies and company culture. Some companies preferred to limit their staff's contact with competitors, while others were more open to such interactions. For example, Allen Kryger of Florida Flavors reimbursed his employees for local IFT meeting expenses, believing the benefits outweighed the risks.

Publicly-supported research efforts in Florida also helped the industry, including activities at the University of Florida, the USDA and the Florida Department of Citrus. Collectively, these organizations supported over 150 scientists working on diverse topics related to citrus, ranging from genetics to horticultural practices, pest control, fresh fruit handling, and juice processing[59]. A handful of these scientists worked on projects directly relevant to the commercial flavor industry, particularly in citrus processing, byproduct, and flavor research. This work was primarily conducted at the University of Florida's Citrus Research and Education Center (CREC) in Lake Alfred, FL, and the USDA's Citrus and Subtropical Products Laboratory in Winter Haven, FL, both of which have long histories in Florida. At the CREC, Robert Braddock continued his longstanding leadership role in byproducts research, focusing on citrus oils, aromas and related processing techniques (see pg. 188). Another significant UF/CREC scientist at this time was Russell Rouseff, a chemist who had joined the CREC in the early 1970s. Although he initially focused on non-flavor aspects of orange juice, he had shifted his focus to citrus flavor chemistry, studying the important flavor-active trace chemicals found in citrus. At the USDA, Phil Shaw continued his longstanding research on citrus flavors (see pg. 187), retiring in the year 2000[60]. These scientists, along with others occasionally working on a project of interest to the flavor industry, made important contributions. They served not only through their specific research work but also as neutral, non-commercial technical experts. When industry-wide problems arose, these academics could gather information, conduct research, and propose possible solutions transparently. They were particularly valuable when information needed to be provided to regulatory agencies, as there were no complicating commercial interests involved. Unlike industry employees, their careers were rewarded by creating and disseminating knowledge, and their reputations were advanced by doing good science. They also acted as reservoirs of industry and technical information. In return, the industry supported their work through financial and material support, and occasional technical advice in areas where industry expertise was more advanced.

One industry-wide issue that emerged in this decade was the discovery of halogenated hydrocarbons in citrus oils around 1999[61]. Pesticides had generally been a minor concern for the industry, although they were increasingly worrying to consumers. Pesticides were applied to the exterior of citrus fruits during the growing season, but after harvesting, washing, and juicing the orange, little pesticide residue remained in the juice. However, the situation was more complex with peel oils, as some pesticides dissolved into the oils from the fruit's surface. Fortunately, since peel oils are used at very low levels in flavoring foods (typically 10–200 ppm), even high contamination levels of pesticides in peel oil result in very low contributions to the final food product. A similar situation arose for fungicides applied to fruits initially intended for sale as fresh fruit, but later processed for juice. For the US government, citrus peel oils did not constitute a large enough food category to warrant specific pesticide limits; instead, regulatory standards for whole citrus fruits were usually applied. However, testing and monitoring pesticide content in citrus oils were costly and not routinely performed, as the low usage rates of these oils generally ensured food safety.

However, as analytical chemistry methods improved, and consumers interest in "chemical-free" foods grew, food and beverage companies were vigilant about any contaminants that might catch consumer attention. One example of such a contaminant was the discovery of the halogenated hydrocarbons in some citrus oils. The details of the discovery are murky, likely intentionally so to avoid drawing unnecessary attention to the issue. One version of the discovery relates that a major soft-drink company conducting chemical analyses of citrus oils using a new, highly sensitive detector for halogen elements (chlorine, bromine, etc.) unexpectedly found several very low-level halogenated hydrocarbons in some oils. Knowing these chemicals were unlikely to be natural citrus components, it was important to identify their structures and sources. Robert Braddock from UF soon became the leading public researcher on this topic in Florida. By shifting the research to a university researcher, along with providing necessary funding and equipment, the issue could be swiftly studied without drawing undue attention to specific consumer products or brands. Soon, new analytical methods were developed and shared with both citrus processing companies and the users of their essential oils, including the Florida flavor industry. Dr. Braddock determined that the trace contaminants resulted from chemical reactions between citrus oil limonene and over-chlorinated process water used to separate the oils from the fruit peel[62, 63, 64]. In addition, by monitoring the process water chlorine levels, the citrus processing plants could prevent the problem.

The Terpene Market

By this time, the d-limonene and related terpene market, crucial to the Florida citrus flavor industry, had significantly matured into a global enterprise. Originally developed by Bert Schulz at Florida Chemical Company, d-limonene was now routinely collected and sold by all the Florida citrus plants. Local flavor companies also utilized this market to sell their excess distilled terpenes. However, Brazil was now the largest producer of these chemicals due to its larger processed citrus crop, and end-use customers were spread around the globe. In Florida, Florida Chemical Company maintained its dominant market position, with Bert Schulz transitioning the company leadership to his son, Paul Schulz, and other non-family management. Joining Florida Chemical were several small companies, including Interstate Commodities and Florachem, which bought, sold, or brokered limonene and terpenes. Interstate Commodities was founded by David Cline in 1986, and Florachem by Steve McAlister in 1988.

Limonene and terpenes had achieved a variety of regular uses, including as a chemical feedstock for resin production, an environmentally friendly solvent, degreaser, cleaning agent, and in a few food-related applications. However, the entire market for these products remained relatively small and was suceptible to rapid price fluctuations related to citrus crop sizes in both Florida and Brazil, or the behavior of large customers. During the 1980s and 1990s, the average terpene price was around \$1/pound, but it could easily double or halve due to a freeze or changes in crop estimates. Even so, the terpene market remained a fundamental part of the business dynamics for the citrus flavor industry. In manufacturing their folded oils, FTNF flavors, and various flavor isolates they produced large quantities of distilled terpenes. By selling these terpenes into a ready market, their main products could be produced more economically.

A Century of Citrus Flavors in Florida

As the year 1999 came to a close and the world fretted about the impending Y2K computer problem, the citrus flavor industry in Florida was enjoying remarkably favorable conditions. It had been nearly 90 years since F. A. McDermott first studied the use of Florida citrus oils as flavoring ingredients, having been contracted by the Florida Citrus Exchange, 70 years since Wilbur Pipkin invented a peel oil recovery machine and set up a company with J. J. R. Bristow in Tampa to sell citrus oils, 55 years since the launch of Florida's famous FCOJ product, and 40 years since the invention of the TASTE evaporator and successful essence recovery. Within this environment, a local flavor industry had successfully developed, tracing its roots back to James Redd and his eponymous company, Redd Laboratories, started in 1961. Redd's career largely overlapped with the remarkably successful Florida orange juice industry, but the local flavor industry he inspired eventually expanded far beyond the boundaries of Florida and orange juice. Combining the unique know-how of Florida citrus experts with the technological expertise and sales reach of leading international flavor companies, a small ecosystem of competing companies in Florida went on to provide citrus flavors and flavor ingredients for the enjoyment of consumers worldwide.

This niche industry had reached global importance. Before the turn of the century, the world's most sophisticated citrus flavors and fragrances were made in Europe, drawing on the technological expertise of European flavor and fragrance houses using citrus ingredients from around the Mediterranean and, to a lesser extent, elsewhere. Now, the world's production of citrus flavors was squarely centered in Florida, where vast quantities of citrus oils and essences were processed into highly specialized flavors and flavoring fractions and sold to nearly every continent. The European flavor houses, transformed into international companies, were active participants in Florida. Over the course of 100 years, the world's leading technology in the production of citrus flavors had relocated to a rural, southern state in the US with little intrinsic chemical infrastructure.

In terms of size, the Florida citrus flavor industry was much smaller than the broader fresh fruit and juice industry. Florida's many citrus growers had long been romanticized in the state's OJ lore and advertising, and together with the large juice processors and their many employees, they formed a potent economic block in the state. Their representatives and interests largely drove the state's Department of Citrus and the broader citrus agenda. The niche flavor industry, quite small in size and employing perhaps a total of 500 people by the year 2000, operated largely under the radar. The broader citrus industry was well aware of their existence; they bought the processing plants' byproducts and sold flavors to all of the juice manufacturers, but it was largely done quietly with little outward attention. This silence served both the industry and its corporate customers well. Juice manufacturers wanted their customers to think about fresh oranges, not scientifically-designed FTNF flavors, when they purchased orange juice. International flavor companies were interested in being known as experts in *all* citrus, not just Florida specialists. And for the very profitable Florida flavor industry, less attention often meant less interference in their operations.

The flavor industry offered its employees many benefits, not the least of which were excellent-paying jobs. For a high-tech industry, it was unusual that many of these jobs required only aptitude and on-the-job training, disregarding the growing trend of requiring college credentials. Hiring both locally and attracting professionals from outside Florida and the US, the industry offered engaging work with opportunities for national and global travel. Moreover, the regionally-concentrated nature of the industry allowed employees to offer their services to multiple employers. Additionally, the industry provided excellent training for jobs in the broader flavor industry beyond Florida. By the 1990s, major flavor companies were routinely transferring employees into and out of their Florida operations, almost always to the benefit of the individuals involved. The industry was also an attractive employer for chemistry, chemical engineering, and food science graduates within the state.

One attribute that could never be associated with this niche industry was "static." Since the days of Redd Laboratories, it had been an environment of near-constant change, reflecting the agricultural roots of the raw materials and their subsequent weather dependence; corporate acquisitions and entrepreneurial startups; the competition for key suppliers, customers, and employees; the growth of the Brazilian citrus industry; and the strong personalities of many industry leaders. Moreover, more change, of a quite predictable nature, was on the horizon. Other large flavor companies continued to shop for acquisition targets, and industry regulation was increasing as worldwide safety "experts" identified additional concerns about flavors used in their markets. Another predictable transition was underway as the industry pioneers aged into retirement and a new generation of leadership emerged. Dr. Redd himself had retired earlier in the decade, and many other early industry participants were in or nearing retirement. A number of companies, including Firmenich's Florida operation, Florida Chemical, and Florida Flavors, employed second-generation children of early leaders. More importantly, an influx of new talent from outside Florida and recent university graduates were arriving, learning on the job and making their contributions.

Change was something the industry was accustomed to, and all these changes appeared very manageable. In fact, the future looked very bright. The EU market was growing rapidly, with the adoption of a unified currency nearly complete. Asian and Chinese markets were exploding with consumer wealth growing rapidly. All signs pointed to these consumers adopting more flavored food and beverage products that required citrus flavors. An emphasis on free trade was driving economic trade agreements and subsequently easing the international exchange of flavor products. As a result of these and other trends, worldwide flavor sales continued to grow at a healthy pace, and there was international optimism. Closer to Florida, the state's citrus crop was producing fruit at record yields, as was Brazil's crop. Citrus was also being planted in other areas, including Mexico and Central America, to support growth projections. All of this fruit ensured excellent raw materials would be available for the industry looking forward.

And in this way a very remarkable century of Florida citrus came to a close with optimism in the air.

References

[1] "A Novel Experience." In: *Tampa Morning Tribune* (Jan. 14, 1950), p. 4.

[2] Mark Brown, Tom Spreen, and Renee Goodrich. "Trends in the NFC Orange Juice Segment." In: *Citrus Industry* (Jan. 2000), pp. 18–19.

[3] "This and That." In: *Citrus Industry* (Feb. 2000), p. 10.

[4] Robert A. Morris. *The U.S. Orange and Grapefruit Juice Markets: History, Development, Growth, and Change.* EDIS Document FE834. IFAS, University of Florida, Gainesville, FL, June 2010. URL: https://journals.flvc.org/edis/article/download/118658/116582/ (visited on 07/23/2024).

[5] Constance L. Hays. "Pepsico to Pay $3.3 Billion For Tropicana." In: *The New York Times* (July 21, 1998), p. D1.

[6] Karen McEver. "Minute Maid Advertising Plans Presented at FOM Meeting." In: *Citrus Industry* (May 1995), p. 14.

[7] Jerry Sachs. *Interview by Robert Kryger.* By Phone. Nov. 19, 2020.

[8] Jerry Sachs. *Interview by Robert Kryger.* By Phone. May 17, 2021.

[9] Nancy Hardy. "Minute Maid Talks Strategy." In: *Citrus Industry* (May 1997), p. 57.

[10] Susan Martin. *Interview by Robert Kryger.* By Phone. Aug. 18, 2022.

[11] Susan Martin. *E-mail to Robert Kryger.* Aug. 23, 2022.

[12] Ernie Neff. "Imagine No Orange Juice." In: *Citrus Industry Magazine* (Mar. 1998), pp. 9–11.

[13] Susan Webb. "Citrus World, Inc. 1980 - 2015. An Examination of Adaptation in a Long-Enduring U.S. Agricultural Marketing Cooperative." Masters Thesis. University of Missouri - Columbia, 2016.

[14] Paul Power Jr. "Lykes Squeezed in Juice Market." In: *Tampa Tribune* (Apr. 12, 1998). Section: Business & Finance, p. 1.

[15] *FCPA Statistical Summary 1992-93 Season.* Copy in UF CREC Library, Lake Alfred, FL. Florida Citrus Processors Association, 1993.

[16] John Reinan. "Getting Squeezed Out." In: *The Tampa Tribune* (July 23, 1998). Section: Business & Finance, pp. 1, 8.

[17] Paul Power Jr. "Brazilian Firm Purchases 2 Juice Plants." In: *Tampa Tribune* (July 24, 1996), pp. 1, 8.

[18] *2010 Citrus Reference Book.* Florida Department of Citrus, Aug. 2010. URL: https://app.box.com/embed/s/dt42f2c7kk (visited on 10/01/2023).

[19] *USDA NASS Citrus Summary 1999 - 2000.* United States Department of Agriculture, Jan. 22, 2001. URL: https://www.nass.usda.gov/Statistics_by_State/Florida/Publications/Citrus/Citrus_Summary/index.php (visited on 07/01/2023).

[20] Peary Marro. *Interview by Robert Kryger.* By Phone. Jan. 16, 2023.

[21] Beverly Bateman and Rex Harper. *Interview by Robert Kryger.* Lakeland, FL. Feb. 11, 2021.

[22] Wesley Beck. *Interview by Robert Kryger.* Lakeland, FL. Apr. 12, 2023.

[23] Laszlo Unger. "Basic Business Trends in The Worldwide Flavor and Fragrance Industry 1987–1990." In: *Perfumer & Flavorist* Vol. 14 (May/June 1989), pp. 42–45.

[24] Hans Abderhalden. "The Future of the Flavor Business." In: *Perfumer & Flavorist* Vol. 16 (Nov./Dec. 1991), pp. 31–34.

[25] Johannes Buchel. "Flavoring with Citrus Oils." In: *Perfumer & Flavorist* Vol. 14 (Jan./Feb. 1989), pp. 22–26.

[26] David Rosen. *Interview by Robert Kryger.* By Phone. Dec. 13, 2022.

[27] *Hercules Inc. 1992 Annual Report.* 1993.

[28] Marc Reisch. "Hercules, Imcera in Flavors Joint Venture." In: *Chemical and Engineering News* Vol. 69 (Issue 50 Dec. 16, 1991), p. 5.

[29] Dick Rawe. "Flavor-makers in Joint Effort Here." In: *The Cincinnati Post* (Dec. 12, 1991), p. 5.

REFERENCES

[30] "Joint Venture Approved." In: *The Cincinnati Post* (Feb. 25, 1992), p. 12.

[31] "Name Chosen for Flavor Firm." In: *Springfield News-Sun* (May 24, 1992), p. D2.

[32] "P&F News." In: *Perfumer & Flavorist* Vol. 17 (Mar./April 1992), p. 58.

[33] Jeff Dodson. *Interview by Robert Kryger*. By Zoom. Dec. 1, 2022.

[34] Chris Aregood. "Hercules will sell Tastemaker Holding." In: *The News Journal* (Feb. 6, 1997), p. B7.

[35] "Flavor Firm Sold." In: *The Los Angeles Times* (Sept. 12, 1991), p. D5.

[36] Donald Hendrix. *Interview by Robert Kryger*. By Phone. Apr. 13, 2023.

[37] Beverly Bateman. *E-mail to Robert Kryger*. May 23, 2023.

[38] J. D. Vora. *Interview by Robert Kryger*. By Phone. Apr. 4, 2023.

[39] Tom Antonik. *Memorandum on Sunpure Marketing Strategy 1992*. Unpublished. Oct. 1991.

[40] Bruce Flickinger. "Quality Effort Bears Fruit." In: *Food Quality* (Mar. 1998), pp. 28–30.

[41] Ed Baranski. *E-mail to Robert Kryger*. Oct. 9, 2023.

[42] Kris Hudson. "Becker Sells FP Plant to Sunpure." In: *Fort Pierce News* (Aug. 29, 1997), p. A7.

[43] "Juice Processors Join Forces." In: *The Tampa Tribune* (Sept. 20, 2000). Section: Business & Finance, p. 6.

[44] *Settlement Agreement Between Tastemaker, Florex Flavors Inc., and Allen Kryger*. Unpublished. July 12, 1995.

[45] Robert Kryger. "Role of Polymethoxylated Flavones in Citrus Flavor." In: *Natural Flavors and Fragrances - Chemistry, Analysis and Production*. ACS Symposium Series 908. American Chemical Society, 2005, pp. 161–172.

[46] Flavourtech. *Company Website*. URL: https://flavourtech.com/ (visited on 10/06/2023).

[47] *Takasago Centenary Book: 1920 - 2020*. Takasago, 2020.

[48] Kenji Yagi. *E-mail to Mark Walsh.* Aug. 17, 2022.

[49] E. Gildemeister and Fr. Hoffmann. *The Volatile Oils.* Trans. by Edward Kremers. 2nd ed. Vol. 2. New York, NY: John Wiley and Sons, 1916.

[50] K. C. D. Hickman. "High-Vacuum Short-Path Distillation - A Review." In: *Chemical Reviews* Vol. 34 (Issue 1 Feb. 1, 1944), pp. 51–106.

[51] Harapanahalli Muraldihara. "Removal of Pesticides from Citrus Peel Oil." Pat. 5,558,893. Assignee: Cargill, Inc. United States Patent. Sept. 24, 1996.

[52] Ed Baranski. *E-mail to Robert Kryger.* Oct. 11, 2023.

[53] Alexander Fleisher. "The Poroplast Extraction Technique in the Flavor and Fragrance Industry." In: *Perfumer & Flavorist* Vol. 15 (Sept./Oct. 1990), pp. 27–36.

[54] Alexander Fleisher. "Citrus Hydrocarbon-Free Essential Oils." In: *Perfumer & Flavorist* Vol. 19 (Jan./Feb. 1994), pp. 11–15.

[55] M. H. Auerbach. "A Novel Membrane Process for Folding Essential Oils." In: *Flavor Technology.* ACS Symposium Series 610. American Chemical Society, 1997, pp. 127–138.

[56] Ingo Blume and Richard W. Baker. "Treatment of Evaporator Condensates by Pervaporation." Pat. 4,952,751. United States Patent. Aug. 28, 1990.

[57] Tony Dennis. "Biogeneration of Flavors." In: *Citrus Processing - Present and Future.* Food Industry Short Course. Gainesville, FL: University of Florida Department of Food Science, 1992, pp. 85–100.

[58] Barry Wilson and Adrienne Wilson. "History of the Short Course." In: UF International Citrus and Beverage Conference. Clearwater, FL, Sept. 2012.

[59] "Citrus Research Personnel." In: *Citrus Industry* (Annual Citrus Guide 2000), pp. 23–24.

[60] "Obituary - Philip E. Shaw." In: *The Tampa Tribune* (Nov. 5, 2013), p. B6.

[61] R. J. Braddock and E. Weiss. "Preventing or Minimizing The Formation of Limonene Chlorohydrins in Citrus Oils." In: USDA Winter Haven Citrus Processor's Day. Lake Alfred, FL, Oct. 17, 2002, pp. 1–4.

[62] E. R. Weiss et al. "Occurrence and Preclusion of Terpene Chlorohydrins in Citrus Essential Oils." In: *Journal of Food Science* Vol. 68 (Issue 6 2003), pp. 2146–2149.

[63] Eve R. Weiss, Jana Pika, and Robert J. Braddock. "Isolation and Identification of Terpene Chlorohydrins Found in Cold-Pressed Orange Oil." In: *Journal of Agricultural and Food Chemistry* Vol. 51 (Issue 8 2003), pp. 2277–2282.

[64] Robert J. Braddock and Renee M. Goodrich. "Reduction of Limonene Chlorohydrins in Commercial Citrus Oils." In: *Journal of Food Science* Vol. 70 (Issue 1 2005), pp. C104–C107.

9

Looking Ahead into the Next Century

"I envy you young people just starting out, for I can foresee that the next 50 years can be just as exciting as the last 50 have been for me!"

—James Redd, 1988[1].

It is fitting to note that Jim Redd, so intertwined with many of the flavor industry developments in Florida, passed away on July 13, 1999, just as the 20th century was closing[2]. He had consulted for a few years after selling his company to Firmenich in 1988, but soon retired. Unfortunately, he lost his wife a few years later to cancer. Redd suffered a stroke at age 80 and died soon after, surrounded by his family and some close friends. The funeral was private, with Redd requesting no obituary or public service.

Given his quiet passing, there was no opportunity for the citrus flavor industry to come together and celebrate his life. Redd, as far as any individual can be identified, was instrumental to the growth of this Florida industry. As a young man, he was present at the start of the FCOJ industry, and he closed his life having seen the largest citrus crop ever grown in Florida, a booming worldwide citrus juice industry, and a thriving flavor industry in Florida. Even twenty years later, many of his former colleagues were happy to share stories about his sharp intellect, friendly personality, and love of storytelling when interviewed.

Outside the orbit of his personal friends, he is universally recognized for his unique role in the formation of the citrus flavor industry. In 1988, Redd himself noted that his generation was passing along, and a new generation of professionals would carry the industry forward[1]. The author is one of those "young people" who has thoroughly enjoyed his time in this fascinating profession. And in some way, this written history is a tribute to his accomplishments.

Many of the industry trends described in the previous chapter continued into the new millennium. In 2001, Danisco, an international food company, purchased Allen Kryger's company Florida Flavors as part of its strategy to create a flavor division through acquisitions. Sunpure was acquired by Kerry Foods in 2003, who also sought to build a flavor division by acquisition. In 2007, Firmenich acquired Danisco's flavor business, uniting what remained of Jim Redd's Intercit operation with his old Redd Laboratories trainee Allen Kryger's company. While earlier acquisitions generally increased resources, headcount, and expertise in Florida, Firmenich's 2007 acquisition of Danisco marked the arrival of consolidation pressure. Following this, Firmenich managed two major citrus manufacturing facilities in Florida, one based in Safety Harbor, where Intercit had been founded, and another in Lakeland. Within a few years, Firmenich closed the Safety Harbor site and consolidated operations into Lakeland. Despite the consolidation trend, the industry still saw small, new entrants including Citrasource, started by two industry veterans, and Molecular Separation Specialists, founded by the author. The limonene and terpene company, Florida Chemical, also made a major expansion into citrus oils, fractions, and flavors.

Other trends were less positive for the industry. First, consumers were becoming wary of the sugar and calorie content in orange juice and sensitive to the technological processing of foods. Coca Cola's creation of the brand *Simply Orange* in 2001 was one attempt to address these consumer concerns. These trends combined to slow and eventually reverse the growth of orange juice sales, putting pressure on flavor sales and margins in the citrus flavor industry. Second, due to the history and specialized nature of the citrus flavoring business, Florida-based citrus operations had largely operated independently, even when owned by out-of-state corporations. However, there was now significant pressure on larger flavor companies to consolidate some of their Florida operations for strategic purposes or cost-savings. As one example, in the early 2000s, Givaudan relocated most of their technical and sales staff in Florida to Cincinnati, their US headquarters. Third, a growing non-food based application for limonene upset the traditional supply/demand balance for citrus oils, causing raw material prices to spike. Starting in the mid 2000s, the oil-fracking business in the US grew considerably. That industry discovered that limonene was particularly useful for certain drilling applications, driving up demand. In 2010, the Deepwater Horizon oil spill caused an additional spike in demand as the solvent was found useful in the clean-up effort. Consequently, Florida citrus oils experienced historic price levels which drove up the cost of natural citrus flavors and encouraged customers to seek non-citrus alternatives.

All of these problems were manageable, but the greatest threat to the industry arrived unseen. In the early 2000s, a bacteriological disease known as citrus greening was accidentally introduced into Florida, likely through the Port of Miami. The disease, spread by small insects called citrus psyllids, infected trees, which showed few symptoms initially. Over time, the bacteria impede the nutrient flow within the trunk, effectively starving the tree. The first infected trees were discovered in 2005, but there was no known cure or treatment. Efforts to isolate the infection by destroying nearby trees failed, and within a few short years, greening escalated into the largest agricultural disaster ever to hit Florida, far surpassing the impacts of any previous disease or freeze.

The industry invested heavily in intensive research, supported by both federal and state resources. However, more than twenty years later, the disease continues to devastate the state and has spread to Texas and California. By the 2022/23 season, the Florida citrus crop size had declined to less than a tenth of its pre-greening peak. The impact on the Florida citrus industry has been catastrophic. Besides the reduced availability of citrus oils and essences, the disease has altered the flavor qualities of these raw materials, posing challenges for both the Florida juice and flavor industries. How the industry will ultimately manage and recover from this disease remains to be seen, a story that will be written by the next generation of citrus specialists.

References

[1] James B. Redd. "The Volatile Flavors of Orange Juice." In: ASME 1988 Citrus Engineering Conference. Lakeland, FL: American Society of Mechanical Engineers Digital Collection, Mar. 24, 1988, pp. 79–93.

[2] Beverly Bateman and Rex Harper. *Interview by Robert Kryger.* Lakeland, FL. Feb. 11, 2021.

Index

A. E. Staley Manufacturing Company, 142, 163–170, 175–177, 182, 183, 217
Adams Packing Association, 64
Agricultural Experimentation Station, State of New York, 116
Alcoma Corp., 137, 161
Alexander the Great, 1
AM Todd Company, 208, 210
American Extract and Vinegar Company, 30
Anglea, Tim, 210, 211, 214, 215, 241, 242
Antonik, Tom, 249
Archdiocese of Cincinnati, 95, 96
Arizona Chemical Co., 209, 215
Armour & Co., 141
Atkins, Cedric Donald, 43, 59–61, 66–68, 139, 142
Atlantic Coast Line Railroad, 154
Attaway, John A., 139, 142, 197
Automatic Citrus Juice Extractor Inc., 21

Baier, Willard E., 99
Basic Research Laboratory, University of Cincinnati, 51, 95
Bateman, Beverly, 218–220
Beatrice Foods, 197, 200
Beavens, E. A., 121
Beck, Wesley, 233, 234, 246, 247
Birdseye, Clarence, 50
Bireley Citro-Mat Extractor, 21
Bireley's Inc., 18, 50, 81, 103, 120
Bireley, Frank, 21, 50, 120
Black Hand, 27
Borden Inc., 19, 51, 53
Bordo Citrus Co., 161
Bovill, Hugo, 222
Braddock, Robert, 188, 257, 259
Brannan, Charles, 67
Brent, Jewell Allen, 127, 137
Bristow, James Jefferson Ricker, 21, 30, 31, 53–57, 59, 65–68, 96, 114, 132, 260
Bristow, Louis L., 53

Brokaw, Charles, 127, 154
Bruce's Juices Inc., 18, 29, 48, 65
Bruce, J. Adams, 18
Bucek, Wesley, 173, 174, 230
Buflo-Vak Co., 82
Bureau of Alcohol, Tobacco, Firearms and Explosives, US Department of Justice, 161
Bureau of Plant Industry, US Department of Agriculture, 26, 28
Burkart, Francis, 17, 18
Burns, Warren, 28
Bussenius, Harold, 217
By-Products and Sales Co., 30, 53, 55
Byer, Ellis, 126, 137

C. E. Rodgers Company, 47
California Citrus Fruit Exchange, 98
California Crushed Fruit Company, 47
California Fruit Growers Exchange, 10, 11, 19, 103, 114
California Fruit Juice Company, 47
Campbell, H. A., 120
Canada Dry Ginger Ale Co., 48
Capasso, Phil, 210
Carbide & Carbon Chemicals Corporation, 60
Cargill Inc., 245, 254
Carpenter, D. C., 116
CES, *see* Citrus Experiment Station, University of Florida
Chace, E. M., 32, 52
Citrasource Co., 270
Citrosuco Paulista S. A., 231
Citrus & Subtropical Fruit Research, US Department of Agriculture, 67
Citrus and Subtropical Products Laboratory, US Department of Agriculture, 257
Citrus Central Cooperative, 165, 179, 183, 184
Citrus Concentrates Inc., 55–59, 62–65, 80
Citrus Engineering Conference, 219
Citrus Experiment Station, University of Florida, 20, 52, 97, 98, 101, 123, 138, 141–143, 155, 186, 188
Citrus Fruit Laboratory, 55
Citrus Industry Magazine, 60
Citrus Research and Education Center, University of Florida, 257
Citrus School, Florida Southern College, 155, 156
Citrus Short Course, University of Florida, 257
Citrus World Inc., 230, 256
Claffey, Joseph B., 133
Clearwater High School, 132
Cline, David, 259
Clinton Industries, 65, 155
Coca-Cola Special Products,

INDEX

171–175, 187, 200, 210, 228–230, 247
Collins Canning Company, 16
Collins, H. L., 16
Columbus, Christopher, 1
Commander, C. C., 47, 48
Commission of Agriculture, State of Florida, 11
Commonwealth Engineering Corporation, 95
Compagnie Morana, 24, 29, 104
Concentradora de Puerto Rico, 136
Cook, Ralph, 132–134, 136, 143
Cotton, R. H., 67
CREC, *see* Citrus Research and Education Center, University of Florida
Crist, Raymond, 11
Crosby, Bing, 64, 97
Cross, Joe, 67
Crump, J. E., 50
Curl, A. Lawrence, 67

Danisco A/S, 248, 270
Deepwater Horizon Oil Spill, 271
Del Monte Co., 160
Department of Agriculture, State of Florida, 14, 123, 127, 131
Department of Citrus, State of Florida, 44, 68, 139, 143, 168, 186, 201, 257, 261
Department of Food Science, University of Florida, 186, 188
Dillard, A. N., 49

Dilpako Canning and Packing Company, 49, 54
Dixie Canning and Preserving Company, 16
Dodge & Olcott Co., 24, 104
Dr. P. Phillips Company, 18
Du Bois, Clarence, 127, 137
Duke University, 187

E. J. Kelly and Associates, 123
Eagle Lake Cannery, 17, 18, 47
Earl Silzle Company, 31
Eastern Regional Research Laboratory, US Department of Agriculture, 117
Eckes Co., 160
Edison, Thomas, 27
Eisenhardt, Nelson H., 133
Escobar, Gil, 210, 211, 214, 215, 246, 247
Eskew, R. K., 117, 118, 120, 121, 124, 132–134, 137, 143
Essential Oils Company of America, 29, 30, 53
Exchange Lemon Products Company, 103
Exchange Orange Products Company, 103

Faulds Extractor, 21
Faulds, Norval Merritt, 21
FCC, *see* Florida Citrus Commission
FCC-CES Essence Unit, 138
FDOC, *see* Department of Citrus, State of Florida
Firmenich S. A., 104, 176, 183, 184, 212, 219, 220, 230,

233, 236, 238, 240,
242–244, 247, 249, 256,
262, 269, 270
Florachem Co., 259
Florence Citrus Growers
Association, 64
Florex Flavors Inc., 199–201,
207–212, 214–216, 218,
221, 222, 236, 238, 239,
242, 244–248
Florida Agricultural
Experimental Station,
University of Florida,
14
Florida Agriculture Hall of
Fame, 44
Florida Canners Association,
18, 57
Florida Chemical Company, 99,
166, 169–171, 175, 207,
209, 259, 262, 270
Florida Citrus Canners
Association, 18, 63
Florida Citrus Canners
Cooperative, 57, 61,
62, 64, 65, 67, 81, 123
Florida Citrus Code, 93
Florida Citrus Commission, 11,
43, 44, 57–64, 66–69,
81, 89, 93, 94, 96, 99,
101, 123, 137–139, 142,
143, 186, 187
Florida Citrus Exchange, 7, 11,
12, 17–19, 27, 47, 51,
59, 60, 260
Florida Citrus Hall of Fame,
43, 68
Florida Citrus Oils Company,
29

Florida Department of Citrus,
see Department of
Citrus, State of Florida
Florida Flavors Inc., 233, 234,
246–249, 256, 257, 262,
270
Florida Foods Inc., 63
Florida Fruit Products
Company, 15
Florida Gold Cannery, 31
Florida Grapefruit Canners
Association, 18, 19
Florida Grapefruit Juice
Company, 15
Florida Molasses Corporation,
99, 100
Florida Process, 116, 118, 120
Florida Southern College, 60,
155, 156
Florida Treatt Inc., 221, 222,
248, 249, 256
Florida WorldWide Citrus
Products Company,
222
FMC In-Line Extractor, 82
Food Machinery Corporation,
82, 132
Fraser-Brace Extractor, 101
Freyfogle, E. B., 165, 167, 177
Fries & Fries Co., 104, 219,
237, 239, 240
Fritzsche Brothers Co., 24,
101–104
Fruit Industries Inc., 94, 96
Fruit Products Company of
Florida, 47
Fruit Products Laboratory,
University of
California, 20, 51

INDEX 277

Frutarom Ltd., 182

Gallesio, M. George, 1
General Foods Corporation, 19,
    50, 52, 67, 80, 81, 103,
    120, 126, 137, 160, 180,
    197
Giampietro, Aristide W., 26, 27
Gildemeister, E., 24, 114
Givaudan Co., 104, 210, 230,
    237, 242, 248, 255, 256,
    270
Golden Gem Citrus Processors,
    184
Golden Gift Co., 96
Grierson, William, 79
Groover, F. C., 15
Guenther, Ernest, 32, 102, 103
Gulf Machinery Corporation,
    96, 128, 132, 134, 136,
    156, 157, 159, 164, 183,
    184, 218

Hall, J. Alfred, 114
Hamilton, Alissa A., 124, 131
Harper, Rex, 159, 164, 219, 220
Harvey, Rodney, 55
Hawaiian Pineapple Company,
    118, 124
Hawkins, J. E., 154
Hawkins, Orville, 47
Hawthorne, H. W., 9
Hayes, Norman, 67
Heid, J. L., 32, 57, 61, 63, 67,
    119
Hendrickson, R., 102
Hendrix, Charlie, 125, 156, 158,
    160, 165, 219
Hendrix, Don, 219, 220

Hercules Food and Flavor
    Ingredients Group,
    211, 212, 239
Hercules Inc., 177, 182–184,
    210–217, 219–221, 236,
    237, 239, 244–246
Hercules Redd Citrus
    Specialties, 182, 183,
    185, 199, 200, 206–216,
    218–220, 222, 233,
    238–240, 242, 243
Herlong, A. S., 61
Hi-Ester Corporation, 96, 97,
    156
Hill Bros. Inc., 18, 48
Hoffman, F., 24, 114
Hoffman-LaRoche Co., 105
Holland & Knight LLP, 247
Holland, H. W., 65
Hood, S. C., 28, 30, 31
Hopkins, James T., 7, 64, 65
Huff, O. P., 28, 114
Huffman, Carl, 127, 137, 173,
    230
Hull, William Q., 103

IFF, see International Flavors
    and Fragrance Inc.
INA Trading Co., 160
Indian River Foods Co., 245,
    249
Institute of Food Technologists,
    256, 257
Institutum Divi Thomae
    Foundation, 95, 96
Intercit Inc., 164, 169, 183–185,
    206–210, 212, 214, 215,
    217–220, 222, 234, 236,
    238, 242, 243, 270

Internal Revenue Service, 128, 131
International Flavors and Fragrance Inc., 104, 176
International Food Products Company, 27
International Pure Fruit Juice & By-Products Co., 26, 27
Interstate Commodities Co., 259

J. Manheimer Inc., 176
Jefferson, Jon, 159, 160
Johnson, Joe, 179–182, 210, 212, 215, 218
Joint Problems Board on Citrus Research, Florida Division, 57
Jones, Paul, 210
Joslyn, M. A., 51
Judd, 50
Juice Industries Inc., 64, 65, 80

Kansas State Agricultural College, 29
Kaufman, Charles W., 67, 120
Keller, G. J., 121–123, 126
Kelly Co., 82
Kelly, E. J., 118, 123–125, 142
Kerry Group plc, 270
Kesterson, James Walter, 101, 103, 186, 188
King Juice Company, 176
Knight & Middleton Co., 58, 59
Knight, Marvin, 58
Kraft Foods, 197, 202
Kruger, Albert, 173, 174, 230

Kryger, Allen, 169, 175–178, 180, 208–211, 221, 242, 244, 246–248, 254, 257, 270
Kujawski, Dennis, 179, 212, 216

Lakeland Highlands Canning Co., 64
Lang, Alfred, 126, 137
Langley, Charles E., 16
Lashkajani, Hadi, 179, 208–212, 221, 244–246
LEX Process, 177
Li, Chris, 212
Libby, McNeill & Libby Co., 81, 123–126, 128, 137, 138, 141, 142, 153, 160
Lillard, Johnny, 184
Lund, C. E., 30
LUWA Falling-Film Evaporator, 183
Lykes Pasco Inc., 230

M&O Company Inc., 136, 159
MacDowell, Louis G., 43, 44, 57–62, 66–68, 142, 143
Madsen, H. S., 67
Mallinckrodt Specialty Chemical Co., 219, 239
Marsh, Frances, 159, 162
Mashonas, Manual, 187
Massachusetts Institute of Technology, 53
Massachusetts State College, 60
Mazetis, Jim, 245
McAlister, Steve, 259
McDermott, F. Alex, 12, 13, 26, 46, 47, 260
McDonald, William, 155

McDuff, O. R., 101
McKeithan, David, 247
McNair, James Birtley, 12, 46
MCP Industrial Foods, 243
McPhee, John, 79
Mellon Institute of Industrial Research, 60
Mellon Institute of Pittsburgh, 12
Messenheimer, Margrit, 220
Michigan State University, 188
Middleton, Clyde, 58
Milleville, H. P., 117–119
Millsaps, Tom, 113, 139, 142
Minute Maid Co., 62, 64, 65, 67, 81, 95, 97, 98, 127, 128, 137, 153–155, 160, 168, 171–174, 187, 197–201, 211, 213, 216, 228–231, 256
Mitchell, David, 167
Mojonnier Brothers Co., 63, 67, 82
Mojonnier Thermal Recompression Production Evaporator, 125, 127
Molecular Separation Specialists Co., 270
Moore, Edwin, 43, 59–61, 66–68
Moore, Eunice Wiederhold, 67
Morgan, Donald A., 120
Morse, Richard S., 63, 66
Moscrip, John, 58, 59
Myakka Processors Inc., 161, 218

National Dairy Products Corporation, 51
National Juice Company, 51
National Research Corporation, 63, 66, 97
Natural Foods Products Company, 18, 21
Naval Consulting Board, US Navy, 27
Nu Grape Co., 49

Odio, Carlos, 183
Otterbein, Robert, 220

Pasco Packing Company, 62, 64, 65, 138, 156
Patrick, Roger, 67
Peoples Drug Stores, 58
PepsiCo Inc., 212, 229
Perry, Clyde, 50
Pfaudler Company, 116, 117
PFW, *see* Polak's Frutal Works
Pine Derivatives Marketing Co., 170
Pipkin Juice Extractor, 101
Pipkin Roll, 101
Pipkin, Wilbur, 30, 31, 260
Pipkins Dairy, 135, 157
Plymouth Citrus Growers Association, 64, 65
Polak's Frutal Works, 104, 177–179, 182, 183, 208, 210–212, 214–216, 220, 237, 239, 240
Polk County Public Schools, 31
Polk Juice Extractor, 21
Polk, Ralph Jr., 22
Polk, Ralph Sr., 17, 22, 50
Pontifical Academy of Sciences, 95

Poore, H. D., 52
Poynter, Nelson, 56, 57
Prevatt, Rubert W., 156
Procter & Gamble Co., 53, 198–202, 211–213, 216, 228
Product Brand
    Snow Crop, 155
    Aroma Plus, 180
    Birdseye, 80, 120, 128
    Bireley's Orangeade, 49, 50, 120
    Cal-Ade, 49
    Campbell's, 228
    Citrus Hill, 198, 228
    Coca-Cola Classic, 228
    Cocoa Puffs, 105
    Dair-E, 49
    Dari-O, 49
    Donald Duck, 63
    Dromedary, 18
    Durarome, 243
    Fig Newton, 154
    Five-Alive, 200
    Florida's Natural, 230, 245
    Golden Orangeade, 23, 48
    Green Spot, 49
    Kool-aid, 105
    LUWA Falling-Film Evaporator, 184, 185
    Langley's Grapefruit Extract for Flavoring Purposes, 16
    Langley's Guava Jelly, 16
    Langley's Guava Marmalade, 16
    Langley's Orange Jelly, 16
    Langley's Orange Marmalade, 16
    Langley's Special Fruit Salad, 16
    Langley's Special Processed Grapefruit, 16
    Lash, 49
    Libby, 124
    Mellapak, 181
    Minute Maid, 80, 245
    Mission, 49
    Orange Crush, 23, 48
    Orange Juice Carbonyls, 181
    Orange Plus, 180
    Orange Tetrarome, 176
    Pepsi Cola, 228
    Preparation H, 95
    Pure Premium, 228
    REDD Natural Orange Flavor, 167
    REDD Special Orange Oil Concentrate, 166
    REDD, 160, 163, 164, 182
    Rose's Lime Juice, 221
    Seald-Sweet, 18
    Simply Orange, 229, 270
    Snow Crop, 65, 80, 81, 97
    Southland, 16
    Sumoro Orange, 48
    Sun-Filled, 59
    Sunkist, 230
    Tropicana Twisters, 228
    Tropicana, 94, 245
    Valen'ju, 49
    Virginia Dare, 49
Pure Fruit Products Company, 27, 28

R. C. Treatt Co., 221, 222, 247
Rapp, Jim, 214

INDEX 281

Rector, Thomas A., 80, 120
Redd Citrus Specialties, *see* Hercules Redd Citrus Specialties
Redd Laboratories Inc., 3, 158–171, 173–185, 187, 203, 208, 210, 217, 219, 230, 240, 246, 247, 254, 260, 262, 270
Redd Orange Concentrates Inc., 161, 162, 164, 165, 176, 177
Redd, Allen Toy, 154
Redd, Ella Pitts, 154
Redd, James Beverly, 3, 125, 126, 132–137, 141–143, 153–169, 174, 175, 182–185, 188, 198, 203, 204, 207, 210, 214, 217–220, 222, 240, 254, 260, 262, 269, 270
Redd, Lillian Michaels, 163
Reddy Flavors, 217, 220
Rice University, 187
Rice, Randall G., 121, 122
Robatel Inc., 255
Roser, Charles, 154
Roser, Eleanor Marian, 154, 156
Rossi, Anthony, 94, 157
Rotary Juice Press Extractor, 21, 82, 155
Rotary Juice Press Inc., 21, 132
Rouseff, Russell, 257
Rousselet Robatel Inc., 255

Santa Barbara Juice Company, 18
Sargeant, J. Stanley, 162

Sargent Concentrates Inc., 65
Schaffner, Robert, 123, 124
Schimmel & Co., 23, 24, 103, 104
Schulz, H. E., 99, 100, 169–171, 259
Schulz, Paul, 207, 259
Schulz, William H. Jr., 99
Scott, Colin, 215, 216, 220
Seagram Company Ltd., 228, 229
Shaw, Philip, 187, 188, 257
Shoemaker, Jack, 14, 16, 17
Sigma Phi Epsilon Fraternity, 154
Silzle, Earl, 31
Singleton, F. G., 60
Skinner Falling-Film Evaporator, 54
Skinner Machinery Company, 53
Skinner, Bronson C., 21, 53–56, 59, 65, 67, 68, 96, 114, 132
Skinner, Bruce, 65
Skinner, Lee Bronson, 53
Slayton, M. M., 20, 47
Smith, E. C., 116
Snively Citrus Association, 65
Sokoloff, Boris, 155
Soudijn, Jan, 222
Southern California Fruit Exchange, 10
Southern Drug Company, 15
Southland Citrus Products Company, 17
Sperti Citrus Inc., 65, 96
Sperti, George, 51, 95–97, 156
Spinning Cone Column

Concentrator, 249, 254
Spivey, Ludd, 155
Stahl, Arthur L., 52, 59, 60, 62, 67, 155
Step Freeze Corporation of Florida Inc., 95
Step Freeze Process, 95
Stephens, Henry C., 21
Stevens Institute of Technology, 53
Street, Claude C., 14, 15
Street, Claude E., 14–17
Sucocitrico Cutrale Ltda., 200, 221, 222, 231
Suconasa, 136, 142, 158, 159
Sulzer Corporation, 181
Sunkist Growers Inc., 10, 98, 99, 103, 114
Sunny Orange Concentrates Inc., 158, 161, 162
Sunpure Ltd., 221, 244–247, 249, 256, 270
Sunstar Foods Inc., 177

Takasago International Corp., 249
Tampa Union Terminal Company, 51
Tarquinio, Nick, 243
TASTE, see Thermally-Accelerated Short Time Evaporator

Tastemaker Co., 230, 234, 238–244, 246–249, 255
Taylor, Mike, 175, 176, 179, 182, 207, 213–216, 239, 240, 242, 246
The Coca-Cola Company, 3, 127, 171–175, 179, 183, 210, 211, 222, 229, 242, 256, 270
Thermally-Accelerated Short Time Evaporator, 134–136, 143, 157, 158, 160, 162, 249, 260
Timmons, D. E., 13–15, 17, 18, 47, 48, 50, 64
Todd, U. G., 117
Treesweet Products Co., 123, 137, 161
Tropicana Co., 94, 157, 197, 198, 200, 201, 210, 213, 216, 222, 228, 229, 247, 256
Trousdale, L. L., 26
Trumm, Howard, 123, 124, 160
Turlington, J. E., 9

Union Carbide Co., 95, 97
Universal Food Products Co., 162
University of Central Florida, 174
University of Cincinnati, 95
University of Florida, 13, 28, 59, 60, 62, 81, 98, 99, 114, 132, 154, 155, 184, 186, 188, 257, 259
University of Minnesota, 55
US Department of Agriculture, 8, 19, 28, 32, 43, 52, 60, 61, 63, 67, 68, 81, 93, 97–99, 103, 114, 115, 118–122, 129–133, 136, 139, 141–143, 174, 175, 186, 188, 255, 257
US Lend Lease Program, 56,

INDEX

57, 59, 63, 68
US Patent Office, 43
US Pharmacopeia, 28, 101–103
US Vitamin Corporation, 156
USDA, *see* US Department of Agriculture

Vacuum Foods Inc., 62, 64, 67, 80, 98, 168
Van Ameringen-Haebler Inc., 104
van Houten, Peter, 219, 220
van Iperen, Jean, 221, 222
Veldhuis, Matthew K., 67, 120
Vitamerican Oil Corporation, 155
von Loesecke, Harry W., 19, 32, 114
Vora, J. D., 181, 182, 212, 219

Wagner Excello Co., 217
Wagner Fruit Juice Industries, 163, 176
Wagner, Frank, 163, 217
Walker, Charles, 21, 96, 132–134, 136, 156–159, 162, 164, 169, 183–185, 218
Walker, Seth, 14–17, 29, 31, 47, 51, 57
Welch Grape Juice Company, 15
Welch, Paul R., 15, 16
Welch, Standford Brett, 218
Wenzel, F. W., 138, 141
Will, R. T., 12, 25, 26, 45
Wilson, C. P., 114
Winter Garden Citrus Cooperative, 100, 125, 156, 158
Winter Haven Citrus Products Laboratory, US Department of Agriculture, 186, 187
Wm. P. McDonald Corp., 64, 155, 157
Wolford, R. W., 123, 138, 139, 142, 187

Zoeller, Harper F., 29

www.ingramcontent.com/pod-product-compliance
Lightning Source LLC
Chambersburg PA
CBHW042028050526
44107CB00103B/744